D1593069

PARIS IS NOT DEAD

PARIS IS NOT DEAD

SURVIVING HYPERGENTRIFICATION IN THE CITY OF LIGHT

COLE STANGLER

NEW YORK
LONDON

Requests for permission to reproduce selections from this book should be made
through our website: https://thenewpress.com/contact.

Published in the United States by The New Press, New York, 2023
Distributed by Two Rivers Distribution

ISBN 978-1-62097-782-8 (hc)
ISBN 978-1-62097-828-3 (ebook)
CIP data is available

The New Press publishes books that promote and enrich public discussion and
understanding of the issues vital to our democracy and to a more equitable world.
These books are made possible by the enthusiasm of our readers; the support of a
committed group of donors, large and small; the collaboration of our many partners
in the independent media and the not-for-profit sector; booksellers, who often
hand-sell New Press books; librarians; and above all by our authors.
www.thenewpress.com

Book design and composition by Bookbright Media
This book was set in Wolfgang and Gotham

Printed in the United States of America

10 9 8 7 6 5 4 3 2 1

CONTENTS

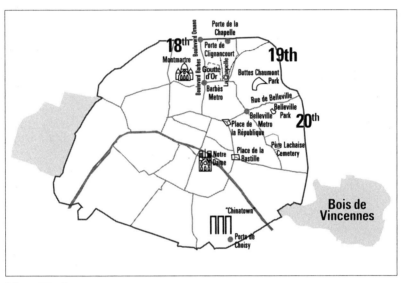

Map of Paris

INTRODUCTION

Tourists visiting the Sacré-Coeur Basilica tend to descend the Butte Montmartre the way they came up. After visiting the cathedral, they might make a stop at the Place du Tertre, the historic square of Montmartre encircled by restaurants whose multilingual menus promise authentic French cuisine at unauthentically French prices. They might admire the dozens of street artists churning out quick sketches of passersby and peddling hastily made watercolors of Paris. They might even jostle to the edge of the square to sneak a final glance at the city from one of its highest points. But once they've had enough, they'll likely make their way down the south side of the hill, following the path of the funicular toward the red-light district of Pigalle and the recognizable sights of central Paris.

A stroll down the north or eastern side does not offer the promise of more tourist attractions, even if these walks come with their own charms: the slopes formed by the summits of the densely packed limestone buildings; the maze of narrow cobblestone streets; the stairways lined with lampposts and the occasional plane or maple tree helping guide the way. But once one reaches the very bottom of the hill—the bustling boulevards Barbès and Ornano—a very different kind of city takes shape.

While the buildings flanking this busy thoroughfare retain the bourgeois grandeur that inspired their construction in the late nineteenth century, the action on the avenue is distinctively working-class. The street traffic moves faster and the corridor's storefronts bear the traces of the area's immigrant population: all-service tech stores hawk cell phones, SIM cards, and pay-by-the-minute internet connections; halal butcheries offer a dizzying display of just about every meat besides pork; an array of corner stores sell everything from yams and palm oil to candy bars and cheap gin; hole-in-the-wall eateries churn out greasy kebabs and fries until the early morning hours. This neighborhood is not built for visits. It is not designed for wistful reflection about former residents. It is made for living today.

This is especially evident at the market surrounding the metro station Château Rouge, known as the Marché Dejean. It's not a street market in the strict sense of the term, since there aren't any temporary stands. Instead, the small businesses here have more or less claimed the sidewalks of the Rue Dejean for themselves, forcing pedestrians onto a five-meter-wide cobblestone street that any sensible motorist wouldn't dare try to navigate. Even during the week, the traffic can be intense. But on a nice weekend afternoon, it can grind to a halt altogether, with pedestrians flocking to the butchers, fishmongers, and fruit and vegetable vendors.

The shops here cater to the population of the neighborhood, much of which has roots in sub-Saharan Africa, from Senegal and Mali to Cameroon and the Congo. On a practical level, this means plenty of specialty foods hard to find elsewhere. Not only do stores offer up the typical array of fresh seafood: salmon, trout, cod, bream, mussels, and scallops, but other, more unusual products are also on ice to seduce the passersby: plump and juicy catfish with their long, extraterrestrial-looking whiskers; slender barracuda with their menacingly sharp teeth (with skin that can have dangerous toxins, depending on where the fish have been caught); and oval-shaped tilapia, which, despite being a mainstay in Africa and Latin America, aren't actually consumed that often in France.

The most exotic offerings are all frozen. If you stick your head into one of the unassuming freezers, you'll find an assortment of raw fish hailing from well beyond French shores: rose-colored blackspot sea bream from Mauritania; from Senegal, flat-as-a-pancake sole and nasty-looking white grouper, which the Senegalese call *thiof*; the spotted *sompatte*, another variant of sea bream, also from Senegal; the radiant Angolan dentex; and Nile perch, known in French as *capitaine*, which also comes in the form of finely cut steaks. Watchful shopkeepers patrol the scene in rain boots, helping consumers out, waving away the occasional seagulls, and adjusting the music accordingly.

The butcheries on the block aren't for the faint of heart. They stock the classics: goat shoulders; legs of lamb; chicken gizzards; goat belly. The stranger cuts include beef rump; slick, scarlet beef kidney; hulking pig feet that, when uncooked, have a disturbing air of overgrown human teeth but are beloved by a certain generation of the French and West Africans alike. Multiple kinds of tripe are on offer, too—mostly beef, though sometimes sheep—their vague resemblance to untreated leather belied by the sponge-like undersides. There are cuts of beef cheek, thin sandwich-like layers of skin, fat, and muscle. And lastly, the famous sheep heads, used for a dish eaten around Eid al-Adha, mainly by Moroccans and Algerians. Heads on display mark the butchers' territory, as if they were sending a message to the uninitiated: *Don't come here unless you know what you're getting into.*

The fruit and vegetables on display at the end of the street and around the corner are maybe the most impressive of all. This is one of the only spots in Paris where you can find okra— *gombo* in French—the gooey, pepper-like vegetable that gives the famous Louisiana dish its thick sauce (and probably its name, too). There are assorted chili peppers, a rarity in metropolitan France where people's tolerance for spiciness tends to run low. There's a panoply of starchy African root vegetables: earthy, light-brown cassavas; bright orange sweet potatoes that glimmer in the sun; yams from Ghana, stacked up like firewood; their hairier, more exotic-looking cousins from Cameroon, taros; and lesser-known white sweet potatoes. There are also plantains and African eggplants—sometimes dubbed "garden eggs" in English but known in Paris, as in West Africa, as *djakatou*, a fruit that looks like a cross between an heirloom green tomato and a miniature pumpkin.

The Rue Dejean is the gateway to the Goutte d'Or, one of the city's most famous working-class neighborhoods—what the French call *quartiers populaires*. Goutte d'Or has managed to retain that distinction over the years, even as the geographic origins of residents have evolved, with the center of gravity moving from metropolitan France to the Maghreb to sub-Saharan Africa in the space of the last forty years or so. In this small section of the city—about a half-square-kilometer expanse that can be traversed north–south by foot in about fifteen minutes, from Rue Ordener to Boulevard de la Chapelle, and east–west in just five minutes, from Rue Stephenson to Rue Poissonniers—the streets hum with the energy created by residents and workers as they busily go about their routines.

While hundreds might be running errands in the Goutte d'Or at any given moment, hunting for products they couldn't possibly find just ten minutes away in either direction, hundreds more are at work, giving life to a constellation of small stores. They're weighing fruits at the cashier; they're cooking up grilled *thiof* and rice at a Senegalese restaurant as mbalax music buzzes out from an old TV mounted to the ceiling, the syncopated rhythms and horns reminding customers they're in a friendly place; they're stocking the shelves at a stuffy import-export establishment where the paint on the wall is cracking but which still manages to scrape by; they're toiling away at one of the textile stores that you see just about everywhere.

Hundreds more in the Goutte d'Or are sitting around idly, not doing much at all. On any given day of the week, young men hang around the Place de l'Assommoir, chatting in Arabic, chain-smoking, playing games on their phones, calling out to friends and acquaintances, and eyeing the not-infrequent police patrols coming from the station down the road. When the weather's nice, people hang around the Square Léon, one of the area's rare green spaces.

There always seems to be a group of people at a café just off Rue Poissonniers. The place can get pretty packed on weekend afternoons. On one such day, a group of older men were playing cards toward the back of the room. Another group was reading their newspapers. Others stood at the zinc countertop, sipping espresso for €1.10, and gesturing with their hands as the conversation got more animated. Sugar packets lined the floor just under the countertop. One of the butchers from around the corner came in and asked the bartender for change, both of them acting like they're familiar with the transaction. A man got up from a table next to the bar to show the bartender a meme on his phone, chortling with laughter, before the latter politely smiled. Sitting by himself, a dazed-looking older man in a djellaba stared off into the distance.

Neighborhoods are complex organisms, strange beasts that feed off geographical quirks, public policy, and a web of inter-personal relations that can't really be understood unless you're a part of it. But more than anything else, the bustle of the Goutte d'Or is sustained by the fact that low-income people can still afford to live here. According to the popular French real estate site SeLoger, the average sales price per square meter in the Goutte d'Or is nearly 20 percent less than the Parisian average—and that's based on a very generous interpretation of where the neighborhood begins.[1] One can still find small studios to rent for €500 or €600 a month here, especially in the easternmost streets.

Deals like these still exist, though it's unclear for how much longer. All signs suggest the screws are tightening.

In addition to the cramped space, bargain apartments come with some serious strings attached: a shared bathroom in the hallway; a shower door that opens up right next to a pair of charred hot plates; a single window overlooking a courtyard that captures just a few hours' worth of natural light; a ground floor apartment on a busy thoroughfare. These conditions are on the edge of what many would-be residents can tolerate. They automatically disqualify other would-be residents who simply can't handle the neighborhood itself—and yet, like just about every resident in Paris, they are subjected to skyrocketing rents. From 2015 to 2020, housing prices shot up in the Goutte d'Or by about 40 percent.[2]

The warning signs of an even deeper transformation can be found on the streets. There's a new all-organic vegan restaurant by the fruit and vegetable stands near the metro station, and a spiffy-looking music hall and bar a few blocks from the Square Léon; the plaza in front of the neo-Gothic Saint-Bernard-de-la-Chapelle church now hosts a couple of restaurants that cater to a very different population from the café by the Marché Dejean. Instead of old Algerian men drinking coffee and playing cards, young professionals tap away on their laptops. Some put on headphones and take work calls, tuning out their surroundings as if they were nowhere in particular.

The contrasts are even more striking around the Barbès-Rochechouart metro station, just at the southern edge of the Goutte d'Or. Another spot infamous for young men idling around—and with an unfortunate reputation for petty crime—the intersection known simply as Barbès sits under an elevated metro line. On one side of the boulevard sits the corpse of the shuttered department store Tati, a neighborhood landmark known for affordable clothing that didn't manage to survive the Covid-19 pandemic. On the other sits Brasserie Barbès, a two-story behemoth that opened a few years ago and is topped with an ostentatious neon sign that looks like it was designed in Las Vegas. It has the prices to boot: you can enjoy €15 cheeseburgers with a €5.50 glass of Coca-Cola.

* * *

Many people living in cities are familiar with the script: land-lords and developers swoop into previously affordable neighborhoods with fresh investment dollars; they drive up housing costs, revamp many of the businesses, and eventually alter the fabric of the place as lower-income residents are forced to flee. The process is especially brutal in the wealthiest urban centers in North America, Europe, and Asia—magnets for white-collar professionals with savings, wealthy investors with cash to plunk down, and developers looking for a piece of the action. By now, most of these so-called global cities have seen this cycle of investment and displacement play out multiple times over, leaving many low-income residents on the brink.

The same wave of gentrification is hitting Paris, too—and it's hitting hard.

While the numbers can be mind-numbing to anyone familiar with price hikes in their own communities, they're worth focusing on because the spike here is especially massive. Between 2006 and 2018, the median sales price per square meter for an apartment in the city grew by a whopping 73 percent—and in late 2019, average prices surpassed the symbolic threshold of €10,000 per square meter.[3] They're now just below €11,000, according to the website SeLoger.[4]

At this point, home ownership has essentially become a privilege reserved for the wealthy or the lucky who manage to squirrel away their savings for a chance at the bottom of the barrel. In a 2020 analysis, housing experts from the government's statistics agency, the National Institute of Statistics and Economic Studies (INSEE), declared that home ownership in Paris had become "nearly inaccessible" for a majority of renters—a goal intertwined with some amount of personal sacrifice: "For many renters in the region," they wrote, "becoming a homeowner effectively implies leaving one's neighborhood."

Under the authors' model, there is not a single arrondissement in the French capital where median-income renters under the age of forty-five can afford to purchase an apartment.[5]

But Paris has long been a city of tenants—and of course, the rents have become punishing too. At a cost of €24 per square meter, the average monthly rent for a privately owned apartment in Paris now hovers at around €1,200, or the equivalent of $1,270 and £1,057.[6] While those figures may not impress on the streets of Manhattan or West London, they're staggering when you consider the size of what's on offer and how much French people tend to earn: the average Parisian apartment measures just fifty square meters and the median French wage-earner in the private sector takes home a monthly paycheck of just €2,000 after social security contributions.[7] Parisians without some amount of financial means are spending extraordinary amounts of their earnings to live in extraordinarily small spaces.

Even when compared with other hubs of international capital, Paris is on the upper end of the spectrum with respect to housing costs. In a 2022 annual report on global housing prices, the bank UBS ranked Paris thirteenth worldwide for costs—just outside the category it defines as the "bubble risk" zone and ahead of competitors like Dubai, Geneva, London, and New York.[8]

The city's price-to-income ratio is off the charts, too. In that same 2022 report, UBS estimated it would take a "skilled service worker" fifteen years to save enough money to buy a sixty-square-meter flat—the greatest length of time among any of the cities analyzed with the exception of famously cramped Hong Kong. In large part for the same reason, Paris regularly competes for the dubious top spot in the Economist Intelligence Unit's Worldwide Cost of Living Index, an annual ranking of the world's most expensive cities. In the 2021 edition, the French capital finished second, just behind Tel Aviv.[9]

Under these pressures, many residents don't have the endurance to stick around. Since 2014, Paris has been losing about 12,000 inhabitants every year, the vast majority of the emigrants taking up residence in the suburbs and staying within the broader capital region known as Île-de-France.[10] Before the outbreak of Covid, France's INSEE reported that it expected the population decline to continue until at least the middle of the decade—a trend that has proven resilient throughout the pandemic.[11] Unlike London and New York, population loss isn't just a fear.[12] Paris is already losing its population today, expelling its residents to a sprawling, suburban mass that's now much more inhabited than the city itself. According to the official figures, the larger Paris metropolitan area now has a whopping 11 million inhabitants, nearly 9 million of whom live in the suburbs—the *banlieue*, in French.[13]

This means the face of the city is changing. The share of Parisian residents who fit the traditional census definitions of working class[14] has declined from 35 percent in 1999 to just 26 percent today—a stark contrast to the 51 percent of the total labor force such workers represent nationally.[15] By contrast, the white-collar professional population has surged—investment bankers, consultants, publicists for luxury fashion brands, and armies of mid-level managers at companies listed on the CAC 40 stock exchange such as Total, Dannon, and Orange. Known in French as *cadres*, this group now makes up 45 percent of the Parisian workforce, up from 35 percent in 1999. That's well above their share of the national labor force.

How did this happen? How did a place whose working masses were long feared for their capacity for violent revolt end up emptied of so many of them? How did a city that acquired a well-earned reputation as a creative refuge and artistic mecca, a hub for the avant-garde for much of the twentieth century, become overwhelmingly populated by some of the dullest professions that capitalism has to offer? It's the product of particular political choices made by France's ruling elites, fueled by globalization, tourism, and foreign investors looking for a place to park their cash. That's part of the story.

At the same time, I don't want to fall into the trap of a wistful tale of woe, wallowing in nostalgia for a city that no longer exists—as tempting of an exercise that might be. Because the fact is, without exaggerating its size or influence, this other Paris isn't quite dead yet. It exists mostly outside the gaze of the tourists, the bankers, and the consultants, but with a little bit of time and patience, you can still find it. It's alive in the Goutte d'Or, on the slopes of Belleville, across the alleyways and the streets snaking around the northeast of the city, and in the public housing towers scattered toward the peripheries. This shadow city is still around today, as real as the cobblestones, gray zinc roofs, and dusty railyards cutting through its neighborhoods.

These parts of the city can be loud, they can be messy, and every once in a while, they can be just a bit dangerous, defying the image that real estate developers have crafted for the city over the last few decades—refusing to abide by the half-theme-park, half-museum ambiance that prevails in much of central Paris. Unlike the ossified quarters downtown, long ago colonized by the wealthy and hordes of short-term visitors, working-class Paris does not run on nostalgia. Residents are focused on getting by, on making it today.

There's still a lot to play for too. Housing activists are organizing and putting pressure on authorities to help keep the city affordable. In the meantime, the growing exodus to the other side of the ring-road highway separating Paris from its suburbs has only highlighted what's long been apparent: the need for more egalitarian policies that treat the metropolitan area as a unified whole. Tearing down the borders between the capital and banlieue once and for all likely holds the key to a more fair and livable urban area.

This book is separated into three major parts: The first focuses on the working-class Paris of today, the northeastern patch of the city where most low-income residents are still living. In some cases, they're facing immense financial pressures, but many are still holding on. The second part focuses on the ghosts: the people who preceded them, the battles they fought, and the city they built. From the Revolution of 1789 to the Paris Commune of 1871, poor and working-class Parisians fought not just for dignity and material gains, but for actual political control of the neighborhoods in which they lived. And while they ultimately lost that war, their power and influence paved the way for a string of tenant-friendly policies that enabled the city to remain affordable and to emerge as a global hub for the arts. The third and final part focuses on what the future holds: the battle to deliver affordable housing and life in the working-class suburbs, a swarm of cities that often look very different from Paris, but where people deserve something closer to the standards of living that can be found in the capital.

This is not meant to be a sob story. It's meant as a portrait of a city that, while on the ropes, is still very much around. In the end, I hope it's also, in some way, a call to action.

1

THE OTHER SIDE OF THE HILL

The first time we met, in the summer of 2020, just after the first lockdown, then thirty-four-year-old Soumia Chohra called her ground floor apartment on the Rue Marcadet a "rathole."[1] She was careful to insist she meant this literally. At night, Soumia described how she could hear the rats scurrying in the courtyard, which lies just outside the only window of her twenty-square-meter flat. "They're as big as this," she told me, drawing a line from her fingertips to a third of the way down her forearm. "They're everywhere."

To deal with the problem, she and her partner Amin, a warehouse worker who earns minimum wage at a Carrefour supermarket at Place de la Nation, almost always sleep with the windows closed. Even in the summer, they prefer the heat and humidity to the risk of nocturnal visitors. The two sleep on a mattress tucked away on a mezzanine accessible by a ladder that comes unnervingly close to the ceiling. That's also where they've placed containers to store their clothes and other belongings.

A small table sits just beneath this area, though taller guests need to be careful to sit on the side closest to the door to avoid banging their heads on the makeshift stairs. There are hot plates and a microwave, but no oven. Sometimes the couple also hosts Amin's ten-year-old daughter, who sleeps on a separate mattress on the floor, just next to the entrance. Soumia feels for her: "At her mom's, she has a big room, but when the poor thing comes here, she has to sleep here. She doesn't like it."

Soumia has gotten to know this space very well. After starting her career with a string of service jobs, she recently dropped out of a training program to become a medical secretary for health reasons—the result of a condition known as "intracranial hypertension" that produces debilitating headaches. With Covid ushering in lockdowns across France for much of the last two years, she's had little choice but to spend most of her waking hours inside this apartment. In spite of it all, she gives off a disarmingly cheery vibe, deploying a bright smile and the occasional dose of self-deprecating humor.

When I saw her again, about nine months after our first meeting, her friend Fatima, also from Algeria, passed by the apartment and offered to make some coffee. Soumia lit up a cigarette and smoke quickly filled the studio, enveloping all of us in what feels like a matter of seconds. "You live in a cave!" exclaimed Fatima, with Soumia letting out a hearty laugh as she translated from Arabic. Then she sighed, as if to acknowledge the much less funny subtext of the joke: this space costs €800 a month to rent.

It's a ridiculously steep price, but such is the reality today: this is the cost for Soumia to stay in the neighborhood she grew up in, ever since immigrating from Algeria with her mother twenty-two years ago. It's a very deliberate choice. When Soumia decided to move out of her mother's apartment around three years ago and began to look for a new spot with her partner, there was no doubt where she wanted to go. "My husband found cheaper spots in the suburbs, but it was out of the question for me to leave here. I have an attachment to this arrondissement," she said. "I love the neighborhood, I have my points of reference."

That arrondissement is the 18th. While she lives within the limits of what many think of as the Goutte d'Or, Soumia considers that neighborhood to begin a few blocks further south, near all the fishmongers and butchers at the Marché Dejean. Instead, she says she lives around "Marcadet"—the name of her street. It's about smack dab in the middle of the 18th, itself in the northern reaches of Paris. Around two hundred thousand people are packed into this district's six square kilometers, a rectangle stretching from the picturesque hill of Montmartre to the ring-road highway that marks the city's northern limits, from leafy bourgeois apartments in the west to the railyards and the gritty La Chapelle in the east.

Of the city's twenty arrondissements, you'd be hard pressed to find one more representative of Paris as a whole: the western section features spellbindingly elegant apartments overlooking squares and green spaces, and on the slopes of Montmartre, tourists commingle with the bourgeois residents. But once you start moving east, down the other side of the hill, toward the train tracks, things start changing quickly. You start picking up languages other than French and English. It's more common to see puffy jackets and sneakers than sightseers in berets and old white ladies in fur.

Soumia's sister has already left all this. She now lives in the eastern suburban *département* of Seine-et-Marne, in a modestly sized single-family home known as a *pavillon*, a residence that in the French collective imagination epitomizes the notion of settling down, with all the comforts and pitfalls that entails. Soumia enjoys the visits out there—there's more air and more space—but she feels out of her element. When she gets off the exit ramp from the highway and reaches a sprawling intersection just within the city limits, it's a source of relief.

"I get stressed when I'm driving, but as soon as I get to the Porte de Clignancourt, I know I'm in the 18th," she said. "It calms me down, strangely. It makes me feel at ease to be in the 18th."

Many of her friends have also decamped to the suburbs over the years, fleeing because of rising rents and the lack of space for raising families. Soumia, though, enjoys the proximity to her mother, to her friends who have stayed, and to the simple pleasures of life in the neighborhood: picnics in the park just below the Sacré-Coeur Basilica, the string of restaurants on the Rue Ordener near the 18th arrondissement city hall, and nights out at bars like L'Ardoise, which her father-in-law used to own a stake in before he sold it a couple years ago. It's all within walking distance of her flat. "I have trouble separating myself from all these habits," she said.

Above all, perhaps, Soumia appreciates the diverse mix of people: "You can see everything here, artists down here, homeless people up there," she said with a smile. "There's a lot of movement. There's people of every race, from every country, white people, Black people, Arabs, Chinese people, people from every nationality."

Soumia herself is a product of the same northern Parisian melting pot.

When she arrived from Saïda, Algeria, in 1999, age thirteen, she spoke little French. Starting middle school at the Collège Georges Clemenceau, about three hundred meters from where she lives today, she was put in a class with other foreign students who needed to improve their language skills—many of them, like her, of North African origin. "I had no friends," she recalled, "I knew nobody. It was really hard to just change everything overnight." She went on to finish middle school at the Collège Roland Dorgelès, just on the other side of Boulevard Barbès.

Things got better in high school. Soumia attended what's known as a *lycée professionnel*, a vocational school for those who don't plan to attend university, in the neighborhood of La Chapelle, just over a kilometer east on the other side of the train tracks. She specialized in international commerce, combining her studies with work experience in a two-year program. She didn't care much for the job portion, which she spent at the supermarket Monoprix. "My mom forced me to do it," Soumia told me. "I wanted to do plumbing, but my mom felt like this was a job for men, so I found myself in commerce."

But she cherishes the friends she made along the way. "Honestly, it was the two best years of my life. If I could go back those two years, I would do it again," Soumia said with a laugh. Among the many fond memories: going to the movies, smoking *shisha* at tea salons (and hiding it from their parents), swimming at city pools, and posting up at cafés, spending lazy afternoons in front of coffees and cocktails.

Life has gotten much harder in recent years. Soumia herself acknowledges her career hasn't gone as planned and she isn't proud of it. Before the secretarial training program, she bounced around in a number of different gigs—working as an employee for the national unemployment agency, as a cleaner, as a housekeeper, and as a sales representative for a nearby real estate broker. Today, she receives modest state welfare benefits and is back on the hunt for a job. She recently applied for a position with the postal service as a mail carrier, but was turned down.

Still, her husband Amin works full-time, and Soumia has held down jobs in the past, enough of them to put thousands of euros in the bank. At an earlier point in the history of the city, this would've been enough to live decently in the neighborhood—if not in extreme comfort, then at least in better conditions than in the cramped apartment they have today. Now, it's just barely enough.

It's near impossible for Soumia to even imagine owning an apartment here someday. A glimpse at real estate listings reveals why the subject isn't even broached: a twenty-three-square-meter studio just a block away is going for €205,000; a thirty-one-square-meter flat around the corner can be purchased for €302,000; a spacious sixty-square-meter apartment goes for €470,000. The best she can hope for is to find affordable rent.

Soumia and Amin have already applied for what's known as social housing, publicly managed flats rented out to tenants whose household incomes fall below a certain level. But the Paris waiting list is famously long and they aren't holding their breath. In 2020, just one in sixteen candidates formally seeking social housing in Paris and its immediate suburbs was awarded a spot.[2] It might be a couple of years before a civil servant even takes a look at their file, inspecting it down to every line and weighing it up against the competition. The reality is a lot of people are in a similar bind—odds are some of them are even brushing up against Soumia and Amin in the neighbor-hood. More than 130,000 Parisians are on the waiting list for social housing, according to the city.[3]

In the meantime, Soumia and Amin are hoping to avail themselves of what's known as their "enforceable right to hous-ing": an option under French law open to those who are home-less, those living in dangerous and unsanitary conditions, and those who have waited "abnormally long" for social housing, among other factors. With the help of a housing rights associa-tion recommended by Soumia's mother-in-law, the couple has put in a formal request to a state mediator to give them access to improved lodging. According to Soumia, the mediator has already ruled in their favor, but they're now waiting for the next step in the process: the Paris police prefecture has to for-mally present a solution within the next six months. "I think we're the next ones on the list," Soumia told me. "We're just waiting for it to get unblocked."

There's no guarantee it'll be in the 18th arrondissement. If they're lucky, they'll be able to stay in Paris.

One of the most striking things about this corner of Paris is the absolute whirlwind of activity packed into such a tight space—the fact that so many distinctly ordered worlds can exist over just a couple dozen blocks, each of them with complex histo-ries and weighty rules of their own, with various landmarks, workplaces, and housing blocks all exerting competing pulls on one another. High-grade vortexes like these have long sus-tained the world's great cities, but they're increasingly hard to find in Europe or North America today. In fact, the density of the 18th arrondissement is closer to something you'd find in India or Southeast Asia.

If it were its own municipality, this arrondissement would be the twelfth-most populated city in France, with nearly as many residents as Salt Lake City, Utah, or Swindon, England—but all of it squeezed into a tiny stretch of land with precious little green space, and pockmarked by train tracks that officials long ago decided were too important to move. Paris and its twenty arrondissements are already famously cramped, denser than Barcelona, central London, New York City, and even Hong Kong. But with over 32,000 inhabitants for every square kilometer, the 18th arrondissement of Paris ranks as one of the densest areas on the entire planet, on par with places like Dhaka, Karachi, and Mumbai.

You can feel it by looking up. The buildings tend not to be higher than seven stories, but they're literally everywhere, dominating the cityscape. Excepting the outer edges of the arrondissement, only one boulevard truly cuts through the swarm of brick and stone: Ornano, which becomes Boulevard Barbès on its lower stretch, a tree-lined artery that boasts four lanes of traffic. The overwhelming majority of streets in the 18th hold only one or two lanes, meekly cut trails in the forest of gray, while pedestrians spend most of their waking hours in the shadows.

It's almost always busy. That's not the case for much of Paris today, where the residential sectors quiet down during work hours, the business districts wind down by early evening, and certain areas only come alive at night. In the 18th, the action is around the clock: people are living, working, and idling around at nearly all hours—and in close proximity to one another. It's overflowing with what American urbanists might a call a "mix of uses"—what journalist Jane Jacobs famously identified as one of the key ingredients to desirable city living in her 1961 classic

The Death and Life of Great American Cities—though the French would just say it's a historically affordable neighborhood with a lot of restaurants and *commerces de proximité*, small businesses providing essential daily services. There are cafés serving up bitter espresso on zinc countertops; barbershops and butcheries; hardware stores and florists; bakeries and pastry shops with delicate North African baklava and *cornes de gazelle*; fast-food joints churning out €5 pizza and the indomitable "French tacos" (always with an *s*, even when there's just one), a gob of cheese-soaked fries and meat stuffed into a tightly compressed flour tortilla that has become popular in recent years; bars that cater to punks, drunks, students, pensioners, and gamblers. Not everything is nice, but there's a lot to be had.

Certain blocks are shaped more heavily by the presence of specific industries and institutions. In the heart of the Goutte d'Or, near the metro station Château Rouge, it's clearly the textile sector that dominates, with dozens of stores advertising "African tissue." That catch-all term refers to cotton-based fabric with colorful designs and elaborate patterns that can be cut and worn in a variety of ways. Sometimes one can find fabrics like *bazin*, *bogolan*, *kita*, and *kente*—but the most popular, by far, is *wax*, first brought to West Africa by Dutch merchants from Java in the nineteenth century, now a mainstay of the region and beloved by expats abroad.

"You see all this enthusiasm?" Saloum Abdallahy (or as he's commonly known, Monsieur Fadel), the slim, bespectacled designer and founder of Fadel Couture, asked me in his workshop as the sound of sewing machines whirred in the background. "This enthusiasm is created simply because Africans like to live together. When someone gets here for the first time, the first thing they ask for is Château Rouge, because they know they'll find Africans. His problems are almost resolved. He'll have a place to sleep, he'll have financial help, he'll have moral help. . . . It's why when designers get here, their first base they get settled in is the 18th arrondissement. It's very important."

If that sense of generosity and penchant for collaboration sound slightly overstated, it's because Abdallahy heads an organization aiming to harness both in pursuit of the garment sector's development. Back in 2014, he helped create the designers' cooperative, La Fabrique de la Goutte d'Or, an organization that pools resources in order to improve access to clients, some of them big-ticket European brands. "We needed to listen to everybody and that's what we did, to better serve everybody's needs," he explained.

According to Abdallahy, there are 151 different fashion designers in the neighborhood—and they run the gamut in terms of quality and labor practices. In addition to small boutiques like his own that offer prêt-à-porter at steep prices, large wholesalers churn out custom orders, while hundreds work in lower-tier shops for bosses who seem to have a very loose interpretation of the fire code, toiling away on sewing machines surrounded by stacks and stacks of fabric. It's a rough and uneven industry, sustained by ambitious entrepreneurs and heavy demand.

"When you have a store there, you can earn a lot," Yolande Loboko, a designer who first arrived in France from the Congo in 2001, told me. She joined the Goutte d'Or cooperative in 2016 before recently opening her own store about twenty minutes away, which specializes in custom-made patterned dresses. "It's not just the people from the 18th—you have other people coming from outside of Paris, they're coming from everywhere. It's a good neighborhood for business."

A few blocks north, with the garment district faded from view, the Ornano Market engulfs the boulevard every Tuesday, Friday, and Sunday morning—and it's far from picturesque. Among the non-perishable goods, the plastic and the practical predominate. As with any supermarket, the produce is emphatically mediocre; the fishmongers are totally fine but unremarkable; the cheese perfectly acceptable. The main attraction of the market is that it's inexpensive, which means it tends to get very crowded. For reasons that nobody can fully explain, many of the stands spilling onto the sidewalk are staffed by Egyptians who lack French-language skills, but who overcome the hurdles in the diverging Arabic dialects to communicate with the many North African customers and deploy a select few words in the language of Molière when needed—*bananes*, *tomates*, *oignons*, *oranges*, *céleri*, and *euro*—rolling the *r*'s as if they were speaking Spanish.

Just a couple blocks east, it's the Serbian language that reigns supreme. The Rue du Simplon hosts a Serbian restaurant and a couple of general food stores selling specialty foods from the Balkans. Storefronts advertise trips to Belgrade. An early-opening bar hosts older men who drink and chain-smoke from around 10 a.m. onward. But the obvious center of the action is Saint-Sava, the main church for the diocese of the Serbian Orthodox Church of Western Europe. It counts more than two thousand regular worshippers, according to Father Slavisa Sanjic, a priest who's been at the institution since 2003. On Sundays, the street fills with families.

Inside, Sanjic showed me a fresco designed to demonstrate the tolerance of the church, whose nationalist political ties came under scrutiny after the ethnic violence of the Yugoslav Wars of the 1990s. "We're proud of what we have in our culture but we're not closed off," Sanjic said to me before gesturing at the mural depicting people of different origins enclosed in a golden semi-circle. "Every person is a source of richness, whatever their origins may be. All these human categories are going to disappear after the Final Judgment, no? . . . It means nothing afterwards. What matters is, have we been nice to people around us and loyal to the word of Christ?"

He told me that in the neighborhood he's been confused for a devout Muslim, because of his black robe and beard. One time, a man who appeared intoxicated saluted him on the street: "My brother! You are a real Muslim!" the man said. "I am not," Sanjic replied. "And neither are you."

Around the corner is the realm of the Paris transit authority. The Simplon bus depot is the largest within city limits, a four-hectare zone closed to the public that is packed with more than two hundred buses every night. It's why people mill around a nearby café at unusual hours, swilling coffee or sipping pints of *blonde* depending on whether they're beginning or ending a shift. Union delegates linger around, talking shop with drivers and boosting their presence when it's time to elect workplace representatives or organize strikes. The arrivals and departures of buses structure the days, the squeaking of the brakes and hissing air releases providing a rhythmic backdrop that residents have no choice but to get used to.

Then there's the Wild West of the Porte de Clignancourt, the intersection at the northern edge of Paris where the boulevard ends and where Soumia Chohra feels relieved to come back to after trips to the suburbs. It sits right next to the elevated highway that surrounds Paris proper. At this spot along the fortification, the neighboring town of Saint-Ouen also happens to host a massive, world-famous flea market, a draw that only adds to the flow of traffic that begins in early rush hour and continues into the early evening.

Against a hazy backdrop of exhaust, men loiter throughout the day around the tramway station and by the stairs leading down to the underground metro stop. Some set up pop-up food stands, selling peanuts and bananas without permits. Another crew has been hosting a game of three-card monte for what seems like years, with a crowd hulking around and placing "bets" in the hopes of catching gullible takers. Others sell knockoff cigarettes, delivering their ubiquitous, rapid-fire sales pitch of "Marlboro, Marlboro, Marlboro" in a second or less. Others peddle harder stuff, crisscrossing the tramway tracks to make deals virtually in plain view, as though they were in the backyard of their friends' place. Despite the regular interventions of law enforcement, these illicit sales are part of a cat-and-mouse game that's been going on for decades. The police come in, sometimes they issue citations or make arrests. But once they clear out, the vendors come back.

This is what the heart of working-class Paris—or what's left of it—looks like today. And it goes well beyond the 18th. Starting from around Boulevard Ornano and extending eastward into the 19th arrondissement, then south into the 20th arrondissement, through La Villette and Belleville, this northeastern patch of the city is home to most of the last remaining affordable neighborhoods. There are pockets of public housing scattered elsewhere on the edges of Paris: enclaves that line what are known as the Boulevards des Maréchaux, wide thoroughfares named for Napoleonic-era generals that encircle the city, as well as an ensemble of towers in the southern limits of the 13th arrondissement, but these areas are cut off from their

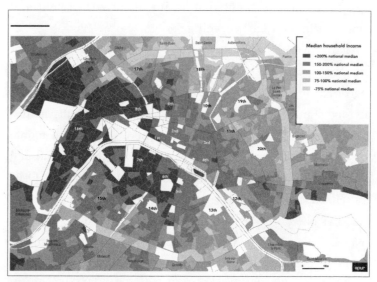

Neighborhoods classified by average income levels. *Map courtesy of Anne Servais, Paris Urbanism Agency, 2022, based on 2019 data.*

immediate surroundings. In the northeast, there is continuity, a form of interconnectedness and interdependence. You can walk for twenty minutes and still feel like you're in the same part of the city.

These neighborhoods have complex identities of their own—particular characters and secrets; innumerable flaws and scars; rites and traditions that may apply only to a few blocks—but their territories still manage to flow into one another, united by the hectic pace of life, diverse street activity, and the fact that most of their residents are earning on the lower end of the spectrum in an increasingly wealthy and expensive city. These areas aren't always pretty. The hustle and bustle can take time to get adjusted to—and even, then, they're not for everybody. But for hundreds of thousands of Parisians, it's what home looks like.

In many ways, the northeastern quarters are the front lines for the battle over the future of Paris. Other more centrally located parts of the city have fallen before them, with rent hikes displacing residents as the gentrifiers remake, renovate, and erase the more unsightly features of city life over the years. But the real estate boom hasn't fully extended its stranglehold over the northeast, at least not yet.

The word "gentrification" was coined by British sociologist Ruth Glass. In 1964, she noted how certain historically low-income neighborhoods in London were seeing an influx of new, middle-class residents. Once the process begins, she wrote, "it goes on rapidly until all or most of the original working-class occupiers are displaced, and the whole social character of the district is changed."[4] Her explanation appears in a short piece that only uses the g-word once—but Glass laid down the foundations for a topic that would go on to attract generations of sociologists, geographers, and economists.

Perhaps the most influential of them was Neil Smith, a Scottish-born American geographer who studied under fellow British Marxist David Harvey and who argued this process was not the product of individual consumer choices; rather, it was bound up in the very nature of capitalism. Gentrification is embedded into the economic system—it is "a structural product of the land and housing markets," as Smith put it in his landmark 1979 paper.[5] Since housing, like the power of labor, is a commodity, city streets naturally attract landlords and developers looking to make the right investment in the right place at the right time.

But he also developed a theory for why it happens. According to Smith, the driving force was what he called the "rent

gap": the difference between existing rental incomes on a giv-
en apartment or a plot of land and what presumptive owners
think they might be able to charge at a future date for the property in question. The core argument is disarmingly simple: if
there are opportunities to turn a profit on a piece of land, then
investment will follow. Over time, this process reshapes whole
city neighborhoods, as developers swoop in to get a piece of the
action.

Investments may very well be welcomed on the ground, especially when existing land prices are low. Few would complain
about, say, a bookstore that replaces a sketchy-looking massage
parlor that only opens after 7 p.m., or a small Mexican restaurant with neon lights that fills an empty storefront where the
gutter punks and their Rottweilers used to hang out. But when
existing land prices are higher, the changes can be harder to
swallow—think an independent bookstore transformed into a
bank, or an old neighborhood haunt that becomes a bland retail
clothing outlet. By the time new condominiums go up and
nearby residents start trickling out, most people with a sense of
decency feel like something has gone wrong. In any case, each
of these scenarios represents a form of capital accumulation,
driven by the pursuit of profit.

Smith's framework remains a helpful way of thinking about
gentrification, which has evolved into a buzzword whose
true meaning can feel murky. As with the "culture wars" or
"identity politics," nearly everyone agrees that gentrification
is everywhere—and yet, it's not always clear exactly what it
is they're talking about. A gluten-free bakery that opens on a
sketchy-looking street? Bike lanes? Young artists showing up
in poor neighborhoods? Smith's rent gap thesis, refined over
time and backed up with reams of data, helps cut through the

noise.[6] In the end, gentrification is about the increase of property values in urban areas. Rather than a temporary trend that hinges on the shifting preferences of young creative professionals, it is a trait of profit-seeking investment—a fundamental part of how cities work in contemporary capitalism.

Of course, the transformations don't happen overnight, and they often differ a great deal—even within the same city. When trying to make sense of this famously unwieldy term, it can also be helpful to think of it as a process with multiple stages. In this sense, the framework developed by American researcher Phillip Clay can bring some clarity.

In 1979, Clay identified four different phases of gentrification: in the first phase, "pioneers" move to run-down areas in search of low rents; they're soon followed by members of the middle class in Phase Two; in the third phase, the area's original working-class population can't keep up with costs and starts leaving; in the fourth and final phase, the wealthy come in and fully claim the neighborhood for themselves.[7] A taxonomy like this can make it easier to discuss what's happening in certain regional cities today—say, to identify the different phases of gentrification underway in New Orleans and Denver or Leeds and Liverpool. It even works for thinking about certain parts of northeastern Paris.

More recently, though, the American journalist P.E. Moskowitz—among others—has suggested maybe the framework needs an additional fifth stage to capture the process underway in the world's wealthiest cities. In certain parts of Manhattan, as Moskowitz astutely noted, real estate prices are so out of control that even wealthy residents and top-tier shops are having trouble keeping up.[8] At this stage of the game, architects and bankers are being replaced by executives and oil heiresses.

Brand-name retailers are giving way to even higher-end luxury brands.

This fifth-stage madness applies to parts of central Paris, too. Between lockdowns and waves of the pandemic, iconic bookseller Gibert Jeune announced it'd be shuttering two of its stores in the Latin Quarter. The rents here have long been out of control—this is the land of Airbnb and students relying on support from wealthy parents—but it was a brutal reminder that nobody's spared. Today's real estate market holds no prisoners, even if the victim happens to be the biggest bookstore in Paris by square footage and even if its stores have been in the same location near the Sorbonne since the late nineteenth century. In January 2022, reports suggested a new Five Guys might replace one of the old bookstores.[9] It'd be an eyesore for sure, tragic even—on the other hand, it'd fit in fine with the Chipotle and Starbucks just around the corner, on the Boulevard Saint-Germain.

Toward the end of his career, Neil Smith himself had recognized that globalization was ratcheting up gentrification to another level.[10] Not only were growing cities in the Global South also seeing spikes in land values and the displacement of low-income residents, but by the early twenty-first century, these trends had reached dizzying new heights in the most economically powerful global cities. Hubs for international finance and magnets for lucrative, interconnected industries, cities like London, New York, and Paris had begun to experience even more aggressive forms of gentrification, booms fueled by global cash flows.

This is true on a visceral level—if you stroll around inner London these days, Ruth Glass's descriptions of Islington in the mid-1960s can seem almost quaint. Just imagine a unit in any one of the new condominium complexes that spring up today in Shoreditch or in the City of London: the complex might have been built by an American developer and designed by a Swiss architect; the unit could belong to an Emirati construction scion, and if so, he probably accrued his wealth on the backs of immigrant labor from Southeast Asia; at the end of the day, a British bank likely drew up his mortgage. His work is globalized, his fortune is globalized, and so is his worldview. When he started thinking about buying a new apartment, he probably wasn't even considering Manchester or Liverpool—the alternatives were Dubai or Paris.

Other fundamental changes in global capitalism may be accelerating the trend. As the urbanist Samuel Stein has argued, another big reason why gentrification has intensified over the last couple decades is the increasingly central role played by real estate in the world's wealthiest urban economies. Stein's work *Capital City* focuses on New York and the U.S., where state support for renters is far more limited than in Europe, but his arguments provide a valuable frame of reference.[11]

For the first half of the twentieth century, the expansion of cities relied heavily on the growth of industry. Slowly but surely, that began to change in the postwar years, with advances in technology and new international treaties encouraging investors to move supply chains away from where large concentrations of consumers were located. Certain cities have navigated this shift in economic activity more successfully than others—with sectors like the arts, entertainment, media, tech, consulting, and low-wage services all plugging the gap. But as Stein shows, finance and real estate tend to do much of the heavy lifting.

Today, real estate holdings make up a majority of the world's assets. Valued at more than $320 trillion, they're worth far more than gold, equities, or debt securities—and much of that sum is concentrated in the world's wealthiest cities.[12] According to calculations from French housing experts, Paris real estate alone is worth over €700 billion, on par with the annual GDP of Turkey or Switzerland.[13] Luxury apartments may not be the most productive investments, but these highly valued assets generate a lot of revenue for city coffers, since both homeowners and businesses in France pay land taxes to municipal authorities.

As Stein underlines, public authorities have generally come to accept this trade-off as well. The tax revenues are too good to pass up; the model has proven to be acceptable politically; and once it's in place, it's often not worth burning bridges over with key economic players. Urban planners aren't necessarily dead set on inflating property values or kicking out low-income people. This just happens to be an effective mode of governance for de-industrialized cities. If a new developer is promising to deliver millions in fresh tax revenue and there's little pushback on the ground, why not green-light the project, even if it means cost-of-living hikes for nearby residents? As Stein puts it, "gentrification is what happens when real estate rules and planners follow."[14]

The effects of this process tend to resemble one another, regardless of the continent: As property values rise, many residents' wages can't keep up. Some of them hold on in subpar conditions, scraping by as their neighborhoods are transformed. Others are pushed to the peripheries of major metropolitan areas. Some simply flee cities altogether.

In these respects, what's happening in Paris isn't unique.

Displacement is particularly brutal in the U.S., where housing markets are lightly regulated and the state rarely steps in to provide support. With New York City now boasting the highest average rent costs in the U.S., low-income residents are mostly confined to upper Manhattan and the outer boroughs. While Los Angeles has a smaller population spread out over a larger area, it has seen housing prices ramp up significantly in recent years, pushing more and more low-income residents inland, away from the Pacific coast.[15]

In Asia, Tokyo has managed to keep housing prices somewhat in check through innovative public policies—a reminder that state regulation can ensure a modicum of affordability if the political will exists.[16] But the housing crisis is dire in Hong Kong, where exorbitant prices have forced more than two hundred thousand residents into what are known as "subdivided" flats—units cut up to squeeze in a mix of low-wage workers, poor retirees, and families who can't afford to live elsewhere. These include the infamous "coffin homes," plywood cubicles that measure around two feet wide and less than six feet long, home to the most down-and-out.[17]

In Europe, the business hubs of Milan and Frankfurt are both experiencing painful housing booms of their own, while historically affordable cities like Barcelona and Berlin have also witnessed displacement of residents who can't afford to keep up with the changes. The housing crisis is especially bleak in London, the global city par excellence. As foreign cash has poured into developments across the city center—a real estate bonanza apparently undeterred by Brexit—the working-class and poor are increasingly pushed to the city's north and eastern peripheries.

The transformation of Paris echoes many of these stories. And yet, there are other, more specific factors at play, additional pressures exacerbating the crisis.

The first factor has to do with geography.

Paris and its 2.16 million inhabitants are packed into a very small amount of space—an area that's roughly fifteen times smaller than Greater London, or twelve times as small as the five boroughs of New York City. To think of it another way, Paris has about as many residents as Houston, Texas, but occupies about one-sixteenth the space. While the city limits have expanded several times over in the past—growing outward in concentric circles ever since the Romans decided to build a trading post on the banks of the Seine—they practically haven't budged since 1860, the time of the last major expansion.

Since that time, most of the metropolitan area's population growth has taken place in the suburbs, which extend outward in all directions, covering hundreds of different municipalities. When France's then-brand-new Third Republic conducted its 1881 census, about 1.5 million people lived in the Parisian suburbs. While the population of the city proper has actually declined slightly since then, more people live in the suburban region than ever before—close to 9 million, according to official census figures. The metro area dwarves the actual city, and it's not even close.

In North American cities, housing woes are often exacerbated by a lack of density. Places like Los Angeles and Toronto were built around a cult of the automobile, which was seen as the life-sustaining connection between school, work, and single-family residences.[18] Developments in middle-class neighborhoods were broadly opposed by residents, with the

NIMBY agenda ("not in my backyard") carrying the day. Only more recently has the consensus begun to shift in the other direction. As some say, "build more and build higher."[19] There may be something to the YIMBY logic ("yes in my backyard") on the other side of the Atlantic, but it's less appealing in western Europe, where governments regularly intervene in housing markets and where density tends to be relatively high in the first place. In the case of Paris, it's unclear where new housing developments would go. Since the end of the last major expansion in the late nineteenth century, there's not much space to build within the current boundaries.

Height restrictions limit most apartment buildings at around seven stories, and there's already a lot of people living in them. At some point, it's either physically impossible to build more or downright undesirable to tear up the existing urban landscape, because—like Rome—it contains a great deal of beauty and historical value. Unlike Berlin, London, or Rotterdam, Paris wasn't bombed heavily in the last world war, leaving its churches, monuments, public buildings, and old housing stock intact. The open spaces that do exist tend to be valued by residents precisely because there aren't many of them or because they're already serving other purposes. Who would want to build in the Tuileries or the Luxembourg Gardens?

While the prescriptions may vary considerably, just about everyone agrees the housing market in Paris is marked by a colossal shortage—a situation in which demand far outstrips supply. Fortunately, authorities have an array of weapons to address the problem that go beyond simply "building more and building higher." As chapter 5 shows, there's plenty to be done: more conversions of apartments into public housing units, improved rent controls, and more crackdowns on vacant housing, among other measures. Activists are putting pressure on the city and state to do all of the above.

Nevertheless, there is a basic supply crunch that is helping to drive the boom underway, an environment in which apartments tend to go to the highest bidder and in which prices seem to inch relentlessly upward. Along with the other structural factors fueling hypergentrification worldwide, the housing shortage means that Parisian real estate has become—to put it bluntly—an attractive investment for those who can afford it.

As people like Soumia and Amin are scraping by to make rent, the city is being bought up by a very different crop of people.

That starts with the white-collar professionals from some of the CAC 40's well-established industries like finance, insurance, luxury goods, and defense, and who, until recently, may have preferred owning a home in the suburbs. Some of them might work in La Défense, the carefully planned and vaguely dystopic business district that sits just outside the city limits. This is home to France's biggest skyscrapers: the Tour First, a mind-numbingly boring building that is the country's tallest; the Tour Total, a cluster of windows that makes the former seem like a daring piece of architectural bravado; and the heinous Tour Majunga, an awkward attempt to break up the monotony and which looks like a glassblower sneezed on their creation in progress.

Another big chunk of investment comes from the flourishing tech, fashion, and tourism sectors that have flooded the city with cash in recent years. These homeowners are joined by older, more middle-class residents who have some extra savings to plunk down and have decided there's money to be made from renovating or renting out space. And there are younger first-time buyers who've saved up and can count on parental support to snatch modest apartments at the bottom of the market. All of them are riding the wave and driving up prices.

But another factor behind the boom—one that carries a lot of weight because of the astronomical sums of money in question—is the fantastically lucrative market for luxury real estate, a domain for which Paris has become celebrated internationally in recent years. If the success of the blissfully unserious Netflix series *Emily in Paris* shows the resilience of a certain image of Paris—a city of romance, art, and spontaneity where dreams come true—its dark cousin is *The Parisian Agency: Exclusive Properties*. Hosted on the same streaming platform, this show follows around members of a top-end housing agency as they seek to cash in on sumptuous multi-million-euro apartments meant to make viewers slobber. The true star here is the real estate and there's no shame about it. Paris did not used to be like this.

To try and better understand these upper tiers of the market, I reached out to Marie-Hélène Lundgreen, manager of Belles demeures de France, the international wing of the Paris-based luxury agency Daniel Féau.

As she explained over the phone, the term "luxury real estate" tends to refer to properties in "desirable locations" and that are worth at least €1 million. Her agency, which has a partnership with Christie's International Real Estate, distinguishes between apartments that fetch €1 to €3 million and those selling for €3 to €35 million.

Foreign investors play a fundamental role. In 2019, they made up just over four-tenths of sales in that uppermost tranche, according to the Féau agency. Despite a slight dip during the pandemic, Lundgreen said that the overall luxury market has remained largely stable.

Not only are the returns on investment too enticing to ignore, but, as Lundgreen explained, the City of Light also comes with cultural cachet that's hard to match anywhere else. "There are beautiful cities around the world, 'global cities' as we say, but Paris offers everything," she told me. "It's history, culture, food, fashion. It's a bit of a dream for everyone." Some of her foreign clients come from the Middle East, but she said the two biggest groups come from the U.S. and China. Unlike their French counterparts, Lundgreen explained, it's rare for these international investors to seek a primary residence in the city.

The Americans "often already have two, three, or more [residences]," she said. "Maybe they live in New York or in Los Angeles. It could be in Turks and Caicos, it could be in Connecticut, it could be in Florida . . . but it's people with a certain culture. It's not just the money that counts. It's a love for France, for history and for French culture."

It's a bit different with the Chinese, Lundgreen said, for whom an investment in Paris is more firmly tied to hopes of upward social mobility. It might not be their first choice on the list of global cities—New York and London are more attractive for business reasons and because of the predominance of English—but the French capital does come with advantages.

"Having a pied-à-terre in Paris puts you at a different social level. It's often people that are already in international circles at home," Lundgreen continued. "It's not something that they absolutely need—it's not for their business or for educating their children. It's to enjoy for themselves, for the culture, for the *art de vivre*, for all this."

Wherever their origins may be, foreign investors tend to be drawn to the same parts of the city. Known as the *beaux quartiers*, these are neighborhoods in central and western Paris where, in some cases, moneyed classes have been living for generations: the prestigious 8th and 16th arrondissements; the calm streets near the green spaces of Parc Monceau, the Luxembourg Gardens, or the Champ de Mars and the Eiffel Tower; swanky flats near the city center built in the late nineteenth century under the modernizing plans of the Baron de Haussmann.

All of this may be far from the more rough-and-tumble swaths of the northeast, but as Michel Mouillart, a housing economist at the University of Paris Nanterre has argued, the pressure at the upper bounds of the market is having a ripple effect across the city. With the upper gamut effectively off-limits to all but the super-rich, people that might otherwise have sought an apartment in the *beaux quartiers* have gradually adjusted their expectations.

"It's not that the residents of the *beaux quartiers* are moving," Mouillart told me, "but it means that those who wanted to go to the *beaux quartiers* are moving elsewhere."

This process has already transformed the Marais, a formerly dilapidated aristocratic quarter that once served as a hub for Jewish immigrants from eastern Europe and a center for LGBT cultural life before being overtaken by luxury clothing stores and cafés catering to tourists. More recently, it has remade the area around the Canal Saint-Martin and the busy thoroughfares of the central 10th and 11th arrondissements, sweeping into Montmartre and the hill around Sacré-Coeur. As prices mount in all these areas, the boom extends further to the northeast, inching into swaths of the city the bankers and consultants moving in today would have considered off-limits until just recently.

On a gorgeous spring morning, I met David Rivelin, a real estate agent with Daniel Féau whose area of focus includes the 18th arrondissement. After months of receiving my inquiries about luxury sales in the north of the city, the agency finally invited me to a tour a flat on the Place Charles Dullin, a leafy square toward the southern edge of the district that's home to the historic Théâtre de l'Atelier. Largely hidden from the street and extending over an amount of space that feels unreal for an apartment in Paris, this 245-square-meter, five-bedroom apartment was going for €2.99 million. It had a charming library, multiple walk-in closets, an American-style kitchen that connected to a spacious living room—and, most impressively, a whole separate upstairs level with a terrace that was itself three times the size of Soumia and Amin's apartment.

"There are new neighborhoods that are coming up, where there are expensive sales," Rivelin said as we sat down at a table on the patio. "Yes, the west is still very expensive, very chic, very luxurious. Here, we don't have the same sublime common areas, it's not quite the same structural foundations, but at the same time, we have very beautiful *hôtels particuliers* [freestanding residential buildings]. . . . There are fewer apartments or buildings that make you go 'Wow!' but there are still very beautiful things, hidden spaces, and outside areas."

Rivelin has the business casual style typical of a certain Parisian man in his late thirties to early fifties, sporting a slim cut jacket over a dress shirt that has one more button undone than is customary in the U.S. or U.K. He speaks quickly and assuredly, with a slightly gravely smoker's voice, telling me that while he has worked at the agency for thirteen years, the 18th has only started to emerge more recently.

"The neighborhood has changed immensely over the last ten years, it's crazy. The prices take that into consideration. The buildings are more and more cleaned up. The underlying structures are pretty. These were rough neighborhoods even ten, fifteen years ago," he said. "It's become very gentrified."

He said many clients drawn to the 18th today are attracted to a certain vision of city life—precisely the sort of mixed-use development that one used to find in the Marais or in the central parts of the Left Bank before the housing boom swept it away.

"These small, local businesses are what make our neighborhoods," said Rivelin, who's lived here himself for the last eighteen years. "It's what defines our neighborhoods compared to others. A quality of life that you can't find elsewhere—five butcheries here, two fishmongers there. That's what's great. We're really in a village."

I asked him if he thought the housing boom would have the same effects as it did in those other, more central areas. Does the gentrification underway not risk turning the entire neighborhood and its distinctive trappings into a museum?

"Yes, completely," he said without hesitating, starting to answer before I even finished formulating the question. "That's how it is. Yes, absolutely. We need to be careful what we're doing. I don't want Paris to become Disneyland."

For now, he said he doesn't try to sell properties in certain parts of the 18th: the areas of Marx Dormoy and La Chapelle that have yet to shed their seedy reputations. But he told me he does manage to sell individual homes tucked away around Barbès and the Goutte d'Or. The biggest challenge is the public schools, which he said discourage certain families from buying.

"At the moment, the Goutte d'Or remains a bit tense," Rivelin said. "But we've been saying for years that the Goutte d'Or or Barbès is going to explode. Is it good they're not exploding? It's not for me to judge."

In fact, the prices already are exploding. That may not be perceptible to the sorts of clientele that agents like Rivelin cater to: families and investors who aren't interested in acquiring homes in neighborhoods until they've already reached a certain level of gentrification—say, the final stages of Phillip Clay's classification system. But in reality the pressure is already being felt at the lower end of the market and across the northeast.

Soumia and Amin's "rathole" is just a twenty-minute walk from that €3 million flat. Many have already left the area or consider themselves definitively priced out. Then, there are inhabitants who literally can't afford to make rent at all—like thirty-one-year-old Omar Diko. Along with other migrants and refugees, the native of Mali has spent countless weeks sleeping outside at the Porte de la Chapelle, where the 18th arrondissement meets the ring-road highway.

Born in the war-torn region of Gao, and a member of the ethnic Tuareg minority, Omar was shocked at what he saw when he first arrived in Paris in 2017. "In my life, I had never, ever slept in the street until I came to France," he told me over coffee at my apartment. "Even in Africa, people don't do it."

It's a common occurrence in these parts: with no means and no connections, thousands of migrants like Omar have flocked to La Chapelle in recent years, setting up sprawling tent cities that have been demolished repeatedly by police, only to spring up anew weeks later—a cycle that's been more or less on repeat since 2015, even during the pandemic. The living conditions here are atrocious and unstable, but the shantytowns continue to draw residents via word of mouth.

Dozens of camps have come and gone, but the scene is usually the same: tents are concentrated as far as possible from the public walkways; trash piles up on the edges of the living space toward the sidewalks; the pungent smell of dried sweat fills the air; men—and it's almost exclusively men—wait in line nearby as volunteer groups distribute food and water; during the cooler months, plumes of smoke waft outward from modest fires built to warm residents.

Their homelessness is bound up with a deep failure of public policy. Many of the migrants sleeping in the streets have either applied for asylum or even already obtained refugee status—and in theory, the French government is supposed to accommodate both groups and ensure they find work and lodging throughout the process. But in practice, neither milestone comes with long-term housing guarantees, and it's extremely common for migrants in Paris to spend at least one night on the street. Even once they obtain their refugee status, the state system is so poorly run and the private housing market in Paris so punishing that they sometimes resort to living on the street—as Omar did.

Arriving wasn't easy, either. As Omar recounted in detail, the voyage itself took more than a year. After a grueling journey from his native village in northern Mali, through the sweltering Algerian Sahara to the Libyan coast, across the Mediterranean on a raft, up through Italy to the French Riviera, by train from Marseille, he finally arrived in Paris on a chilly night in November.

"I thought I was in a dream. Is this real?" he remembered

thinking as he got off the train at the Gare de Lyon, with its massive clocktower that looks like a more elegant version of Big Ben. But there were more practical concerns. He had nowhere to sleep and knew nobody who could help.

Omar tried asking people for assistance in French—to no avail. Eventually, he said he stumbled upon an Egyptian, asking him in Arabic, "Where do the migrants sleep?"

The man gave him directions to Porte de la Chapelle and handed him a metro ticket: Get on the subway, he told him, stay on it for a few stops, then get off the train: "Go ask when you get to the top, and you'll find lots of people."

Omar doesn't read very well, but he committed the directions to memory and followed them precisely. After ascending the stairs out of the metro and finding someone who lent him a tent, he posted up under a bridge near the intersection. It was his first night in the streets and he hardly slept at all. "I could hear everything, the people around me, the cars," he said.

Eventually, the anxiety subsided: "I started to calm down, I realized there wasn't a solution. You have to sleep here until the problems are resolved," Omar recalled telling himself. "You need to demand asylum, you need to wait."

That's precisely what he did. After spending four nights under a bridge at La Chapelle, Omar went to the nearest police prefecture, stood patiently in line, and filed a formal request for asylum. A few days later, he was assigned a spot in a shelter for asylum seekers in a small village in eastern France. Omar liked the town, but he sensed there were few opportunities for him there. As he waited for the state to process his case, Omar opted to return to La Chapelle, gradually getting to know volunteers from the various humanitarian groups that give out sustenance and legal advice.

Omar is friendly, gregarious, and multilingual. He speaks Arabic, Tourag, French, and Bambara, making him a valuable asset for camp residents struggling to communicate among themselves and for NGOs to reach them. He's even developed into something of a leader in his own right, getting involved with one of the regular groups distributing food and sharing information with people on-site. Despite all the connections, he's spent much of the last few years in Paris sleeping outside at La Chapelle, even after obtaining asylum in June 2018.

There wasn't much of an alternative, he told me. All the opportunities are in Paris.

"Many of us want to stay in France," he said. "I want to live like everybody. I want a job, I want housing, I'd like to get married. I just want to live like everybody."

Recently, he took a big step in that direction.

Omar entered a training program to work in construction, which, thankfully, comes with guaranteed lodging for the duration of the six-month program—a housing complex in a small town in the southern suburban *département* of Essonne, about an hour from central Paris on the commuter rail line. He said he hoped it would pave the way for him to find his own place somewhere in the region—and eventually make it possible to bring over his eleven-year-old child, now living with his grandparents in Mali.

"If they give me work, I'll start a job and I'll find housing," he told me. "If there's no work, then there's no choice. I'll go back to the street."

2

THE MELTING POT

If you get on the line 2 metro at Barbès–Rochechouart, right at the southern edge of the Goutte d'Or, there's a chance you'll cross paths with one of its regular passengers at work. He's short and slender, with a Casio mini-keyboard strung over his shoulder. When he starts playing, the first few notes on the keys may sound unremarkable, like any street musician. But once Mohamed Lamouri starts singing, his otherworldly voice is impossible to ignore. Rough and gravelly—right on the cusp of raspiness—it has a way of drawing you in with its strangeness and poignancy. It's also capable of a tremendous amount of versatility, moving from the high drama of Algerian *raï* to a deftly arranged Arabic-language cover of "Billie Jean."

From Barbès, it's only a ten-minute metro ride east to the neighborhood of Belleville. From the moment one emerges from the metro here, the energy in the air is palpable: young men peddling knockoff cigarettes; giant Chinese letters above a restaurant overlooking the plaza and a French translation in neon lights that reads "LE PRÉSIDENT"; sex workers lining the main boulevard from the early afternoon onward; café terraces filled with patrons of different ages and ethnic backgrounds; more action bustling on a thin street winding its way up a steep hill. Belleville is many things, but one of its distinguishing qualities is that it remains a holdout to the wave of uniformization sweeping through Paris, a neighborhood that has managed to hold on to something that can't be found elsewhere.

It needn't be idealized too much. There are all the familiar signs of gentrification—a sleek new organic food store; an expensive wine and liquor store; an art gallery—spaces that invite certain clients and exclude others. The rents are becoming ludicrously high. The divide between those who live in social housing and those who don't is growing by the year. And yet, certain facets of life in Belleville carry on: a willingness to embrace difference; a streak of rebelliousness; perhaps above all, in certain places and at certain times, a recognition of the fact that multiple populations share this space—that this neighborhood has never belonged to any one group in particular and that therein lies its charm.

One such spot is Le Zorba. It's technically what's known as a PMU, a café that doubles as a place to gamble on horse races. (The abbreviation comes from Pari Mutuel Urbain, the company with a monopoly on equestrian bookmaking in France, known for its emblematic green-and-red signs sticking out of cafés nationwide.) In the mornings, the café draws workers making quick stops for coffee breaks: construction crews, bus and subway conductors, sanitation workers. In the afternoons, it's mostly dominated by the old-timers who come to watch the races. About a dozen men fill the back of the café, their eyes transfixed on the flat-screen TV. But the decor suggests something else happens here, too. A smattering of concert posters covers the wall. A pair of thin, pink neon lights run across the ceiling.

In the evenings—and especially Friday and Saturday nights— Le Zorba is a popular spot for a crew of twenty- and thirty-somethings who come here to party, dance, and get drunk until it closes, like most bars in Paris, at two in the morning. A fourth and final wave of patrons—the most obliterated of all— tends to arrive when Le Zorba opens back up at 5 a.m. It's one of the few places around to keep the party going.

On a windy Saturday night in March, well before midnight, much of this younger crowd was braving the cool air to smoke cigarettes outside, spilling out onto the sidewalk. Inside, a group of four men in their thirties speaking Latin American Spanish shared a table, pounding down pints of La Chouffe beer and laughing loudly. An older guy wearing a suit and a beige scarf stood alone at the countertop sipping a gin and tonic, nodding along to the classic disco playlist with his eyes closed. A couple was making out at a table where the horse-race bettors were a few hours ago.

One of the defining figures of gentrification in Paris is the "bobo"—a portmanteau word derived from *bourgeois-bohème*. The term was always vague, but it's been overused to the point that it means almost nothing today, not unlike "hipster" in the U.S. It's employed almost exclusively in jest or as a form of derision. Nobody would call the guys betting on horses "bobos," but in cases where there's doubt over someone's status, the subject is near-impossible to broach because there is no consensus over what the defining traits are. Is it wealth? Family money? Home ownership? Whiteness? Cultural capital? Certain tastes in art and music? If the lawyers and consultants buying up apartments in Montmartre are bobos, then how does one distinguish them from the sort of people who come to Le Zorba? Some would probably call them bobos anyway—the predominance of piercings and jean and leather jackets is enough to make the call. In any case, they're here because they want to be here.

Downstairs was packed. A couple dozen people were huddled together in a small underground space—a *cave* in French—listening to a self-described "queer emo trap duo." The synth is booming. There's a drum machine, and the singing alternates between spoken word and soaring vocals that seem to come out of nowhere. The floor is sticky and the room smells like sweat. The disco ball seems to move in slow motion as the crowd sways back and forth, absorbing the pink lights and dreamy ambiance. Then, a bearded guy in a hoodie comes bumbling down the stairs, angling for a spot at the back of the cave, miraculously keeping his freshly poured beer from spilling. He turns to his left. "Wow, there's a lot of people," he says to his neighbor who lifts his eyes in recognition but doesn't respond verbally. A few seconds later, he turns to the girl to his right, "Wow, there's a lot of people."

The next day, the regulars were back. The music was off. The TV was back on, broadcasting a horse race from the South of France. Nearly all the patrons were on coffee, not beer. At around two in the afternoon, the bar's manager walked in the door, forty-two-year-old Ferhat Becheur.

"We have different clienteles," Ferhat said over espresso on the sunlit terrace, pausing for drags on a cigarette. "The morning, it's people who work. In the afternoon to early evening, it's people for the PMU. And then after that, it's the young people. It's sort of *branché* [hip]. I think we're one of the rare cafés that does this."

Ferhat has helped run the bar since 2016, taking over the job from his father, who opened Le Zorba in 1990. (Before that the space, which had been around for decades, was known as La Comète.) Many of the regulars—the guys who come for the horses—are from Belleville. Other clients just spend a lot of time in the neighborhood, like the legendary metro singer Mohamed Lamouri, who's been known to post up inside Le Zorba at night after singing on line 2. He usually orders a peach or strawberry Diabolo, a non-alcoholic cocktail made of syrup and lemonade. Then he takes the night bus back to his home in the northeastern suburbs.

Becheur said the churn around him is visible: "A lot of my clients have left Paris because of the rent." He says he knows of a few other café owners nearby who've shuttered their doors in recent years—they were either unable to make ends meet or tired of hustling. But he says he's doing all right.

It seems to me there are profound, perhaps even mystical, ties between Le Zorba and the neighborhood, but when I ask Ferhat about this, he's much more grounded, much more to the point. "That's Belleville for you. I like this neighborhood a lot," he smiled after my overwrought attempt at getting him to muse about where he lives.

"It's the mix," he continued. "I feel like I'm at home [in Algeria], but I also feel like I'm in France."

* * *

Ferhat Becheur is perhaps too modest to point it out himself, but he's also representative of another tradition deeply ingrained in the fabric of the city and Belleville in particular: the success of immigrant entrepreneurs.

People born abroad have long left their marks on Paris, sometimes through the arts, but most often through underappreciated low-wage labor, working behind the scenes to keep the city running and business flowing. They've tanned leather, repaired shoes, sewed clothes, refined chemicals, built cars, swept streets, run subways, cleaned dishes, and served food. Since they started arriving in more significant numbers from the late nineteenth century onward, this share of the Parisian population has tended to go woefully unrecognized.

Of this larger group, a small subset has gone on to open small businesses of their own—shops, restaurants, and cafés—with varying degrees of success. Networks of fellow immigrants often play a vital role in sustaining these enterprises, especially in the early days. But sometimes—through enough work, perseverance, and some luck—they break through to the native-born population. In a place where the foreign-born have never received their due credit, these high-visibility businesses don't just provide vital services. Their very presence sends a worthwhile message: don't forget who built this city.

It can be overlooked given all the flashiness that envelops the French capital today, but the fact is Paris has always been a city of immigrants. Nearly a fifth of the greater Paris region today is made up of immigrants—that is, people born as foreigners on foreign soil, according to INSEE—a figure that is double the share in metropolitan France as a whole.[1] While many today are increasingly moving to the banlieue—either priced out of Paris proper or attracted to the suburbs from the onset—a large

share still lives in Paris, where they make up about 20 percent
of the total population.

Today's political obsessions notwithstanding, this is not a
new phenomenon. The French capital and its eastern neighborhoods in particular have long been home to foreigners seeking economic opportunities for themselves and their families.
What's changed, above all, is where they come from. For much
of the twentieth century, immigrant workers hailed from
eastern or southern Europe: Poland and Italy in the first few
decades, then Spain and Portugal. Most today can point to roots
in the Maghreb or sub-Saharan Africa, countries that were
once holdings of France's colonial empire.

Think of Paris today as a palimpsest. Some of the page may
be torn. Certain sections may be downright missing. What you
do see has been rewritten by generations multiple times over—
in different scripts and in different languages. Belleville is far
from the only passage worthy of attention, but what's remarkable is how closely today's version resembles previous versions
of the text. In many respects, Belleville is still a working-class
neighborhood, and it's still an immigrant neighborhood.

In the early twentieth century, the slopes of this then-peripheral
neighborhood began to welcome in waves of Jewish migrants,
many of them fleeing pogroms in Poland and Russia. While the
more religiously devout gravitated toward the Marais, Belleville developed a secular, left-leaning reputation—especially
in the 1920s and 1930s. Around the same time, these eastern
Europeans were joined by an influx of residents fleeing violence in Greece and Armenia, many of them taking jobs in the
area's shoemaking industry.[2] (The two writers perhaps most
associated with Belleville both trace their roots back to this

era: Clément Lépidis and Georges Perec were born to families from Armenia and Poland, respectively.) Tragically, much of the neighborhood's Jewish population was wiped out in World War II—and especially those without French citizenship. With the complicity of the French state, fifty thousand Jews from Paris were deported and exterminated in the concentration camps.[3] In the aftermath of this atrocity, in the 1950s and 1960s, Belleville saw a new influx of residents from France's former colonial holdings in Algeria and Tunisia. Many came from Algeria's northern Berber-speaking region of Kabylia, but a large share were Sephardic Jews, a group with very different languages and customs than the largely Ashkenazi population that had been tragically lost decades prior.

The heritage of this North African immigration is still very much visible today. There are a few kosher butcheries, right around the metro station. Many of the area's cafés and restaurants are run by Kabyles, like the Becheur family at Le Zorba. Just up the Rue de Belleville sits Aux Folies, another Kabyle-managed institution known for its giant, sprawling terrace, four or five rows of seats deep. Much smaller cafés dot the neighborhood, extending into the neighboring quarter of Ménilmontant. (It's long been debated where exactly Belleville ends and Ménilmontant begins, with some simply calling all of it Belleville-Ménilmontant.)

In the 1980s and 1990s, yet another wave of immigration began to arrive from China. In some ways, it's the most visible one today, with a few Asian supermarkets and restaurants clustered around the main intersection by the Belleville metro station. There are thousands of residents with roots in China, and they're often out and about on the streets. Looking up the Rue de Belleville, running up the hill from the main intersection, the succession of vertically aligned signs with Chinese characters sticking out from the buildings is hard to miss.

One of them belongs to Alexandre Xu, the forty-seven-year-old owner of Chez Alex.

Like much of the Chinese-born population of Belleville, Xu was born in Wenzhou, a city in southeastern China. His restaurant serves up many of the area's specialties: raw crab, eels, fried pork tripe, vegetable fried rice with dried beef. There are also non-regional classics like dumplings and fried eggplants with garlic. The food is top-notch and affordable.

"Wenzhou cuisine is turned toward the sea," he explained on a Thursday afternoon, the one day of the week the restaurant is closed. "It's not too spicy, compared to Sichuan [cuisine], but it's true there's a lot of vinegar. Not in everything, but, for example, with noodles with Wenzhou sauce we use a lot of vinegar soy sauce. . . . When you're growing up, you're very attached to it, but it's true that there's a lot of vinegar."

Sporting a buzz cut and a short-sleeve shirt that shows off his muscular arms, Xu explained his place is something like a time capsule from when he and his family emigrated to France. "The China of 1984 isn't the same as the China today," he said. "Even in China, you can hardly find *tripes aux carrés de sang* [pork tripe over bits of blood sausage]. The restaurant is like you took a photo from 1984. Time hasn't moved here, but it's moved over there. Coming here is like a trip back in time."

Xu's rise to success is emblematic of many immigrant entrepreneurs in the city, a road paved by a rough start and shattered illusions. He moved to Paris in 1987, at age twelve, three years after his parents first came to France. Before arriving, his mental image of the city had been shaped by his uncle, the first to go to the French capital. When his uncle triumphantly returned to visit Wenzhou, he was wearing nice clothes and a fancy-looking belt, and carried a flashy umbrella—all of it impressive for what was then a fairly poor city.

"A lot of immigrant families do the same thing," Alex recalled. "They don't tell the people in their town that they've been working sixteen hours a day, they don't say they're struggling, they don't say it's not easy. They just want to show the good side and show their prosperity."

Xu still remembers one of his first days out in the streets of Paris, walking in the February snow with his brother and thinking they were going to find gold bars—literally. At some point, they thought they'd spotted some and crouched down to pick up the mysterious-looking material, only to be shrieked at by their mother. It was dog poop. "We were shocked because in China there was no dog poop. Zero!" he said. "It completely changed our image."

In those early days, the family all lived in a tiny apartment in the 10th arrondissement, on the building's fifth and final floor, without an elevator. The apartment was what's known in French as a *chambre de bonne*, a room that refers to the maid's chambers. These spaces are designed for just one person, and even then, it's tight. The whole apartment measured eighteen square meters.

"It was pretty crowded," Xu said, chuckling. "At the time, my parents worked at home, so there were two sewing machines. At night, we cleaned everything up and put the mattress on the ground. We rolled up the mattress in the morning."

The family later moved to a larger space in the same arrondissement, with two bedrooms spanning a relatively spacious thirty-five square meters. Eventually, by 1992, his parents had saved up enough cash to open a restaurant in a neighborhood that many of the Wenzhou-born Chinese had begun moving to. Alex took it over in 2001.

Since then, the restaurant has developed a solid reputation among the neighborhood's Wenzhou population—though over the same stretch, Belleville has seen an influx of immigrants from the opposite side of China, in the northeast. They're often referred to as the "Dongbeis." Many have settled in the sub-urbs, but a sizable number still reside in Belleville.

They, too, are part of the mix at Chez Alex. On a given night, there may be patrons speaking the Wenzhou dialect. Others might be speaking Mandarin. They're joined by a French cli-entele that, according to Alex, has been growing over the years. When I asked about the latter, he raised his eyebrows: "Ah, the bobos?"

"There are a lot of journalists, artists, architects. They tend to have open minds. If you don't have an open mind, you don't come to Belleville," Xu said. "There are often people who've traveled a lot. . . . Sometimes I have to be careful, because there are French clients who understand Chinese—they've lived in China or they've been to China—and they're waiting for cui-sine from there. They want something authentic. They don't want [Westernized] cuisine."

Xu himself is well accustomed to navigating the different worlds of his clients. Not unlike many in Belleville, he's com-bined a deep desire to become French with an effort to main-tain links to his home country—the end product reflecting a strange synthesis that's not really one or the other. Using a pop-ular French expression, Xu said he has his "ass between two chairs." For years, he said, he struggled with that in-between status, swinging back and forth between French and Chinese "mentalities," as he put it—sometimes abruptly so. By now, he's embraced both.

"To integrate, I tried to cut links with everything that was Chinese," Xu said, recalling his first French-language classes in elementary school. "I didn't want to be with the Chinese. I always went with the people who made me speak French, people from Algeria or Yugoslavia, but I wanted to avoid the Chinese."

He argued a lot with his parents in his late teens and early twenties. At the heart of the tensions were conflicting expectations. "[In France], the individual comes before the family. It means, if you're happy, you feel good, then you're the center of the world," he said. "The Chinese mentality is all about the family. The family comes before the individual. It means you need to do things for the family to do well, even if you need to sacrifice your time or something else, and this changes everything. All your behavior."

"When I was young, I would hang out with my friends after class," Xu continued. "When my parents needed me, they'd call and I absolutely hated it. They'd say, 'We need you at the restaurant.' It made me so angry. I thought the philosophy was, 'When I'm happy, that's the most important thing, I'm the center of the world.' But then when the family needs you, you need to drop everything for the family."

"At the time, it was hard," Xu recalled. "I either had to act Chinese or French. It was difficult to make decisions."

That sense of whiplash and the hard feelings have faded over time. Xu's wife is Chinese and their daughter has grown up speaking French and Mandarin—the latter thanks to classes on the weekend. Xu's parents are retired and live just a few minutes away, down the main boulevard. They both like to go to the nearby Parc de Belleville. His father plays ping-pong and his mother does synchronized gymnastic dancing every morning, alongside many other elderly Chinese women. Xu eats dinner with them once a week. They're French and Chinese, though above all, they're Parisians.

The melting-pot attributes of the French capital don't get much recognition from the powers that be. Unlike New York City, the city of Paris does not officially celebrate its ability to absorb foreigners and make them into Parisians. That fact has little to do with demographics or the actual historical record of migration. As with New York, millions of immigrants have flocked here over the years, struggling with discrimination, language barriers, and low-wage labor to provide for their families and generations to come. The main reason for the city's reticence is that a narrative of this sort—one that draws attention to people's status as foreigners and deviations from the French norm—fits awkwardly with the country's national mythology.

Officially, La République does not recognize ethnic or religious difference. The state does not collect statistics on racial backgrounds or religious faiths. The only numbers it does gather concern nationalities. In other words, one can tally up the number of Algerians, Portuguese, and Chinese living in France—but not the second-, third-, or fourth-generation French citizens who might think of themselves as being Franco-Algerian, Franco-Portuguese, or Franco-Chinese. That's because, in theory, these distinctions don't matter. Once you're French, you're French.

It doesn't mean people with foreign backgrounds are shunned publicly. There's a long list of French celebrities with immigrant origins. But this recognition usually comes at the expense of their non-French backgrounds. Frank Sinatra and Joe DiMaggio are sometimes described as Italian American, but it would be odd to call Charles Aznavour or Zinédine Zidane anything other than French. Successful integration hinges on dropping the foreign-ness, embracing the French-ness. That's the whole point.

Language plays a pivotal role in erasing these differences. In France, you won't find official government documents published in Arabic, Chinese, or Peul; you won't find TV stations on basic cable broadcasting in foreign languages; in Paris, you're unlikely to find street signs or plaques in anything other than the official language, which is French and only French.

This hardhanded approach extends to languages that developed within the borders of metropolitan France as well. The country's historic regional languages have been largely erased, and live on largely thanks to the work of mid- to late twentieth-century activists who successfully fought to include them in special school programs. They're sometimes on street signs in provincial capitals, but Alsatian, Breton, Basque, and Occitan aren't spoken anywhere close to the same levels as, say, Basque, Catalan, and Galician in Spain. Even the regional distinctions of French have been flattened out over the years. They're marginal when compared with the varieties of Italian and German spoken in different parts of those countries.

Much of these practices were enshrined into law by the Third Republic, the system of government that followed the downfall of Napoleon III in 1870 and which coincided with similar nation-building processes across Europe. With political leaders selectively tapping into the memory of the French Revolution, this was the era in which primary schooling was made free and obligatory; it was the period in which the country's variant of secularism, *laïcité*, was adopted. And it was also a crucial period for French colonial expansion, inextricably binding the creation of the modern French nation to imperial conquest in Africa and Asia.

Not unlike the American national project—with which it shares Enlightenment-era influence and similarly universalist aspirations—French republicanism has been deeply fraught from the onset, full of contradictions, and marred by an inability to live up to its egalitarian promise. It's also been subject to competing interpretations and political goals. A force of progressive state intervention against the conservative influence of the Catholic Church, the Republic was at the same time invoked to justify brutal wars of aggression against populations abroad that needed to be "civilized." While so-called Republican values have long been referenced in the fight against racism and discrimination, they are roundly weaponized these days against minorities, especially those of the Muslim faith.

A common charge is that the country's Muslim population, widely accepted as the largest in Europe despite the lack of official figures, isn't doing enough to respect the pillar of *laïcité*. It's an overwhelmingly baseless accusation, but one amplified by a string of brutal terrorist attacks, some of which were committed by French nationals, as well as the spread of conservative Islam in certain low-income, suburban neighborhoods. Neither question concerns the vast majority of Muslims living in France, but they're often called upon to denounce and distance themselves from these problems—to show their loyalties to the Republic in ways that non-Muslims aren't asked to do.

A related directive, lobbed not just at Muslims but rather foreigners at large, is to avoid the snares of "communitarianism": the practice of self-segregation based on ethnic or religious difference, of adhering to group identities instead of integrating into the broader nation. French republicanism is built on erasing difference, not celebrating it. As such, pundits and politicians regularly contrast the pitfalls of "Anglo-Saxon communitarianism" with the bolder ambitions of France's "Republican" model of citizenship. As one might expect, this term is often employed selectively: a bilingual Franco-Moroccan family that eats halal and lives in the suburbs of Paris is far more likely to be accused of "communitarianism" than a group of Catholics living in small-town Burgundy.

Most foreigners who've spent some time in France are familiar with these terms, these debates, and the expectations they generate—the importance of speaking French, of appearing French, of becoming French, and what failure to do so signifies. At the same time, none of this has discouraged foreigners from continuing to move to Paris or from maintaining ties to their home countries once they arrive.

This is the true spirit of Belleville's working-class cosmopolitanism. It's the residue of creolization, exchanges between groups that are the product of exchanges between groups that are the product of exchanges between groups before them. Of course, while residents with roots in China, Algeria, or Côte d'Ivoire spend much of their lives in French—those who are citizens may well be proud to be French—their tastes, their preferences, and their culture bear the traces of this syncretism. This isn't quite the same process of integration that the French Republic calls for on paper. It's not about erasing difference; it's not really about accepting difference, either. It's about how difference generates something new altogether. The world's great cities have always been incubators for this sort of thing.

*   *   *

The question today is how long the melting pot can persist. Even though business is going strong, Alexandre Xu tells me his restaurant's Chinese clientele is shrinking.

He pins it on a few different reasons. Many clients used to make trips to Belleville from outside Paris and from as far as the Benelux countries—Belgium, the Netherlands, and Luxembourg—making grocery runs and eating out. But starting around 2010, Xu said a wave of petty crime started turning people off the neighborhood. Chinese locals and visitors alike were getting robbed at knifepoint—a trend that Xu says was fueled by the notion that many of the victims would be undocumented and therefore wouldn't want to file police reports.

At the same time, traffic has gotten worse. It's a nightmare to try and find parking on the two-lane Rue de Belleville. There are the metro and bus lines, but they take time to navigate, and many of those who don't already live nearby have decided it's not worth the hassle.

Above all, though, there is the problem of rising rents, which is transforming the neighborhood. Quite simply, there are fewer Chinese-born residents around here than when Xu took over the restaurant. That means fewer Chinese-born customers.

When I asked what he thinks it'll look like in ten to twenty years, Xu responded without hesitation. "There will be fewer Chinese people, and more businesses will be in the hands of Europeans."

I asked Xu if he still thinks it's fair to call Belleville a working-class neighborhood—a *quartier populaire* in French. This time, he took a long pause.

"Today, it's less working-class than it used to be. The price has changed. But compared to the rest of Paris, it still is."

* * *

Official statistics paint a similarly nuanced picture.

It's not easy to measure because there is no formal definition for the neighborhood, which sits at the intersection of four
different arrondissements: the 10th, 11th, 19th, and 20th. (As
the writer and editor Éric Hazan once put it, Belleville resembles the Four Corners, the region of the American Southwest
where New Mexico, Arizona, Colorado, and Utah meet.)[4] Still,
one can look at the four administrative quadrants (census-
designated zones that are smaller than the arrondissements)
that join together at the Belleville metro stop—and within
them, residents' earnings range from well below to just below
the Parisian average.

There is another way to quantify the gap. A large chunk of
Belleville is defined by the French government as a "priority
neighborhood for city policy," one of 1,300 socially disadvantaged areas across France and 20 in Paris with the distinction.[5] In the area the state officially considers to be "Greater
Belleville," a patch covering about thirty thousand residents
across the 10th, 11th, and 20th arrondissements, all the key
indicators contradict the narrative of a bobo takeover: median
monthly income hovers at just around €1,390, about half the
citywide rate; a third of residents are below the poverty line;
unemployment is higher than both the citywide and national
levels.

There's not much mystery behind it: the single biggest reason
why most of these people still live here is the large share of public housing. Making up nearly 40 percent of the area's housing stock, the rate of social housing here is nearly double that
of Paris as a whole.[6] Not as glamorous as the mansard-topped
Haussmann-style apartments that dominate the wealthier
neighborhoods (though they provide a far more vital service),

these residences are scattered throughout Belleville: on the Rue Robert-Houdin, just by the metro station; along the Rue des Couronnes; up the hill on the Rue Piat, just next to the Parc de Belleville and its panoramic views.

This Belleville—the one supplying a base of the clients to Le Zorba and Chez Alex—is increasingly detached from the private housing market. According to the website SeLoger, average prices in the neighborhood have soared to nearly €10,000 per square meter, just below the Parisian average.[7] And a gap like that comes with heavy consequences. Whether one prefers the term "gentrification" or the older French term *embourgeoisement*, the price hikes are rippling throughout the neighborhood, driving tensions, pressures, and divisions between residents.

At another bar and neighborhood institution, up the hill on the Rue de Belleville and not far from the plaque that commemorates the home the singer Edith Piaf grew up in in the 1920s, I met up for coffee with Mohammed Ouaddane. The fifty-nine-year-old was wearing a black leather jacket with blue jeans, sporting a graying beard and dreadlocks. A sociologist by training, born in Morocco, Ouaddane is also a longtime community activist with a particular focus on the history of immigration. He adores the neighborhood and has lived here since 1997, but told me there's something very painful going on as well, whatever you choose to call it.

"Yes, there are working-class people here. Yes, there is social housing. But Belleville no longer belongs to the working class," Ouaddane said. "The landscape is being redrawn with a new socioeconomic border."

Ouaddane works a lot with young people, organizing after-school events for at-risk youth in the neighborhood. He said the younger generation is feeling the effects of the housing boom. In addition to the very real material gap that exists between their families and some of the newer residents, many have internalized a deep sense of inferiority.

"Can the kids playing soccer in the park sit down and have a lemonade at the bobo café that opened in front of their place? No. There's a nameless violence taking place and signifying to people that the working class doesn't have its place here and that it doesn't have any power."

"It's even worse because a lot of these young kids can get caught up in the parallel drug trade," Ouaddane continued, speaking calmly though his voice got louder. "They're the little soldiers providing the artificial products for the people who come and set up comfortably on the terraces."

I've witnessed this scene countless times on my own: white twenty-somethings buying low-quality hashish—what the French call *shit*—just in front of one of the public housing projects, where gaggles of Black and brown teens in tracksuits wait to be summoned.

"And when I say 'kids,' they could be forty years old," Ouaddane said. "These people have missed out on school, they've missed out on jobs, and at forty or forty-five, they're up there standing up, waiting around. Then you have the bobo who shows up. Maybe he says 'hi' and maybe he's friendly, it can all be very cordial . . . but the violence there is profound."

From a purely economic point of view, the changes in the neighborhood have produced winners and losers—people who, by chance, have come out on the right side of the housing boom; and others who've been caught on the wrong side. The cruelty of the draw can be found across the northeast of Paris, but for an especially staggering example, one needs only to walk a couple minutes north of the Belleville metro station on the Boulevard de la Villette, past the headquarters of one of the country's two largest labor confederations, past the sex workers, past a couple of cafés. On the left is a small street that serves as a gateway to the micro-neighborhood of Sainte-Marthe. The older residents think of it as its own entity, although, officially, it's considered part of Greater Belleville.

Sainte-Marthe is composed of two narrow one-way streets, with a short passage connecting them in the middle, giving the neighborhood the form of an *H*. It's picturesque, as though it were conjured from a postcard of a western European city. There are bike lines, but almost no cars to be found. The storefronts are painted in different colors—teal, sky blue, light pink, yellow—and the buildings are all relatively short for Paris, no more than four stories high.

If it feels like its own village, cut off from the rest of the city, that's because it was originally conceived as such. Sainte-Marthe was designed as what the French call a *cité ouvrière*, a housing complex for workers. One of the first such compounds to be built in Paris, it opened its doors in the 1850s, the private project of a Catholic philanthropist, Adolphe Joseph Hyacinthe de Madre, who wanted to address the lack of space for the city's growing mass of laborers.[8] The de Madre family held on to ownership of the buildings until World War II.

In 1942, a small developer from Normandy bought the property, and shortly thereafter began offering parts of it for sale. This was never highly desired real estate. But over the following decades, the housing stock fell even further into disrepair—few were interested in buying up decrepit and cramped apartments in what was then a poor part of the city. Manual laborers made up the bulk of residents. Many immigrants moved in, looking for cheap rent. Small-scale garment producers occupied many of the shops on the ground floor, not unlike the Goutte d'Or today.

Cândida Rodrigues remembers what it was like when she first arrived here at age twenty-five in 1986—empty, dirty, dilapidated. "All the storefronts were closed," Rodrigues, now sixty, told me at a nearby café, sharing a table with fellow Saint-Marthe residents Marion Samuel, sixty-nine, and Farida Rouibi, fifty-three. "The garment makers would close the shades to protect their tissue from the light, but still it meant everything was closed. There were no shops, no bars, no nothing."

At the time, Rodrigues was working for a travel insurance company, overseeing the repatriation of clients who needed to be brought home for health reasons. But with little more than that job contract, Rodrigues took out a mortgage and bought an apartment of her own. It cost a grand total of 200,000 francs back then, about €30,000. She was drawn to the idea of having her own spot. "I bought a trash can," she said with a laugh. "I told myself, this way, nobody would be able to kick me out of my place."

Still, the conditions were less than ideal. And in 1991, she and others decided to band together and push for improvements. They formed the Association of Saint Louis–Sainte Marthe, the former of the two names coming from the large public hospital that sits at the other end of the neighborhood. The original goal was to push the city of Paris to improve the shoddy conditions of the streets and the buildings.

"The goal was to eradicate insalubrity and to improve living conditions for people," she said with a hint of *gouaille*, an older

Parisian style of speech, drawing out the *r*'s from the back of her throat. "The housing stock was in such poor condition, it's like the buildings themselves were ill. People had no means to rehabilitate the housing stock."

Joining forces with another small group of activists in the neighborhood, they won a big victory in 2003. That's when the city of Paris agreed to launch a massive new "housing improvement project," an OPAH (Opérations Programmées d'Amélioration de l'Habitat), in French housing policy lingo. The process involves a long and detailed study, a diagnosis of the underlying problems, and most importantly, a hefty sum of public money to improve the overall quality of housing.

From 2005 to 2015, authorities oversaw an immense renovation of the Sainte-Marthe neighborhood, pouring millions of euros into badly needed repairs. They injected cement into deteriorating foundations, repaved the streets, and repainted soot-covered buildings, turning the blocks into a semi-permanent construction zone in the process. Rodrigues says she expected the improvements to lift housing prices a bit—some of her neighbors even sold—but not nearly to the extent they did. At the very same time that authorities had finally undertaken long-neglected renovations, a much bigger housing boom was gaining steam in Paris.

Once the renovations wrapped up, the old property management firm from Normandy moved to sell off its remaining real estate stake in Sainte-Marthe, hoping to cash out at a far more attractive price point. At this point, Rodrigues and other activists pushed for the city of Paris to step in and acquire the property with its "right of preemption"—an authority that exists under French law and one that housing activists regularly call on the public sector to exercise—but it ultimately declined to do so. In 2019, control fell into the hands of private real estate developer Edmond Coignet.

The old firm wasn't exactly beloved given its hands-off approach. But Coignet is a very different kind of animal, born and bred from the housing boom, designed to generate returns from the aggressive price hikes underway. According to Rodrigues, now the developer is remaking the ground floors throughout the neighborhood.

"On the one hand, we think it's great, because the stores used to be ugly and empty," she said. "Now they're beautiful, but at what price?"

Rodrigues believes there's something heinous about the way things have played out. Private speculators have essentially taken advantage of public money to turn a profit. The public sector isn't interested in stepping in. "If this neighborhood was renovated, it was thanks to taxpayer money!" she said. "Public authorities have an obligation to regulate the price of housing."

In so many obvious ways, Rodrigues and company are the lucky ones. They all own homes near the center of town. They're sitting on investments that have paid off handsomely. And yet, there are weird imbalances that come from living in a hypergentrified neighborhood like Sainte-Marthe today, strange fractures in neighborhood life. The group's earnings pale in comparison to many of the newer arrivals'. They can't afford to shop at many of the businesses on their own streets. They're somewhat defensive about what the neighborhood's become and the kind of people who've moved in.

The three of them religiously avoid the trendy cocktail bars around the corner. It's why Cândida proposed meeting at this particular café for our conversation. "It's *populaire* [for the people]!" she said. Even this spot used to open its doors at 7 a.m. to host workers on their first shifts, but now it's usually closed until around 9. They lament the presence of at least two different hairdressers that charge between €60 and €80 for a simple haircut. Even beyond the prices, they feel the decor and clientele of certain businesses send implicit messages about who is and isn't welcome.

"There's also a form of exclusion that comes from telling yourself, 'Oh no, that's not for me,'" said Farida, a documentary filmmaker. "Subjectively, you think that it's not accessible, and you tell yourself, 'I'm not going in there.' I'm sorry, but this is insidious."

"Some people think the kebab places are ugly or, you know, the places with pizza for five euros, with those ugly neon signs," she continued. "But I'm one of the people who thinks, the day we don't have those, it's over!"

One especially clear sign of how much things had changed came during the first Covid lockdown, in the spring of 2020. With restrictions barring people from moving beyond a 1-kilometer radius from their homes, Farida and others thought it might be nice to meet up in the streets' interconnected courtyards. That is, until she realized that the gates are now locked and the various courtyards are separated from one another. "There used to not be barriers and now there are barriers," she said. "It's very concrete."

In the meantime, she's hoping to be able to get a haircut in the neighborhood.

"I sent an email to the hair salon, saying I live in the neighborhood but I don't have the means to pay sixty to eighty euros a haircut," Farida said. "I work part-time and I earn 1,800 euros a month. Would you give me a discount of thirty-five to forty euros so that I can come down and take advantage of a service on my street?"

She has not heard back yet.

Despite those frustrations, Farida said she constantly rebuffs those who tell her she should sell her small thirty-seven-square-meter apartment, now valued at around €360,000. The influx of cash would be nice, but then what? Her friends and her job are in the city.

"People say, 'Oh you can leave Paris.' But I don't want to leave Paris! Why would I want to leave Paris?"

Just a few minutes north on the Boulevard de la Villette sits the Place Colonel Fabien, an intersection firmly outside the limits of Belleville. On oval-shaped junction packed with car traffic, it's arguably best known for hosting the headquarters of the French Communist Party, designed by the modernist Brazilian architect Oscar Niemeyer. Views on the building—a curved box of glass that looks like it's floating above the ground, partially encircling a small white dome with a Space Age aesthetic—span a wide range. Some consider it a daring shake-up to Haussmannian monotony, others a monstrosity that doesn't belong.[9]

This is also where Esther Saadoun comes when she has to take the metro, though she goes out less and less these days. The sixty-eight-year-old and recent retiree is an example of what life's like on the other side of the housing boom—what it's like to live in a city increasingly hostile to people who don't have a certain amount of disposable income and who don't own the flats they live in.

Esther and I first met a couple years ago for coffee at the Place Colonel Fabien, but this time, she graciously welcomed me into her apartment on the Rue de Meaux, just around the corner. She lives in a towering, fourteen-story housing complex that takes up the entire block—the sort of building one'd expect to find in the outer boroughs of New York City rather than Paris. She shares this forty-eight-square-meter apartment with her daughter. The living room has beige-and-white floral wallpaper and dark green carpets. Near the table, there's a black-and-white *Vogue* magazine with Audrey Hepburn on the cover. She serves coffee and *ka'aks*, dry, sugary biscuits with a hint of orange zest.

Then, there's the black leather sofa. Esther has been sleeping on it for the better part of twenty-six years, ever since her daughter was born. She's always preferred to leave the one bedroom for her daughter, who splits her time between a master's program and an entry-level job in digital marketing. Together, they're able to cover the €850 in monthly rent—combining the job earnings, Esther's pension benefits, and a modest state housing subsidy.

Esther, too, is a product of the Parisian melting pot. Born to a Sephardic Jewish family in Tunis, she emigrated to France with her parents and five siblings in 1958, settling in the Parisian suburb of Créteil. Just four years old when she left Tunis, Esther is more French than anything else. She doesn't speak Arabic; she doesn't speak Hebrew. The first two years of her life, Tunisia was still under the control of the French protectorate, part of the country's colonial empire. She's lived the entirety of her life in this city.

Esther has bright blond hair, speaks slowly, and occasionally punctuates her speech with a warm smile. While everybody tells her the apartment isn't expensive for Paris, it doesn't make the costs easier to swallow. She says she's constantly making calculations about the most basic of expenses. She feels the pressure most at the "end of the month," deploying a turn of phrase popularized by France's Yellow Vests, the protest movement that enveloped the country in the fall of 2018. That weight can feel overwhelming, and it demands difficult choices.

"We can't go on vacation. We don't buy new clothes. I don't go to the hairdresser anymore and I used to go all the time," Esther said. "Sometimes my daughter pays, she says, 'Go treat yourself!' But I'm afraid of spending money. My daughter spends more, maybe she's more courageous, but I'm careful. I'm very, very careful."

Most of the expenses go toward food. "It's all about food. We like to eat well," she said. "We buy what we need to eat, voilà."

They rarely eat out at the trendy restaurants located within walking distance, but Esther likes to cook a lot. Sometimes, she does Asian food, but her favorites are couscous and tajine, a North African stew named for the ceramic dish that it's cooked in. As with couscous, there are a thousand different ways to make it. She likes to throw in olives, lemons, and artichokes. For the meat, it's a mix. "I like lamb, though lamb can be pretty strong, so I sometimes do chicken," she said.

Esther also makes crêpes. It's something she does very well, because it's how she made her living. Starting in 1985, Esther ran food stands across the city, following her ex-husband into the trade to sell crêpes and candy in areas with high foot traffic, renting spots each year from the city of Paris. The allotments were sold at auctions, though the vendors shared a mutual interest in never bidding up too high. Those years, Esther worked everywhere from the Boulevard de Montmartre to the Place de Clichy.

Finally, in 2000, she used her savings to buy a stand of her own and moved to a fixed location just outside the Gare de l'Est, a busy train station, a hub for commuter rail lines, and a starting point for many of the night buses that run into the suburbs. It worked well for years, with the spot attracting a broad mix of clients, both locals and tourists. By the very end of her run, her patrons included growing shares of homeless people and others who looked to be going through substance abuse issues: the down-and-out and destitute spending nights in the streets. "It was a pretty varied clientele," she said, "but I kept it together. I don't really know how."

Toward the end of her career, around 2020, tensions mounted with the city of Paris. She says city officials informed her that the crêpe stand had become a "nuisance," contributing to security problems in the neighborhood. Esther believes the deeper issue was the stand's appearance: it was supposed to be dark green, but over the years, it had become covered in graffiti. By 2020, it was enveloped with tags: everything from small white tags to bright purple letters and the symbol from *V for Vendetta*.

"For twenty years, they didn't say anything. I thought that was weird," Esther said. "It's because my stand became ugly. They wanted something that looked newer."

Weeks of Yellow Vest protests in Paris had already put a damper on foot traffic, sending sales plummeting, though Covid delivered the final blow. Locked down inside her apartment, eligible for retirement, and grappling with medical issues that limit her mobility, Esther decided it was the time to call it quits.

She managed to sell the food truck with the help of a family friend, ultimately holding on to just a couple of items that are of practical use: scales for weighing ingredients and a wooden crêpe spatula.

* * *

Esther wears a Star of David necklace. She said she celebrates
the high holidays, but doesn't practice on a regular basis. She
eats kosher on certain occasions—sometimes, when she has
guests over—but said there's an important reason she doesn't
do it more regularly.

"I think it's expensive!" she exclaimed. "I just looked at the
price at the butcher downstairs, twenty-two euros for a little
piece of meat! I usually get bourguignon for two to three people, which I get at the supermarket. If it was at a normal price,
I'd buy [kosher], but I don't have the means."

Others in her building are presumably forking over the extra
cash. According to Esther, something like "three-fourths" of
the building's residents are Jewish. It's a near-impossible thing
to measure given the absence of public data on religious backgrounds, but the presence is easy to spot. Many of the doors in
the complex have mezuzahs, decorative cases inscribed with
verses from the Torah that are meant as a show of faith.

More generally, this part of the 19th arrondissement, stretching up and beyond the Buttes Chaumont Park, is home to what's
almost certainly the largest practicing Jewish population living
in Paris proper today—most of them, like Esther, with roots in
North Africa. There are dozens of private religious schools and
kosher markets, and over twenty different synagogues. Since
Sephardic Jews started settling in the area in the 1970s, it's
grown into a magnet for an array of currents, with Orthodox
variants broadly becoming more popular.[10]

It occurs to me that, sociologically, there's not a whole lot
separating Esther from Farida or Cândida in Sainte-Marthe.
They're all the daughters of immigrants (Cândida herself was

born in Portugal and came to France with her family at age five), they all come from modest family backgrounds, and they all grew up in the Paris region. They went into very different professional fields, but it's not like the two in Sainte-Marthe have been raking in the big bucks, either. The biggest difference in their standard of living is that Farida and Cândida bought apartments in Paris when they were younger; Esther did not. They caught the boom at the right time; Esther missed out.

As a result, Esther is never far from eviction. And she has a morass of paperwork to prove it: threating letters from her landlord; court summonses; correspondence with housing nonprofits over legal aid and monetary support; applications for public housing and state aid. It's a never-ending headache.

When Esther Saadoun and I first met, back in 2020, her landlord was suing her, requesting thousands of euros in overdue rental charges and seeking a court hearing for eviction. Fortunately, a housing aid NGO came to her defense, covering the back payments and staving off the legal troubles.

But that's just keeping her afloat. The temporary aid doesn't resolve the much bigger problem, which is that Esther and her daughter want better housing and they can't find it. Esther has been on the official list for social housing in Paris since 1996, the year her daughter was born. Every year, she has renewed that demand to no avail.

It was only recently—after the eviction threat, at the behest of the housing group—that she finally decided to file a formal demand for emergency housing. Like Soumia Chohra in the 18th arrondissement, Esther formally requested the state find her a place to live under her enforceable "right to housing."

In late 2021, that request was even accepted—the only problem was the apartment offered. It was a tiny apartment in the

18th arrondissement, right near the Porte de Clignancourt. At €450 a month, it would've been almost half the price she's paying today, but it was even smaller—only thirty-four square meters—with just one bedroom. Unlike her current apartment, there was no elevator, which Esther makes frequent use of.

It wasn't an easy decision, but ultimately, they said no. "If the goal is to be sad and unhappy, it's not worth it," she said.

The deciding factor was Esther's daughter getting a raise at work. She now earns around €1,500 a month, which is just enough to make rent in their current apartment. While they can't make another request for emergency housing for another year, they're still on the hunt for an apartment—ideally one with two bedrooms, so that Esther can stop sleeping on the couch.

One of the essential ingredients of the Parisian melting pot—as imperfect as it always was, as flawed as it is today—has been affordable housing. It's not the only reason Belleville became Belleville, but it was an essential precondition. Without cheap housing, the neighborhood would never have welcomed in so many immigrants in the early half of the twentieth century; it would not have been the destination of choice for North Africans in the 1960s and 1970s. It would not have attracted immigrants from Wenzhou from the 1980s onward.

Affordable housing is also the lifeblood of other, lesser-known immigrant-inhabited micro-neighborhoods spread across the city, places where new arrivals with little cash can set down roots.

It's why there's another "Chinatown" in the 13th arrondissement, in the southern edges of the city, near the Boulevard

Périphérique and the Porte de Choisy. Predating Belleville's Chinatown by a couple decades, the area also counts a large share of immigrants from Vietnam, Cambodia, and Laos—the former colonial holdings of French Indochina.

Affordable housing is why there's a large Tamil-speaking population from Sri Lanka that can be found around La Chapelle, in a small stretch between the Gare du Nord train station and the La Chapelle metro stop, with a handful of shops extending upward into the southern reaches of the 18th arrondissement.[11] It's why there are stores advertising elaborate saris and Bollywood DVDs, and it's why the first Hindu temple in France, the Temple Ganesh, can be found here, hidden inside a nondescript apartment building.

Affordable housing is why there's the even smaller Serbian micro-neighborhood around the Rue du Simplon in the 18th, right near the much larger West African hub at Château Rouge.

The long track record of foreign people setting down roots, launching businesses and mixing with existing influences—the creation of that hybrid culture that's sometimes more Parisian than French—has long hinged on the ability to find lodging that is not prohibitively expensive. But what happens when you pull that fundamental element out of the equation?

The damage can only be measured over time. Maybe Belleville will resemble something like Manhattan's Little Italy or the Lower East Side, museumified versions of working-class immigrant neighborhoods where one can visit a couple of landmark businesses to feel a whiff of the past and remind oneself that ordinary people used to live there. Maybe, with enough time, Belleville will look like the Marais? A place where you can reflect on the fact there's still a lot of history if you manage to tune out the armies of tourists and shoppers. Or maybe it'll be closer to Brixton in South London? A place where a few older immigrant-run businesses hold the line against the homogenized coffee shops and wine stores.

Fortunately, Belleville isn't quite at any of these levels yet, and neither is much of the northeast of the city. But deprived of its core ingredient, the melting pot of Paris is under duress and the brutality of the changes can be hard to overstate. Many of its residents are leaving; its balances are out of whack; its soul is being sucked out in real time.

None of this is reassuring.

And yet, in some ways, it can be a source of solace to remember that there is nothing inevitable about the process of gentrification. While rent hikes and displacement may be ingrained into urban housing markets under capitalism, these processes can be slowed down, frozen, and occasionally even reversed—depending on political will and the nature of state intervention. Chapter 5 will focus on the myriad contemporary battles aimed at just that. The larger struggle is far from over.

But it's also worth remembering the broader context: the legacy that looms over it all. They didn't debate these questions in the same terms, but Paris has long been fought over by the rich and the poor, the haves and the have-nots, the fat-cat developers and their bourgeois allies versus the renters and the destitute taking up coveted space. This tension was the central political question for much of the city's modern existence, starting with the Revolution of 1789, the launching pad for what historian Eric Hobsbawm famously dubbed "the long nineteenth century."

Class struggle—and more precisely, the struggle over space,

over who gets to live where—is embedded into the fabric of Paris. As the struggles of the long nineteenth century show, the upper classes do have a tendency of overplaying their hand. Things can seem under control until all of a sudden, they're not.

3

CITY OF BARRICADES

In many ways, it can't be overstated how radically different Paris was more than two centuries ago, on the eve of the Revolution. There are certain aspects of life in that era that can make comparison seem laughable. Average life expectancy was around thirty years old. For the two-thirds who made it past infancy, they could expect to make it to age forty.[1] People died regularly from diseases like smallpox, tuberculosis, and typhus. There were barely any sewers. Residents dumped waste into the river and into cesspits. Divorce was illegal. Tens of thousands of people worked jobs so removed from today's economy that their professions sound almost made-up: water-carriers, ragpickers, woodturners, boilermakers, hatters.

The grand boulevards didn't yet exist. There were still houses on one of the main bridges running across the Seine. Unlike London, there were few paved streets to be found. Brand-new streetlights that ran on vegetable oil had just gone up, replacing the old candle-lit lights, but mud was omnipresent and streets could become downright impassible when it rained. The nobility moved across town in carriages, zipping through the busiest of thoroughfares, while everyone else walked. People ate tiny fish from the Seine.

And yet, as unreal as this version of the city sounds, revisiting the period is a worthy reminder that the battle over space in Paris is not a new phenomenon—class conflict is embedded into the city's DNA. Already, the wealth divide between the moneyed western neighborhoods and more modest eastern quarters had begun to emerge by the mid-to-late eighteenth century—fueling tensions that erupted in spectacular fashion in 1789. Even in the periods of calm that followed, class conflict loomed large, with ruling elites seeking to keep the power and influence of the growing masses in check. While the two most violent conflicts of the long nineteenth century—the French Revolution and the Paris Commune of 1871—were world-historical events, they were also deeply connected to the people in Paris and the neighborhoods they lived in.

The Divide

The city of Paris has had many chroniclers over the years, but one of the early masters was Louis-Sébastien Mercier. He's perhaps best known in English for his weird and daring work of proto-science fiction, *The Year 2440*, about a man who falls asleep and awakens centuries later in a utopian Paris, governed by a philosopher-king. Religion no longer exists. There are no more armies. No more beggars. Not even many books still appear to be around: a small library holds the most important works, and Rousseau is the only one whose entire work has made the cut.

But a few years later, Mercier also chronicled a present-day version of his city, *Tableau de Paris* (Portrait of Paris), a genre-defying mix of personal observation and reportage. Along with Nicolas Restif de la Bretonne's *Les Nuits de Paris* (Parisian Nights), it's beloved by historians because it offers a rare firsthand account of the city on the eve of a world-historical event: the final volume came out a year before the storming of the Bastille. As the son of Parisian shopkeepers—a modest but financially secure fraction of the petty bourgeoisie—Mercier wasn't afraid to set foot into parts of the city that many of his literary bedfellows tended to avoid or decided weren't worth mentioning.

According to Mercier, the best way to understand the geography of the city was to ascend the towers of the cathedral of Notre Dame.[2] From here, the view in the 1780s would have been even more stunning than it is today. The towers were some of the tallest structures in the city, matched only by the ostentatious golden dome of Les Invalides and a cathedral still under construction on the Left Bank, then known as the Church of Saint Geneviève but eventually renamed the Pantheon.

From this vantage point, Mercier was struck by the sight of limestone, the white and black building materials that he estimated made up "two-thirds" of the city. Otherwise, the skyline was marked by church spires. And of course, there was what he calls the "eternal smoke," black fumes spewing forth from chimney tops and homes across the city, as people used wood for heating. About fifty years later, Honoré de Balzac may have had the same image in mind when he described the city in the introduction to *The Girl with the Golden Eyes*, part of his *Human Comedy* cycle: "There all is smoke and fire, everything gleams, crackles, flames, evaporates, dies out, then lights up again, with shooting sparks, and is consumed."[3]

Mercier wasn't interested in Montmartre or Belleville because, frankly, there wasn't a whole lot going on there back then. Looking out to the north from the top of Notre Dame, the former would've been largely undeveloped farmland, a slope dotted with windmills far from the smoky mass of the city. The latter was another sparsely populated hill, a small village just outside the borders of Paris. These official limits wouldn't have been hard to spot either. They were being traced at the time by a brand-new three-meter-high wall, still under construction when Louis XVI convened the States-General at Versailles in the spring of 1789.

Unlike previous fortifications, the Wall of the Farmers-General was not designed to protect the city from invasion. Above all, it was meant to collect taxes. Just under sixty posts were set up along the wall, overseeing the payment of duties on all goods sold within the city—the infamous *octroi*. A few of these structures are still standing today, most notably at the Parc Monceau and the Place de Stalingrad. They would later spawn the creation of *guinguettes*, rowdy eating and drinking establishments outside the city limits where wine was exempt from the levy.

From the top of the bell towers of Notre Dame, one also would've been able to spot the city's wealth divide, especially if they had some knowledge of what to look for. Paris would become even more segregated by income and class in the years to come, but there were already signs of the west-east cleavage in the mid-to-late eighteenth century.

The nobility made up a tiny segment of the city's roughly six hundred thousand residents, but they controlled a dispropor-tionate amount of space.[4] A small share lived near the center of town in the Marais, only about a fifteen-minute walk northeast of Notre Dame. Their presence here was unmistakable owing to the plethora of *hôtel particuliers*, grandiose townhouses walled off from the rest of the street and which typically featured pri-vate gardens and courtyards. Many of these structures are still standing today, from the Hôtel Salé to the Hôtel de Soubise, which has since become the National Archives.

Even by this point, though, the Marais had already fallen out of fashion among the most influential swaths of the French nobility. While it remained popular with the "nobility of the robe," as they were known, a subcategory of nobles specialized in administrative and legal work, most of the elite groups had already moved further west, setting themselves up for easier access to the court in Versailles.[5]

The "nobility of the sword"—the most elite group, which could point to long-standing military ties with the throne—was concentrated in the Left Bank neighborhood known as the Faubourg Saint-Germain. Here, they built *hôtel particuliers* of their own, rivaling the old homes of the Marais. On the other hand, the "nobility of finance"—a group that could purchase its titles of nobility and which also included parts of the growing bourgeoisie—was drawn to the area referred to as the Faubourg Saint-Honoré.[6] While these two categories of nobility were dis-tinct, they often commingled and intermarried.

Looking straight down from Notre Dame, one would find less open space. Buildings and small alleyways clogged the Île de la Cité, the small island and historic heart of the city that had developed a reputation for crime and indigency. But just due

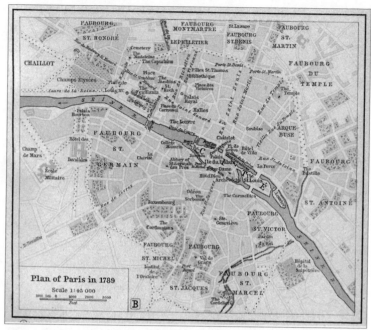

Map of Paris in 1789 from William R. Shepherd's *Historical Atlas*, 1926.

north, the high-density center of Paris would've been unmistakable. The relatively socially mixed neighborhoods here were home to cobblers, masons, carpenters, tailors, butchers, and bakers, all of them rubbing shoulders with lower-paid workers like water-carriers, traveling salesmen, and scrubbers.[7] They also shared the streets with a growing class of middle-class professionals: journalists, lawyers, and doctors who went on to assume much of the political leadership in the coming tumult.

If one looked east, there were the faubourgs. The giant castle and prison of the Bastille marked the beginning of the Faubourg Saint-Antoine, while old farmlands further south were being overtaken by the Faubourg Saint-Marcel. These sprawling neighborhoods were growing rapidly and somewhat chaotically, hosting large shares of the poor arriving from outside the city and looking for work—and they were hotbeds of support for the Revolution.

Originally, the word *faubourg* had referred to villages situated outside the fortifications of Paris. In Old French, *fors le bourg* translates literally as "outside the city." But eventually the term came to describe neighborhoods that were simply on the peripheries of the capital, as it expanded outward. There was an ambiguity to the term that stuck with it for decades: the faubourgs were part of the city, but they were also on their own. They were Parisian, but with an identity that set them apart: a grittier, rowdier, more dangerous version of the city itself.

Victor Hugo was to write this line much later, in *Les Misérables*, but it was inspired, at least in part, by the events that engulfed the city at the end of the eighteenth century: "It is in the faubourgs, above all, that the Parisian race appears."[8]

The Faubourgs

Of the two main faubourgs to the east, the one with the worse reputation was the Faubourg Saint-Marcel, on the Left Bank. In his autobiographical *Confessions*, Jean-Jacques Rousseau described being disappointed when arriving for the first time, in the 1730s:

I had figured to myself a splendid city, beautiful as large, of the most commanding aspect, whose streets were ranges of magnificent palaces, composed of marble and gold. On entering the faubourg St. Marceau [Marcel], I saw nothing but dirty stinking

streets, filthy black houses, an air of slovenliness and
poverty, beggars, carters, butchers, cries of tisane
[herbal tea] and old hats. This struck me so forcibly, that all I have since seen of real magnificence in
Paris could never erase this first impression, which
has ever given me a particular disgust to residing in
that capital.[9]

Even Mercier could barely contain his revulsion. "There is
more money in one single house in the faubourg Saint-Honoré
than the entire faubourg Saint-Marcel," he quipped in his short
chapter on the neighborhood. These lowly people, he stressed,
had nothing in common with the fine inhabitants of Paris.
Nobody has clocks or watches—residents rely on the sun to tell
time—and "particular debates become public debates." It was
a portrait of misery and lewdness. Wives unhappy with their
husbands complained about it openly in the street, getting their
neighbors involved in domestic disputes. Family disagreements
often ended up in sprawling fistfights.

Mercier's account is dripping with condescension, but it does
provide a snapshot of the quarter's image in the public eye. He
writes of residents constantly moving around because they regularly miss rental payments, hauling around their belongings
as they bounce from flat to flat. Lacking financial means, entire
families pack themselves into single rooms. And residents enjoy
drinking excessively. On Sundays, their off day, they head to
the cabarets, dancing without shoes and kicking up "so much
dust that at the end, one can no longer see them." For all the
exaggerations, Mercier may have had a point about the alcohol
consumption. As the social historian Daniel Roche later noted,

there were eight hundred cabarets in the neighborhood by the end of the century, one for every eighty inhabitants.[10]

This is also where Paris's second river used to flow: the Bièvre. Before it was blocked up and paved over in the early twentieth century, its murky waters ran through the heart of the faubourg. Even at this time, it was something like the ugly cousin to the Seine. The Bièvre was thin and famously nasty-looking, as authorities had effectively decided to sacrifice it for early industrial development.[11] That was largely due to the presence of the Royal Gobelins Manufactory, chartered by Louis XIV to specialize in dyeing and tapestry production—a building that is still standing today and, even more remarkably, still operational. The Gobelins employed highly qualified workers who knew the arts of tapestry. But the presence of the Bièvre also spawned a series of smaller workshops devoted to leathermaking, and the neighborhood was home to laborers who occupied different tasks in the production process: tanners; curriers; workers who oversaw tawing and tanning with alum and salt; people charged with adding starch and dye.[12]

Other than leathermaking, much of the faubourg's labor force worked in construction, textiles, and food production. The neighborhood was also home to plenty of day laborers, workers not specialized in anything at all and who were in many cases on the brink of indigency—the "*gagne-deniers*" who were a big reason for the faubourg's miserable reputation. Of the 65,000 people living in the faubourg alone, only two-thirds had actually been born in Paris.[13]

The Faubourg Saint-Antoine was broadly understood as being less destitute than Saint-Marcel. As one observer noted decades after the Revolution, its inhabitants would be "dishonored to be confused with those of the Faubourg St-Marcel."[14] And yet, they had much in common: a massive share of Saint-Antoine's 43,000 residents were immigrants to Paris, with just a third born in the city.[15] The faubourg's defining industry—the one the neighborhood is still associated with even today—was furniture-making. The industry employed nearly a fifth of all men in the Faubourg Saint-Antoine.[16] In one of history's great ironies, these workers were supplying a luxury market driven by demand from nobles: a class whose political power they were about to violently contest.

The vast majority of carpenters and woodworkers employed in the sector worked in small-scale workshops, with only about eight people per boss.[17] But the neighborhood was also home to larger workplaces that hinted at a future mode of production. A few factories known as *manufactures* employed hundreds of workers at a time, churning out glass, wallpaper, and porcelain.[18] One of them hosted a conflict widely seen as a precursor to the Revolution: in April 1789, the director of the Réveillon wallpaper factory allegedly complained about wage rates and contemplated a pay decrease. After word circulated, it spawned a violent riot in the neighborhood, leading to police opening fire and the deaths of dozens.

A couple months later, workers from the Faubourg Saint-Antoine led the assault on the Bastille fortress, a symbol of royal authority and oppression hulking over their neighborhood. Afterward, they formed a group that celebrated their achievement, the "Vanquishers of the Bastille."

It's an impossible task to give the complex events of the French Revolution the attention they merit. Monstrous tomes have been devoted to the power struggle that played out over the span of a decade. But it is worth stressing that the working masses of Paris played a defining role—and especially those in the faubourgs. They were poorly represented in the government's new political institutions, even when the radical Jacobins seized control of the national legislature. They didn't play leading roles in the famous revolutionary clubs. And yet, they were the undeniable motor of events, present at each of the key turning points of the long and tumultuous process that resulted in the overthrow of the monarchy, the installation of a new republican regime, and its gory collapse.

Politically active Parisian masses were represented by the figure of the *sans-culotte*. Before the Revolution, the term referred to people who did not wear knee breeches—an item preferred by the nobility and bourgeoisie. Naturally, this covered a whole swath of the population: manual laborers in small-scale industry, artisans, shopkeepers, day laborers, the unemployed—in other words, the overwhelming majority living in the eastern faubourgs and most of the city center. But as the revolutionary struggle wore on, the most engaged of the bunch infused the term *sans-culotte* with additional political meaning. While they came from a diversity of professions, they had a shared common interest and loyalty to the revolutionary cause, whatever the specific battle or question of the day was.

These were people who drove the Revolution forward.

Months after the fall of the Bastille, in the fall of 1789, thousands of Parisian working women marched to Versailles, demanding authorities tackle the rising cost of bread. Their protest march originated in two places, near the central food market of Les Halles and in the Faubourg Saint-Antoine.[19] After walking for six hours in rain, they burst into the newly formed Constituent National Assembly demanding action, and ultimately dragged King Louis XVI back to Paris with them.

In July 1791, while France was still a constitutional monarchy, an estimated fifty thousand people gathered at the Porte Saint-Antoine and marched toward the Champ de Mars (now home to the Eiffel Tower, then an empty field) to support a petition that questioned the future role of the king. At some point, stones were thrown, and troops commanded by General Marquis de Lafayette shot and killed fifty people. As the work of George Rudé has demonstrated, the dead were the working masses of Paris: small tradesmen, craftsmen, manual laborers, and unemployed workers.

The following year saw further mobilizations against the backdrop of war and rising inflation. In August 1792, a crowd of about twenty thousand stormed the Tuileries Palace, ushering in the fall of the monarchy, the proclamation of the First Republic, and the execution of Louis XVI. But that pivotal day had also resulted in the deaths of nearly four hundred people on the side of the insurgents—many of them shopkeepers, vendors, master craftsmen, and journeymen.[20] The popular faubourgs of Paris accounted for anywhere from one-third to one-half of the casualties.

One of the last great mobilizations of the sans-culottes came in the spring of 1793—when they aligned themselves with more radical clubs dissatisfied with the slow progress of the Republic. As tens of thousands took to the streets, a faction led by the Jacobins seized control of the new legislature and ushered in the most radical phase of the Revolution yet. The new regime imposed price controls, abolished slavery, and approved a radical new constitution guaranteeing the right to work and to public assistance. But it also orchestrated the Reign of Terror, a year of ruthless crackdowns on political opponents and public executions that ultimately resulted in the downfall of the Jacobin leadership itself.

In the end, the sans-culotte dream of building an egalitarian, socially just French Republic failed to materialize. After moderate legislators took control of the state, they abandoned the most radical aims of the Revolution—and eventually, they, too, lost their grip on power. Napoleon Bonaparte orchestrated his successful coup in 1799, taking the title of first consul. Five years later, he proclaimed himself emperor, ushering in an era of non-republican government that lasted the better part of the nineteenth century. As successive empires and monarchies ruled over France throughout these years—the First Empire, the restored Bourbon monarchy, the July Monarchy, the Second Empire—authorities tended to view the Parisian masses with deep suspicion. As the driving force behind republicanism, the city's laborers represented a threat to the authoritarian political order. And as the economy expanded, the changes risked tipping the scales in favor of the capital's ever-growing working population.

The Parisian Working Class: Dirty, Dangerous, and Ready to Revolt

Revolts returned over the course of the nineteenth century, but they were led by a population in deep flux. Paris was growing rapidly, attracting more and more immigrants from nearby regions of France. And the work they came for was increasingly industrialized, as technological advances disrupted many of the old artisanal techniques, replacing some while leaving others intact.

After a slight drop during the Revolution, the city's population doubled in the span of just fifty years, hitting the 1 million mark by 1846. At the time, only London and Beijing were bigger. And as before, the city's growth was fueled by people who came from elsewhere. More than two-thirds—and possibly even more—were born outside Paris.[21] Most of them were poor: according to that year's national census, 650,000 residents were exempt from paying taxes because of a lack of resources.[22] Instead, the city covered the four-franc annual sum they owed, paying it directly to the national government.

In 1848, more than 342,000 Parisians worked in "industrial" jobs, according to a detailed study by the Chamber of Commerce. The organization's definition of "industrial" was vague: it applied to anyone who, through their "work," affected "change" to a product, whereas those who simply sold products "as they had bought them" were considered *commerçants*, employed in commerce.[23] This relatively loose definition of industrial labor applied to much of the population. After accounting for women and children sharing households with workers and business owners in this sector, industrial activity supported about six-tenths of the city's population by mid-century.[24]

This scene was very different from the massive textile mills of Manchester, England, where Friedrich Engels had just been dispatched by his family. Employing hundreds at a time, these sprawling factories and their chimneys towered over the city and the small cottages where workers resided. To be sure, there were a few Parisian sectors undergoing technological advances that had begun to employ relatively large shares of workers per firm. New railroads also employed many, while the construction sector continued to feature a large share of employees per firm, around ten to one. And yet, by the middle of the nineteenth century, the vast majority of jobs were still conducted on a small scale, overseen by a "master worker" in a small workshop, or done at home, sometimes with the help of family members.[25] Many of those using their bodies to make a living would've also thought of themselves as artisans, the distinction blurring with the French word for worker, *ouvrier*. Many of the professions of pre-revolutionary Paris endured, even as the nature of work was evolving.

The notion that these laborers belonged to a class with shared common interests was starting to germinate, sparking theoretical debate and discussion. But no matter how one came down on this question, it was clear the character of the city was becoming increasingly defined by work—and more precisely, by manual labor. This reality would've been visible to anyone visiting midcentury Paris. Not only did a dizzying array of small businesses and workshops continue to line the streets, with bakers, butchers, and cobblers keeping the old medieval scents alive. But technological advances were creating new types of workplaces, with Parisians flocking to freshly built gasworks, railyards, and chemical plants, as a flow of construction jobs sustained the expansion. Migrants were just about everywhere and constantly arriving, a reminder of what the city represented for the rest of the country: this wasn't just the political and cultural capital of France, it was a place to find work and eke out a living.

In 1848, roughly ninety thousand Parisians were employed in clothing production, many of them working independently from home. They made hats, stitched shoes, sewed dresses, knit sweaters, and altered jackets, selling their services for a pittance. The invention of the first sewing machine in 1830 would transform the industry, but it took time for mass industrial practices to kick in. By midcentury, the production of clothing was still painfully time-consuming.

Meanwhile, tens of thousands of Parisians still worked in cabinet-making and furniture production, with the sector remaining clustered around the workshops of the Faubourg Saint-Antoine. A similar number were employed in the almost comically broad category of *articles de Paris*, a sector that corresponds to something like high-quality knickknacks. This included much of what didn't fit into other categories: people churning out jewelry, small bronze statuettes, watches, artificial flowers, musical instruments, umbrellas, ornaments, gloves.[26] There were also nearly seventeen thousand people involved in the printing industry, producing books, newspapers, and pamphlets.

Paris was also home to a myriad of professions not covered by that 1848 study because they were presumably not considered "industrial" enough.[27] Nevertheless, these jobs required a lot of physical labor and offered low pay in return: people working as cooks and servers in restaurants; "artist-sculptors"; fruit and vegetable merchants; ambulant vendors of various kinds, selling everything from lampshades to potatoes; the emblematic *chiffonniers*, or ragpickers, thousands of people who made a living from picking up and reselling waste thrown into the streets. There were even still water-carriers, burly men who transported buckets up and down the stairs for a living. While their numbers had dwindled, there were still thousands by the middle of the nineteenth century, many of them hailing from the central region of Auvergne.[28]

There were also, of course, large numbers of prostitutes, a profession long tolerated by French authorities. It's hard to know just how many. By the end of the eighteenth century,

Nicolas Restif de la Bretonne estimated there were twenty thousand in Paris. In 1832, only 3,600 in Paris were officially registered with the police prefecture, but this underestimated their true number, as it only included those working in brothels, known as *maisons closes*.

The golden era of the *maison close* would arrive later in the century, in the Belle Époque, but nonetheless, there were nearly two hundred of them in Paris at this time.[29] The most prestigious were located in the area of Notre-Dame de Lorette, a neighborhood just south of Montmartre and the Wall of the Farmers-General inhabited by a largely bourgeois and aristocratic population. This gave birth to the term *lorette*, a word used to describe a young, attractive, and elegantly dressed woman offering her services—a figure idealized by many nineteenth-century writers, from Balzac to the Goncourt brothers.[30] The Palais Royal was another famous hub, while plenty of other women worked the streets of central Paris, around the food market at Les Halles, the area around City Hall, and on the Île de la Cité, all neighborhoods that were fairly mixed socioeconomically.[31]

Paris was also home to a large indigent population—that is, people without wealth or income on the margins of the labor market, or who were simply excluded from it altogether. Here, too, there are wide variations in the numbers. Officially, the term "indigent" referred to those who needed assistance from charity, a group that often included single elderly people, the homeless, and orphaned children.[32] The city counted 66,000 such people in 1844, about one in every fourteen inhabitants.[33] But it all depends on one's definition of indigency: the utopian socialist Perreymond (known only by this one-name pseudonym) estimated that three hundred thousand Parisians fit this term in 1848.[34] This would've meant about a third of the city was struggling to get by on a day-to-day basis.

Together, these were Parisians often referred to derisively as the *populace* or the *canaille*: a mix of low-paid laborers working in semi-industrialized sectors, an army of merchants and vendors whose jobs hadn't fundamentally changed since the medieval era, and the truly destitute living on the fringes of society. They had little resources and were far more likely to be born outside the city than their bourgeois or aristocratic counterparts. The latter, meanwhile, were increasingly concerned about living in proximity to the former. In the eyes of France's economic and political elites, the capital's laboring classes came to be associated with three tropes: they were dirty and unhygienic; they were dangerous and criminally minded; and they were prone to violent revolt. The tropes often overlapped with one another—and of course, they were actually grounded in fact, to varying degrees.

The poor and the neighborhoods they inhabited were often literally seen as being sick, as infectious and capable of transmitting deadly illness. Disease had long been a part of city life, but Paris suffered a brutal flare-up of cholera in 1832. From March to September, the malady spread like wildfire, killing some eighteen thousand people in the capital alone.[35] It hit poor neighborhoods much harder than the wealthy ones, corresponding almost perfectly with socioeconomic status.

The parts of the city hit hardest were in the northeast and southeast, in the same faubourgs that had risen up in the Revolution of 1789. There were also a lot of casualties in the center, the areas around the Porte Saint-Denis and Porte Saint-Martin that had welcomed many of the newer arrivals.[36] On the other hand, the west, where the moneyed classes lived largely among themselves, emerged relatively spared. In an episode that sounds eerily familiar, the wealthy took off, leaving Paris to the poor. Then working as a correspondent in Paris for a popular German newspaper, the writer and poet Heinrich Heine reported on the grumbling of the masses: "The people murmured loudly when they saw that that the rich saved themselves and took off, with doctors and pharmacies, on the path toward safer lands. The poor remarked with displeasure that money, too, had become a protection against death."[37]

Back in 1832, there was an understanding that the outbreak was connected to contaminated water, but the disease wasn't yet fully understood—only the fact that it appeared to strike the poorer parts of the city more than the others. In the final report commissioned by authorities and conducted by health experts, authors concluded that the spread of cholera was linked to subpar social conditions: "It is impossible," they wrote, "not to believe there exists a *certain type of population* [emphasis mine], like a certain type of place, that is favorable to the development of cholera, making it more intense and deadlier."[38] The commission's supposed proof was that the disease didn't just hit those neighborhoods close to the River Seine, but also ones further away to the northeast and southeast. The only common denominator was poverty.[39]

Scientists and health experts later discovered that poor hygiene and subpar sanitation practices do, in fact, encourage the development of cholera. The disease is often spread by food and water that have been contaminated by human feces harboring a specific bacterium. But the bacterium wasn't isolated until the 1850s, and it would take time for a public health consensus over the importance of waste and sewage treatment to take hold. When the disease tore through the city, there was simply a sense that the neighborhoods themselves were vaguely responsible for the contagion—the small streets, the overcrowding, the lack of proper air circulation, the habits of residents.[40]

The riffraff were also associated deeply with crime, a subject famously tackled by the historian-demographer Louis Chevalier in his now-classic *Laboring Classes and Dangerous Classes* (1958). In the early decades of the nineteenth century, the Parisian masses were seen as dangerous, capable of stealing, swindling, assaulting, and even killing passersby. There was not a documentable crime wave, and yet the lines between subpar socioeconomic conditions and criminality blurred in the public eye. Chevalier's work can be hard to digest, but it shouldn't be forgotten that he was drawing on the opinion of the state apparatus itself. In 1840, a police administrator named H.A. Frégier wrote a study called *The Dangerous Classes*. For Frégier, "the poor and immoral classes [had] always been the most productive incubator for all kinds of miscreants."[41]

As others have noted, the blurring of these lines was visible in one of the most successful novels of the era, Eugène Sue's *The Mysteries of Paris*. Serialized in a newspaper from 1842 to 1843, Sue's work recounts the escapades of a grand duke disguised as a Parisian worker who gets involved in a series of adventures with the city's lower classes. (The novel opens with the main character saving a prostitute from being beaten on the Île de la Cité, before embarking on a series of improbable twists and turns featuring an orphaned singer, a butcher, a partially blind old lady, and plenty of prisoners.) While his contemporaries Balzac and Stendhal have better stood the test of time, in its day, Sue's work was read far more than either of theirs. *The*

Mysteries of Paris was also, crucially, read by the masses themselves. The son of a celebrated surgeon, Sue later called himself a socialist—it's the upper classes who come across the worst in the book, indifferent to the plight of the people.

If the Parisian masses' propensity for poor hygiene and criminal activity was largely a projection, the other great fear of the ruling elites was, in fact, far more grounded in reality. On several different occasions in the first half of the nineteenth century, the masses of Paris took to the streets and clashed violently with authorities, almost always with national political ramifications. Napoleon's reign as emperor went relatively unchallenged in the capital, but, following his dramatic abdication and a short-lived return to power that unraveled at the Battle of Waterloo in 1815, the Bourbon monarchy took back the machinery of the French state. From this point onward, the French government was notoriously unstable, subject to challenges on a recurring basis by tens of thousands of Parisians.

The nature of the regime, the degree of public sympathy, and the success of the revolts all varied, but common themes ran throughout these early nineteenth-century uprisings. In addition to calls for basic material improvements of varying kinds—price controls and work guarantees were two of the most frequent ones—participants defended broadly liberal-reformist political ideals and invoked the memory of the French Revolution to varying degrees. The demonstrators also adopted a common tactic, which eventually become synonymous with mass uprisings: the barricade. It went up in 1827, 1830, 1832, 1834, 1839, and, of course, in 1848.

The barricade was designed for insurrectionary street combat. It was composed of just about everything its defenders could find and carry: uprooted trees, paving stones, unhinged doors, furniture, planks of wood, windows, hogsheads. While it later became a powerful symbol, it initially had real tactical value, protecting those in revolt and allowing them to hold out for extended periods of time against their better-equipped enemies.[42] Although it had made its first appearance in Paris during a crucial day in the religious wars of the late sixteenth century, the barricade was curiously absent during the revolutionary tumult that forged the first Republic. It only returned in the nineteenth century, with a restored Bourbon monarchy failing to provide economic stability or relinquish its tight grip on political power.

In 1827, a small group of liberals had erected barricades on the Rue Saint-Denis in central Paris, confronting police sent by the government of Charles X to squash a celebration of a minor election victory. But a much larger outpouring came just three years later. Rallied by liberal opposition, thousands took to the streets, erecting a staggering four thousand barricades across the city, and ultimately forcing the abdication of the king. It's these three days of violent confrontation with the police—the July Revolution, or the *Trois Glorieuses* (Three Glorious [Days])—that inspired Eugène Delacroix's famous *Liberty Leading the People*, often mistaken for a depiction of the French Revolution.

A much more ill-fated uprising greeted the newly installed constitutional monarchy of Louis-Philippe shortly thereafter. Just months after the start of the city's deadly cholera wave, a call to arms was pushed by a more motley crew of republicans, disappointed in the lack of reform from a regime that had adopted the tricolor flag. The so-called June Rebellion failed miserably, resulting in scores of deaths and wounded, though it lived on thanks to Victor Hugo's *Les Misérables*. In Hugo's text, a critical scene takes place at a barricade on the Rue de la Chanvrerie, a street that no longer exists just off the Rue Saint-Denis. While this corresponds broadly to one of the central and eastern neighborhoods briefly held by insurgents, there almost certainly wasn't an actual barricade on the Rue de la Chanvrerie in 1832.[43] Hugo's barricade seems instead to be a synthesis of barricades of the nineteenth century, but it offers a valuable description:

> The fact is, that it did not exceed an average height of six or seven feet. It was built in such a manner that the combatants could, at their will, either disappear behind it or dominate the barrier and even scale its crest by means of a quadruple row of paving-stones placed on top of each other and arranged as steps in the interior. On the outside, the front of the barricade, composed of piles of paving-stones and casks bound together by beams and planks, which were entangled in the wheels of Anceau's dray and of the overturned omnibus, had a bristling and inextricable aspect.[44]

Similarly doomed barricade-laden revolts erupted in 1834 and in 1839, both of them led by alliances of working masses and more solidly middle-class republicans. The former resulted in a brutal police massacre, immortalized in a lithograph by Honoré Daumier. Amid a skirmish on the barricades in central Paris, a soldier was allegedly wounded by a bullet that came from inside a nearby house, leading authorities to sweep in and kill a dozen people inside. Shocking for its hyperrealism, the *Massacre de la rue Transnonain* depicts four corpses, with the main subject lying over an infant, and blood curdling on the floor.

A subsequent court investigation produced detailed information about the house itself, providing a snapshot of what the mixed residences of central Paris looked like. Although not as dilapidated as certain buildings in the eastern peripheries, it was cramped and dominated by manual laborers. It hosted shops on the ground floor; more prosperous artisans and small business owners on the first and second floors; workers, apprentices, and day laborers on the third and fourth floors: a jeweler, a hatter, a gilder, a bronzeworker, a specialized leatherworker, a construction painter, a stonecutter, a seamstress, an artist-painter, a painter-glazier, a polisher of clocks, and a repairer.[45]

In terms of sheer numbers and political consequence, the most significant of the revolts came in 1848, the biggest since the wave of tumult that kicked off in 1789. With the monarchy's popularity waning, an alliance of workers, republicans, middle-class liberals, and students took to the streets of Paris, stormed government buildings, put up fifteen hundred barricades in one night, and obtained the resignation of Louis-Philippe. With the backing of bourgeois reformists convinced that the regime was outdated and incapable of modernizing itself, they proclaimed the Second Republic. But it lasted only briefly.

Upon taking power, the new government quickly sought to appease the growing workers' movement, recognizing "the right to work" and creating national workshops designed to provide labor and compensation for the unemployed, concessions that speak to the enormous political weight of the Parisian masses. But the expensive and inefficient policy angered the coalition's bourgeois elements, and the cross-class alliance began to tear at the seams. When authorities disbanded the workshops in June, it triggered yet another workers' revolt—more barricades, more bloodshed—irrevocably alienating the regime.

One of the earliest-ever daguerreotypes captures this moment in the east of the city: *Barricade on the Rue Saint-Maur-Popincourt Before the Attack of General Lamorcière's Troops.* It's an entrancing image, in part because of its surreally old age—it comes from an era that seems like it should be inaccessible through photography. In the row of dirty, soot-layered apartments visible in the image, there were likely residents who had lived through the execution of Louis XVI. But the shot's true force comes from the false sense of hope it conveys on the part

Charles François Thibault, *Barricade on the Rue Saint-Maur-Popincourt Before the Attack of General Lamorcière's Troops*, June 25, 1848.

of the insurrectionists: the barricades are up; the confrontation with the army hasn't happened yet; the battle is looming. Anyone looking at it today knows the movement was doomed to fail, that the political coalition was existentially untenable. There's a second daguerreotype, taken after the attack of the troops: it's less clear, but you can make out people in the streets, surveying the damage.

In any case, the June Days had effectively sealed the Republic's fate, and by the end of the year, voters elected Louis Napoleon as president in a landslide. Three years later, he dispatched with the constraints of the Republic, and in 1852, proclaimed the Second Empire. Once again, popular dreams of an egalitarian republic had been snatched away by a despot supported by commercial elites and conservative forces. This was the historical episode that birthed the famous quip from Marx, reflecting on the parallels between Louis Napoleon's seizure of state power and the dramatic coup of his more famous uncle fifty years earlier: "Hegel remarks somewhere that all great world-historic facts and personages appear, so to speak, twice. He forgot to add: the first time as tragedy, the second time as farce."[46]

Haussmannization: Nineteenth-Century Gentrification

It was the authoritarian regime of Napoleon III that built the Paris most people recognize today: the wide, tree-lined boulevards and giant plazas where they intersect; the uniformized six- to seven-story apartment buildings with their identically colored stone and mansard roofs; the evergreen-colored press kiosks; the elegant streetlamps. While the importance of the renovations can sometimes be exaggerated, they no doubt accelerated trends already in place, casting off the city's remaining medieval heritage, deepening its preexisting wealth divides, and cementing its socioeconomic segregation. From 1853—shortly after Napoleon appointed Georges-Eugène Haussmann to the ultra-important post of prefect of the Seine—until 1870, Paris was transformed into a giant construction site.

It's no doubt a crude oversimplification to suggest the Baron de Haussmann was motivated simply by a desire to eliminate the prospects of street barricades.[47] Haussmann surely had street fighting in mind, but in the end, one could say he was more concerned about controlling the population associated with the barricades than literally eliminating the structures themselves. As well as reducing the risks of political instability, the urban planner was motivated by long-standing concerns over the flow of traffic and by anxieties over public health, the latter of which were amplified by the cholera epidemic, which returned in 1849. But one should also be careful about chalking up the renovations to the ambitions of a single individual. Haussmann was presiding over a city marked by a growing share of bourgeois residents looking for more comfortable places to live and emerging financial capitalists looking for worthwhile investments—core constituencies of the new regime in place. All of this weighed on the massive renovation plans.

On a basic level, the reforms sought to improve the circulation of traffic and air. Under Haussmann's watch, the city embarked upon the construction of wide boulevards: among others, the Boulevard Saint-Michel and the Boulevard Sebastopol forming a crucial north-south axis; the extended Rue de Rivoli and the brand-new Boulevard Saint-Germain running east-west on opposite banks of the Seine; the Boulevard de Magenta and the Rochechouart-Ornano corridor extending north past the city limits; a number of boulevards in the swanky west. All of these new streets were supposed to better connect the city's rail stations to one another and "air out" the city center, making Paris more amendable to travel, business, and public health. (The baron was obsessed with the notion of *aération*.)

That the hyper-dense city center was considered "aired out" after the reforms conveys just how cramped things were before. The author and critic Jules Janin was surely exaggerating in his overview of the city in 1844, but his description of an alleyway off the central Rue du Roule, just a five-minute walk north of the Seine, offers some perspective into how Parisians of a certain social class viewed the maze of alleyways toward the center. On a street "so dark that the lamps burn throughout the day," Janin recounted the tale of one poor bedridden resident who gained so much weight that once she recovered, "it was impossible [for her] to leave" and make it through the narrow passage.[48]

The vast majority of these alleyways and passages were demolished by Haussmann, but a few did manage to escape the renovations, like the sinuous Passage de la Trinité, not far from the spot Janin describes. Irredeemably bleak during the sun-deprived Parisian winters, its eternal shadows still offer a refuge from the summer heat today. There's hardly enough space for two bikes to make it through here at once, let alone packs of pedestrians. And if you stumble into a group of people here, it does have the effect of making you appreciate Janin's anecdote.

Health concerns also drove Haussmann to create a new public water system—one clearly separating potable from non-potable water—as well a brand-new underground sewage system. These innovations were designed to reduce the risks of disease—cholera, in particular. To a lesser extent, health concerns also played a role in the construction of new parks: the massive Bois de Boulogne and the Parc Monceau in the wealthy west, but also the Bois de Vincennes and Buttes Chaumont toward the east.

The reforms also sought to make the city more enjoyable for bourgeois residents, a growing share of the Parisian population with newly disposable income to toss around. The most famous of these projects was the Opéra Garnier, the extravagant, rococo-inspired two-thousand-seat opera house finished shortly after the end of Napoleon III's reign. Its green dome and busy facade, featuring sculptures of electrotyped copper meant to resemble bronze, scream luxury and self-indulgence, while on the inside, the grand staircase and grand foyer hammer home the point. New boulevards nearby gave root to an array of shops catering to the opera's high-paying clientele, including one of the world's first-ever department stores, Printemps. Here, as at the other so-called *grands magasins* that sprung up around the city at the same time, consumers could browse for clothes, kitchen items, and housing products all under the same roof—and in an enjoyable space that encouraged them to take their time. This was the start of mass consumption as an experience of its own, shopping as spectacle.

But as the work of geographer David Harvey shows, Haussmann's reforms also benefited the growing share of bourgeois residents in a far more tangible way: by increasing the value of land.[49] Over the course of two decades, banks and developers pumped enormous sums of money into the transformation of Paris and made out with phenomenal returns. During Napoleon III's reign, from 1852 to 1870, the total value of Parisian property increased from 2.5 to 6 billion francs.[50] A lot of people got filthy rich: while the state laid the foundations and managed the process throughout, a web of private sector actors identified opportunities for profit and extracted value from a market that hadn't been known for being so lucrative.

The state's tool of choice—the mechanism that put the wheels of this early gentrification in motion—was expropriation. Following a December 1852 Senate law that expanded Napoleon III's authoritarian powers, the government was authorized to seize land by simple executive decree. With this new authority, it embarked on a multiyear binge, taking over land from a myriad of low- to middle-grade property owners and selling it to a web of larger developers with which it maintained close relations.[51] As Harvey shows, it was these large-scale developers, backed themselves by a growing financial sector, who oversaw much of the renovation and construction in central Paris.

To ease concerns about all the cash it was burning through, the state also began to sell unused parcels of the land it had expropriated at freshly inflated post-construction values. Since prices were constantly on the rise, the expropriations tended to finance themselves. In other words, the state itself was a high-grade speculator, its day-to-day operations dependent on a relentless increase in land prices.

The expropriation frenzy was slowed by a couple of court rulings that favored resistant property owners toward the end of the decade, delaying construction projects and raising the costs of the state taking over private land. But they didn't stop the bubble from inflating further. From this point onward, Haussmann began to lean more on credit, with new financial institutions stepping up to the plate. Two of the most critical ones were the Crédit Mobilier and the Crédit Foncier, both of

them linked to the politically influential Péreire family. The
state also relied on the Caisse des Travaux, a special public
works fund overseen directly by Haussmann that issued bonds
to fund operations.

It's no coincidence that France's most powerful and well-
known banks also got their start in this era, getting in on
the action in Paris. The Crédit Industriel et Commercial, the
Crédit Lyonnais, and the Banque de Paris, predecessor to BNP
Paribas, were all founded in the 1850s and 1860s.[52] (All in all,
these loans—some of which were taken out at less-than-desired
interest rates—left the city greatly indebted. Paris didn't finish
paying back debt incurred in the Haussmann era until 1929.)[53]

Much of the construction took place in what were already well-
to-do quarters, leaving wealthy residents with new spacious
apartments and verdant boulevards to stroll on. Haussmannization in one of its purest forms can be found in the residential avenues near the Arc de Triomphe. These were already
fairly quiet areas removed from the chaos of the city center, but
they were vastly upgraded under Napoleon III: among others,
the Avenue de Friedland, Avenue Kléber, Boulevard Pereire,
and the crowned jewel, the Avenue Foch.

But the renovations also transformed the center of Paris,
which was home to a much more socially mixed population.
Nowhere was this process more brutal than on the Île de la
Cité, where 25,000 residents were expelled from their homes
and entire blocks razed to the ground. While the Notre Dame
Cathedral and the Sainte-Chapelle survived the devastation,
the surrounding area was transformed from a living and
breathing neighborhood into a barren administrative hub. The
streets described in Eugène Sue's *Mysteries of Paris*—a place

Haussmann derided as being "choked by a mass of shacks . . . inhabited by bad characters and crisscrossed by damp, twisted and filthy streets"—gave way to a collection of government buildings, with a brand-new barracks and courthouse joining the Palais de Justice and a newly expanded hospital.[54] Thanks to the new open-air plaza, the beauty of Notre Dame could be better contemplated from the ground level, freeing sightseers from any brush-ups with odd and undesirable locals. This was something of a precursor to the museumification of Paris.

While Haussmann wasn't motivated solely by dreams of reducing the likelihood of urban revolts, a series of tactical reforms clearly targeted certain neighborhoods known for their political restlessness. In the Faubourg Saint-Antoine, where memories of the 1848 barricades were still fresh, authorities drove the Canal Saint-Martin underground and covered it with the Boulevard Richard-Lenoir, a wide new artery running through the western swath of the neighborhood. This removed a key maritime barrier of defense preferred by insurgents. But as Haussmann later boasted about in his memoirs, his plan also made it possible to "attack the faubourg from the rear."[55] After construction of the Boulevard Voltaire and Boulevard Diderot, the entire Faubourg Saint-Antoine was hemmed in by three broad avenues, theoretically difficult to block with barricades and ready-made for imperial troop movements.

Haussmann also proudly admitted that the new roads he created in the city center marked a "gutting of the old Paris, the neighborhood of riots and barricades with a large central route."[56] In addition to this dominant artery—the Boulevard Sebastopol—the Rue de Turbigo and the Rue Étienne Marcel both cut clear lines through the old jumble of streets, and the Rue Transnonain, site of the 1834 massacre, was lit-

erally removed from the map. (While they aren't explicitly
mentioned by Haussmann as having either strategic or political value, a couple of major projects on the Left Bank can be
viewed through the same lens: the Boulevard Saint-Marcel
cut through the impoverished Faubourg Saint-Marcel, while
the Rue Gay-Lussac and Rue Claude Bernard allowed for easy
access around the Montagne Sainte-Geneviève, another frequent location of street fighting.)

As with the most brutal forms of gentrification, Haussmann's renovations produced mass displacement and helped
transform the geography of the city. Not only were tens of
thousands removed from their homes, but the ensuing price
hikes ensured that class-based spatial segregation would be a
defining part of Parisian life for years to come. Under imperial
rule, the city's east-west wealth divide grew sharper than ever.
While the area around the food market of Les Halles marked a
notable exception, the reforms largely pushed the poor and the
riffraff away from the city center.

Until Haussmann's reign, socially mixed apartments in the
center of Paris were still fairly commonplace. People with radically different levels of wealth and social status were more likely to bump into each other in the stairwell. Like the building
that witnessed the infamous 1832 massacre, shops tended to
occupy the ground floor, while the wealthiest lived on the floor
above it, known as the "noble floor," the largest and easiest to
reach. Residents descended in social class until the very top of
the building, where the poorest lived.[57] After Haussmann, this
model became increasingly rare. To borrow a commonly used
phrase from French historians, vertical segregation gave way to
horizontal segregation.

Another major reform from Haussmann ensured that many

of the displaced would remain (at least nominally) residents of Paris. In 1860, the city opted to demolish the Wall of the Farmers-General and extend the city borders outward in all directions. Overnight, Paris doubled in acreage, increased its population by a third, and grew from twelve to twenty arrondissements. The new frontiers were placed at what were known as the "Thiers fortifications," a wall of defensive barriers installed a couple decades prior. The villages of Montmartre, Belleville, Batignolles, La Villette, and Charonne, among others, were all annexed to Paris. For imperial authorities, the reforms carried the promise of expanded tax revenue and an opportunity to better manage the population in question.[58]

While the former villages were suffused with the resources of new inhabitants and became bustling neighborhoods of their own, the renovations had also dealt an irrevocable blow to the city's medieval core. Baudelaire's oft-cited "The Swan," from 1861, captures the sense of loss felt by those partial to its mystery and dark romance:

> *Old Paris is gone (no human heart*
> *changes half so fast as a city's face)*
> *and only in my mind's eye can I see*
> *the junk laid out to glitter in the booths*
> *among the weeds and splintered capitals,*
> *blocks of marble blackened by the mud; . . .*[59]

Émile Zola's lamentations were more explicitly political.[60] In an 1872 article, one of several he published on Haussmann's renovations, the novelist wrote that the "old Paris" had been "cleansed." To finish "the cleansing," the masses were being pushed out to the hinterlands. They were no longer welcome in the city center.

The Backlash

If the main goal of Haussmannization was to kick out the poor from central Paris, it was an undeniable success. But if it was to make the city barricade-proof, then it was a spectacular failure. The reforms didn't remove poverty or a growing mass of laborers from Paris, but rather displaced both and concentrated them in the same areas, a risky gamble that backfired in dramatic fashion. When France descended into a political crisis in 1870, it provided the impetus for an urban revolt that was far greater and far bloodier than anything since the Revolution.

The Paris Commune of 1871 was many different things: an experiment in worker self-government; a fleeting moment of liberation for women; a backlash against the suffocating and conservative influence of the Catholic Church; a source of inspiration for socialist movements worldwide. But it was also, as the historian Jacques Rougerie has argued, the revenge of those who'd been pushed out to the peripheries of Paris in the preceding decades, the victims of the empire's brutal urban reforms.[61] For a brief two months, the working masses reclaimed central Paris as theirs.

In the run-up to the Commune, residents of the lower-class neighborhoods had been swimming in revolutionary political ideas—and that started with republicanism. While they've since lost much of their anti-establishment luster, the ideals of the French Republic—*liberté, égalité, fraternité*—were imbued with radicalism at a time when the country was ruled by an imperial police state. Against a backdrop of authoritarianism and gaping wealth divides, the Republic represented France's unrealized promise of democratic self-government and social

justice. Critics of Napoleon III's regime were regularly imprisoned, and the most forceful of dissidents were sent off to the
bagnes, a series of penal colonies operating overseas. (Devil's
Island in French Guiana was one of the more notorious ones,
hosting hundreds of political prisoners in the early 1850s, about
a fifth of whom died in the camp.) Calling for basic political
freedoms and equality among citizens could be a risky move,
and there was plenty of sympathy for those who did so.

This rich tradition had been complemented by a rapidly
developing socialist movement, a diverse set of thinkers who
believed in the broad principles of collective ownership and
rational management of resources. They included theorists
like Henri de Saint-Simon and Charles Fourier—the "utopian socialists," as Karl Marx derisively labeled them—as well
as full-fledged politicians like Louis Blanc. The latter took an
especially active role in 1848, elected to the National Assembly alongside Victor Hugo, both of them staunch proponents
of parliamentary democracy. An architect of the failed national workshops, Blanc left for London in exile after the bloody
June Days, though his socialist twist on French republicanism remained a steady source of inspiration for critics of Louis
Napoleon.

Other working Parisians were drawn to the ideas of Auguste
Blanqui. A veteran of the Parisian barricade battles of the
1830s and 1840s who spent much of his life in prison, Blanqui
shared the socialists' commitment to collective ownership and
the redistribution of wealth. But he had a much more hardened
theory of change. Unconvinced by the merits of parliamen-
tarism, Blanqui endorsed the use of revolutionary violence and
the need for a small group of dedicated insurgents to seize power and instill changes from the top down. This wasn't the most

theoretically sophisticated doctrine, but Blanquism had natural appeal at a time when France was governed by an imperial police state backed to the hilt by financial elites.

Some radicals gravitated toward the ideas of Pierre-Joseph Proudhon. A precursor to the anarchist tradition, Proudhon and his allies called for a federation of independent self-governing units—the foundation of what he called "scientific socialism." Despite their disagreements with the Blanquists, these mutualists had participated alongside them in the creation of the International Workingmen's Association in London in 1864. Seven years later, Karl Marx had emerged as one of the leaders of this organization, which was gaining support among a subset of politically conscious Parisians.

As these ideas circulated, rank-and-file Parisian workers had begun to organize themselves on the shop floor, too. Officially, trade unions remained outlawed in France, but an 1864 reform had authorized laborers to go on strike and to form "coalitions," which they did to an impressive degree over the following several years. Also in 1864, a strike led by Parisian bookbinders resulted in wage hikes and a reduction in working hours.[62] In 1869, employees of the new department stores walked off the job to demand Sundays off to rest; they were joined that same year by marble workers, wood workers, and leather workers.[63] By 1869, in Paris alone, at least 165 workers' associations represented some 160,000 members.[64]

Meanwhile, the industrial workforce continued its steady expansion, though relatively few made a living at large factories.[65] A few well-known ones employed upward of a thousand workers—for instance, the Say sugar refinery and the Cail steam engine works, both of which sat on the western banks of the Seine in the southeast of the city—but many Parisians still worked from home or in small workshops. Life expectancy had improved from the previous century, but existence was a grim affair for much of the Parisian working class. Wages were low. Work was often grueling. And there was usually little time left for much else.

The wretched conditions also produced a new generation of leaders. There were people like Eugène Varlin, a bookbinder born to peasants just outside Paris who'd led the 1864 strike and had joined Karl Marx's new International. And Nathalie Lemel, another bookbinder who oversaw a cooperative restaurant for workers, La Marmite.[66] And Louise Michel, a schoolteacher critical of the lack of rights for women and their substandard treatment at home. All of them would become active in the movement that took back control of their city.

Like many other revolutions, the Commune was forged in crisis, a moment of deep uncertainty that allowed otherwise impractical dreams to become realizable. After Louis Napoleon launched a war on Prussia, French troops suffered a brutal defeat at the Battle of Sedan, resulting in the capture of the emperor himself. With German forces on the march westward, a group of legislators seized the moment to proclaim a new French republic, vowing to defend the nation against the foreign invaders. But the German military ultimately proved insurmountable. In the fall of 1870, Prussian troops launched a terrible siege on the French capital, and despite months of stubborn resistance, the new government finally signed an armistice in January that favored the Prussians as victors.

The surrender only widened the gulf between French elites and the city's working masses. Residents of Paris had just resisted a brutal siege only to see the state surrender in their name. Moreover, their new government, though nominally republican, was filled with many of the old foes of the *peuple de Paris*. While the city of Paris elected republicans to the National Assembly in February 1871, the rest of the country voted in a comfortable majority of monarchists, split between those favoring a restoration of the House of Orléans and those for the House of Bourbon. Aware of the simmering hostility in the capital, these legislators opted the following month to govern from Versailles, rather than inside the city itself. On the other side of the city's fortifications, armed neighborhood troops known as the National Guard, a ragtag bunch of conscripts initially formed to defend Paris against the Prussians, remained on watch.

In March came the trigger that set off the insurrection. The government in Versailles dispatched forces to dismantle the National Guard's defensive weapons and, while the process appeared to go well at first, it ran into resistance on the slopes of the Butte Montmartre. Encountering a crowd of angry residents from the recently annexed neighborhood, soldiers ignored the orders of their commanding officer General Claude Lecomte to fire on the civilians. A group of locals then captured Lecomte, executing him alongside another general against a wall in Montmartre. Events only escalated from there. Many of the city's wealthy residents fled over the following days, while the remaining members of the cabinet fled to Versailles, effectively abandoning Paris. Over the next two months, the city belonged to workers.

The Commune found its base of support in the peripheral neighborhoods inhabited by the city's growing working class, a reality illustrated by the municipal elections organized just a week later by the National Guard's central committee. Just under half of the city's roughly 485,000 voters took part, and they were skewed heavily toward northern and eastern neighborhoods: about three-fourths of registered voters showed up in the eastern 20th arrondissement, while less than a fourth voted in the bourgeois 8th arrondissement.[67] Meanwhile, the professions making up the city's laboring class were finally represented in government. Of the eighty officials elected to the new city council, thirty-five were listed as manual laborers, or *ouvriers*; fourteen were service workers, or *employés*; five were small business owners; and there were about a dozen journalists and another dozen lawyers, teachers, artists, and doctors.[68]

As Karl Marx himself wrote in 1871, the Commune was the "first revolution in which the working class was openly acknowledged as the only class capable of social initiative"—but the reality is the governing coalition was unbelievably messy.[69] The newly elected municipal council featured Blanquists, scores of mutualists under the influence of Proudhon, and others aligned with the recently formed International Workingmen's Association. There were also dozens of self-identified Jacobins who saw the revolution as a means to fulfill the unrealized promise of 1793. These men had deeply conflicting views about the objectives and very nature of state power—not a good thing when you're supposed to be exercising it—and spent a lot of time caught up in sweeping theoretical debates.

Nevertheless, they agreed enough with one another to be able to lay out a bold vision of change in a formal Declaration to the French People, published in April 1871. In this public manifesto, the Communards proclaimed their loyalty to the republican form of government, yet also called for the "absolute autonomy of the Commune" to be extended to every locality in France. They declared that the revolution underway marked "the end of the old world of governing," to which "the proletariat owed its serfdom." And they defended themselves against the charge that Paris was trying to impose its will on the rest of France—to the contrary, they wanted everyone to benefit from the sort of autonomy being exercised by the capital, hoping to forge a "voluntary association of local initiatives."[70]

Internal tensions notwithstanding, the Commune did adopt a series of reforms aimed at improving material conditions for the city's working population. One of the very first was the extension of a wartime rent moratorium that the government in Versailles had just moved to repeal. Under the new rules, outstanding rental debt going back to October 1870 was also wiped off the books. The following month, the Commune voted for the requisitioning of unoccupied apartments, a measure designed to provide housing for those whose buildings had been damaged by military hostilities. To further ease the debt burden, the Commune authorized Parisians to reclaim objects sold to pawnshops for less than twenty francs.

The Commune also sought to improve working conditions. Councillors banned night work for bakers, a policy that famously irked Parisians accustomed to fresh bread in the morning.[71] They imposed a maximum salary for municipal employees, prohibited employers from docking pay, and even moved to requisition workshops abandoned by their owners, an ambitious policy that didn't have time to fully take effect.

Education and cultural policy were similarly innovative. Three decades before France's Third Republic did the same, the Commune of Paris imposed a strict separation of church and state, making primary schooling free, mandatory, and secular. Citizenship was opened up to the roughly one hundred thousand foreigners residing in Paris. (The Hungarian-born Jewish

goldsmith Léo Frankel played a leading role in the Commune
government.) An official federation of artists, led by the painter
Gustave Courbet, moved to cut off funding for the city's prestigious Beaux-Arts academy, which it viewed as an elitist institution, and began discussing new ways of supporting the arts.[72]

Women played an important role, too. Although they lacked
the right to vote, a group of supporters formed their own
organization to rally support, the Women's Union to Defend
Paris and Care for the Wounded. Led by Élisabeth Dmitrieff,
a Russian-born representative of the International who'd been
sent to Paris by Karl Marx, the union published a call for wom-
en to "defend and avenge" their brothers, creating committees
to organize work for nursing and canteens and the construction of barricades.[73] When Louise Michel wasn't fighting on
the barricades, she advocated for enhanced divorce rights and
an end to prostitution. It was these politically engaged women
who spawned the myth of the *pétroleuse*, the rebellious, lower-
class Parisienne who doused debris in oil to keep the flames
burning as the Commune battled its enemies.

The streets of Paris were politicized. People strolled through
the bourgeois neighborhoods that were previously off-limits.
The Tuileries Palace, where the emperor had been living, was
opened up to the general public. Workers discussed and debated the issues of the day in a flurry of new political clubs situated not just in the northeast, but in the very center of the city,
often meeting in abandoned churches.[74] While the new government banned critical newspapers, pro-Commune publications flourished, with editors reviving the Revolutionary-era
Père Duchesne and readopting the old Revolutionary calendar.
(They were now in year 79.)

In the end, as with prior uprisings, revolting Parisians proved unable to defend their gains. In late May, troops commanded by France's new chief executive, Adolphe Thiers, finally made their move, easily penetrating the city's defenses from the southwest. While the barricades went up again and gave way to fierce street battles, the enemy government troops, the Versaillais, quickly gained the upper hand over the insurrectionary forces commanded by the Polish-born Jarosław Dąbrowski. As they fell back to their strongholds in the north and east, supporters of the Commune intentionally set fire to the Tuileries Palace and to City Hall. ("Paris will be ours or it will cease to exist," Louise Michel is alleged to have said.) Montmartre fell on May 23. The final barricade, defended by a single Communard on the Rue Ramponeau in the heart of Belleville, fell on May 28.

The repression was brutal. Over the course of what became known as the "Bloody Week"—*la semaine sanglante*—tens of thousands of Communards were summarily executed without trial. Another forty thousand were imprisoned.[75] More than a hundred members of the National Guard were shot against a wall at the Père Lachaise cemetery before their bodies were dumped into a mass grave.

"The ground of Paris is filled with corpses," soon-to-be president Adolphe Thiers wrote in a telegram sent to prefects nationwide. "One hopes this horrible spectacle will be a lesson to the insurgents who dared to declare themselves partisans of the Commune."[76]

Not Dead Yet

Parisians have been gathering to commemorate the Commune for more than a century. Every May, since at least 1880, people have marched to the Communards' Wall to pay their respects.[77] At one recent march, on a perfectly sunny Saturday afternoon, I met up with hundreds romping through the 20th arrondissement—black-clad anarchists mixing with Yellow Vests, trade unionists, and activists from France's panoply of left-wing parties, all of them joyously making their way through one of the Commune's old strongholds. A marching band blared out classics like "Bella Ciao" and "El Pueblo Unido, Jamas Será Vencido" as the crowd sang along and chanted anticapitalist slogans of their own. When the procession reached the gates of the cemetery, the mood became more subdued, and a group of demonstrators sang along to "La Semaine Sanglante," a song penned by the Communard Jean-Baptiste Clément just a few weeks after the wave of repression. Its verses describe the bloodshed and disappointment following the fall of Paris, while the chorus is a call for vengeance:

> *Yes, but things aren't as steady as they seem*
> *The hard times will end*
> *Get ready for revenge*
> *When all the poor get down to it.*[78]

As the crowd made its way to the wall, I caught up with Estelle, a fifty-four-year-old who had a thirty-year career in printing but has been unemployed the last couple of years after losing her job amid mass layoffs. Born and raised in Paris, she told me she'd been coming here for decades, sometimes even stopping by the wall to pay homage when in the neighborhood. "It's in my blood," she told me. "The wall and the Communards and the Commune are part of my history."

How powerful a connection can one truly feel to an event that occurred during an era when most Parisian children were working, when the city's residents were still recovering from a siege that had pushed them to the brink of starvation and resulted in the eating of zoo animals? When the biggest source of jobs was an unregulated textile sector in which people regularly worked twelve hours a day? Estelle quickly mentioned the policy of domestic partnership to which she feels indebted: under the Commune, the city paid benefits to the partners of deceased soldiers, whether they were married or not, as well as to their natural-born or "legitimate" children. But above all, it's the geography of the city that connects the distant past of the Commune to the realities of the present.

"It's the same thing today, we've all been kicked out of Paris," she said. "You look at the neighborhoods we went through today, they used to be working-class neighborhoods. Now they're neighborhoods with people who got rich."

Like many Parisians, she's moved around a lot in the pursuit of affordable rent. Estelle was born in the 6th arrondissement on the Left Bank. Then she moved to the 20th, where her grandmother used to own a bar near Belleville. Next it was on to the northern suburb of Saint-Ouen, and then back within city limits in the 18th, where her son was born. Now she lives just off the A6 highway, in the *département* of Essonne, about fifty kilometers south of the city.

A union activist for ten years, Estelle told me she lost her job in the printing sector when a new firm bought up her company and digitized much of the labor that used to be done manually. "There's no savoir faire left, everything's digital now," she said. "But you know the Commune represents that too—people fighting for their know-how."

The commemoration hit its crescendo as the crowd of several hundred, clenched fists in the air, belted out "The

Internationale," first written as a poem in the midst of the repression. Its author, a Communard named Eugène Pottier, was then holed up in the 18th arrondissement, in the Goutte d'Or. In an impressive display of leftist geek credentials, a majority kept singing beyond the first verse, keeping the anthem going until it subsided into rousing applause. Many milled around afterward, not willing to let go of the thrilling sense of solidarity. High school–aged kids smoked cigarettes, sipping from tin cans of Kronenbourg beer. A crew of antifa supporters from Red Star, the third-division football team that plays in the suburb of Saint-Ouen, not far from the Porte de Clignancourt, hung around. Activists from a plethora of left-wing parties talked about the upcoming legislative elections.

Nearby, a group of older people in a circle sang along to an odder, lesser-known tune from Pottier written years after the Bloody Week, accompanied by an accordion player. Set to the music of a late nineteenth-century song called "T'en Fais Pas, Nicolas," or "Don't Worry About It, Nicolas," the morbid lyrics rattle off a list of the massacred leaders and describe the killings of the Bloody Week in detail. ("They filled up the cemetery, they thought they cut off his arms and emptied out his aorta," goes one verse.) But the melody is disarmingly joyful and the refrain reminds the central subject of the song, the anxiety-prone Nicolas, that "in spite of it all, the Commune isn't dead." The final chorus ends with a defiant look at the future:

> *They're gonna know it soon, damn it.*
> *The Commune isn't dead!*
> *They're gonna know it soon, damn it.*
> *The Commune isn't dead!*[79]

*   *   *

While its rebellious spirit may live on, the fall of the Commune did mark the end of a certain cycle of contestation and violent state repression that had shaped the city up until that point. Over the following decades, the laboring population of Paris led countless strikes and mass protests—increasingly in the banlieue where the city's industrial development extended—though dreams of revolutionary change never again translated into such open confrontation with the government. The class struggle took different forms, with the influence of the growing Parisian workforce helping to usher in a series of new worker rights, regulations on business, and pro-tenant housing prices.

The pressure that working people exerted on authorities helped to define twentieth-century Paris in just about every way, even playing a vital, if underappreciated, role in the city's emergence as a global hub for the arts, starting around World War I. Now part of the Parisian mystique commodified by real estate developers and wealthy investors—yet another piece of the dream they're buying and selling—the heydays of innovation in painting, film, photography, and literature are, in fact, deeply indebted to the struggles of the city's working majority. Without low rents, it's hard to imagine many of the artists coming here in the first place.

4

ART AND AFFORDABILITY

During the glory years of Paris as a global center for the arts and the avant-garde—the roughly fifty-year stretch that starts with the Surrealists around World War I and ends with the development of New Wave cinema in the late 1950s—a common thread runs through it all, one that tends to get over-looked. During this time, the city was, relatively speaking, dirt cheap. While there were a multitude of factors drawing creative-minded types to the French capital, low housing costs played a pivotal role in attracting them and allowing them to stay. As prices continue to spiral upward today, it's worth recalling just how much of the city's great artistic production hinged on affordable living—how inexpensive urban rents delivered benefits far more important than the meager earn-ings going into the pockets of landlords.

They might not all have been aware of it, but the long list of painters, writers, musicians, photographers, and filmmakers who honed their crafts in Paris were the beneficiaries of a strictly regulated real estate market tilted in favor of the city's working masses—a series of tenant-friendly laws and price controls forged by class struggle and sustained by fears of popular revolt. Thanks to a rent freeze imposed at the start of World War I and that was only partially repealed following the liberation from Nazi occupation, Paris was home to some of the cheapest rents in Europe.

Across this period of ferment, the relationship between the artists and the mix of industrial and service workers that made up the city's majority was complicated. These groups weren't always living in the same places, and the worlds inhabited by the latter were often ignored by some of the most renowned and commercially successful artists. And yet, this aspect of the city and its messy expansion attracted the attention of countless others. Their work contains painful truths about what's been lost—it is a minefield of nostalgia—but within it lie reminders of what's still around: a Paris that certain forces would like to extinguish for good, but which, in spite of it all, continues to resist.

When the Left Bank Was Cheap

In 1902, a decrepit-looking residence for the visual arts called "La Ruche," or "The Beehive," opened its doors on the southern edges of the city, offering two types of housing. Ground floor rooms in the main building, a hexagon-shaped tower, went for just 50 francs a month, while rooms on the upper floors and nearby pavilions went for 150 francs a month—both modest sums at the time.[1] The actual lodging conditions were subpar and there was an interminable war against rats and bedbugs, but the low rents allowed people to move in and created a meaningful community.² While many French residents lived by themselves, a wave of émigré artists began to flock to shared living spaces, benefiting from pavilions used for exhibiting work and theater performances on the premises. Born to a Jewish family in Belarus, then part of the Russian Empire, Marc Chagall arrived in 1910; the perpetually penniless Amedeo Modigiliani passed through in 1912; Diego Rivera and Chaïm Soutine arrived in 1913.³ "In those studios lived the artistic Bohemia of every land," Chagall wrote in his memoir.⁴

Others went to the Cité Falguière, a nearby residence that thrived on a similar model. It had opened earlier, in the 1870s, though it underwent a revival in the early twentieth century. From 1913 to 1915, Soutine and Modigliani both lived here as well, as did the Japanese artist Tsuguharu Foujita.⁵ This was a place that was designed to be affordable and devoted to the production of art, blind to the eccentricities of its inhabitants. As the Jewish Lithuanian-born artist Pinchus Kremegne recalled years later in a TV documentary, Modigliani and Soutine were roommates at the Cité. One time he came to pay them a visit around midnight: "They'd thrown away all the furniture because it had been infested with bedbugs. I entered. . . . There was no electricity or gas. They were both lying on the floor and each holding a candle in their hands; Modigliani was reading Dante and Soutine was reading 'Le Petit Parisien [newspaper].'"⁶

These residences had helped pave the way for a deeper shift in the city's artistic center of gravity, a gradual move away from the northern hill of Montmartre and toward the Left Bank neighborhood of Montparnasse—which, at the time, was also quite affordable.⁷ While Picasso lived in comfort at the 242 Boulevard Raspail, Modigliani lived just down the road at number 216. His residence, a glass box located in a small courtyard down a passageway, may or may not have been an abandoned greenhouse.[8] Brooklyn native Man Ray first arrived in the city in 1920, thanks to some financial aid from his sister and a $500 advance from an American art promoter in exchange for a promise to sell everything he painted the following year. He bounced around hotels and studios before settling in Montparnasse the following year.[9]

Around this time, the area also began to attract a collection of Anglophone writers—and Americans, in particular. While the Lost Generation's attraction to the French capital stemmed from the strictures of Prohibition back home and a more general fascination with Europe heightened by the experience of World War I, the low cost of living was undeniably a key factor. Here, they spent little on hotels, apartments, food, and basic services. For Americans, in particular, the favorable exchange rate between the dollar and a depreciating French franc made things even easier.

There is a compelling case to be made that without cheap rents, Paris would never have become the center of the Anglophone literary world in the 1920s. For one, the legendary bookstore Shakespeare and Company—the center of the scene—owed its creation to the city's affordability. As the founder and owner Sylvia Beach recalled in her memoirs, her initial goal was to open a French bookshop in New York, but it was too expensive of an ask for her mother, whose savings would finance the project.[10] Instead, she chose the Left Bank of Paris, setting up shop around the Rue de l'Odéon, just around the corner from fellow book vendor Adrienne Monnier, a doyenne of the French literary scene who became a close friend and lifetime romantic partner. Shakespeare and Company initially attracted visitors with its lending library and a series of literary events, but eventually reached worldwide levels of fame after it published James Joyce's *Ulysses*, a novel that American and British editors were reluctant to publish for fear of breaking anti-obscenity laws.

Once in Paris, the Irish novelist famously lived beyond his means, relying on a supply of friends and supporters to help finance his spacious apartment off the Boulevard Raspail, including Sylvia Beach herself, who worked as a de facto agent in addition to serving as publisher. But the low cost of living played a major role in his original decision to move in the summer of 1920. At this point, Joyce had had some success with *Dubliners*, but was still earning a modest income teaching English in Italy, when Ezra Pound suggested he head to Paris.[11] "Is it not extraordinary the way I enter a city barefoot and end up in a luxurious flat?" Joyce wrote to a friend in December 1920.[12]

Aspiring novelist Ernest Hemingway arrived in late 1921. One of the first pieces he published with the *Toronto Star*, in February 1922, was entitled "Living On $1,000 a Year in Paris." "Paris in the winter is rainy, cold, beautiful and cheap. . . . It is anything you want—and cheap," he wrote in a short article that lists out the price of various items (soup, salad, red wine, and beer) before poking fun at other foreigners for suggesting the city was expensive.[13] "There are several hundred small hotels in all parts of Paris where an American or Canadian can live comfortably, eat at attractive restaurants and find amusement for a total expenditure of two and one half to three dollars a day."

Unlike Joyce, Hemingway chose to live in a low-income neighborhood, moving to the Rue Cardinal Lemoine just around the Place de la Contrescarpe. This was near the heart of the old Faubourg Saint-Jacques, only about a decade after the dingy old River Bièvre had been moved underground. His wife Hadley did receive regular income from a trust fund—a critical fact that Hemingway neglected to mention in his subsequent homage to the city, *A Moveable Feast*—but they weren't exactly living in luxury either. The couple paid just 250 francs (less than $20) a month in rent. And the conditions were sparse, with only two rooms, a tiny kitchen, and a squat toilet.[14] Eventually, the couple upgraded to a nicer spot on the Rue des Notre-Dame-des-Champs, just next to the Luxembourg Gardens.

After World War II, the center of gravity on the Left Bank shifted slightly north to Saint-Germain-des-Près. As in Montparnasse, cheap studios and hotel rooms could be easily found here—a fact that helped to draw in writers and musicians from around the world, as did the prospects of crossing paths with Jean-Paul Sartre and Simone de Beauvoir, the larger-than-life novelist-philosophers. The unrivaled literary power couple had stayed in Paris during the Occupation and emerged from the dark years as model intellectuals, holding court at Les Deux Magots and Café de Flore, two cafés next to the neighborhood's church and main square. Of course, many of the star French writers gravitating around them didn't need to worry about making rent, and as in the prewar era, the Left Bank attracted well-established foreign novelists, including the Hungarian Arthur Koestler and American Richard Wright. But the Saint-Germain crowd also helped promote previously unknown writers: Françoise Sagan published *Bonjour Tristesse* at the age of eighteen, while Jean Genet got his big break when he was noticed by Sartre and Beauvoir—readers who understood the profound moral vision underlying his debut novel about a gay prostitute living on the margins of society.

Several younger, lesser-known American writers bene-fited from the low rents as well: Canadian-born Saul Bellow was awarded a Guggenheim Fellowship and arrived in 1948. While he first lived in a furnished flat with his family near the Champs-Elysées, he also decided to rent a hotel room in Saint-Germain-des-Près, just to be near the cafés and the heart of the action.[15] Norman Mailer arrived with his wife Beatrice Silverman in 1947, right after sending in the manuscript for *The Naked and the Dead*. They found a spot at 11 Rue Bréa, just south of the Luxembourg Gardens, for the tidy sum of less than a dollar a day.[16] The following year, twenty-four-year-old James Baldwin came to town, with just $40 in his pocket and no book contracts to his name.[17]

Baldwin rented a hotel room off the Rue de Verneuil, between the heart of Saint-Germain and the Seine.[18] He got by with the help of friends, and eventually began to write pro-lifically. Working from the Café de Flore, Baldwin wrote his breakthrough novel, the semi-autobiographical *Go Tell It on the Mountain*, then *Giovanni's Room*, a novel recounting the love affair of a bisexual American man in Paris. Like other Black writers and performers in the city, Baldwin relished the fact that Paris offered a shelter from the brutality of American racism—no small thing—but exile offered even deeper advan-tages. In the company of other writers in Paris, Baldwin felt the ability to experiment, innovate, and find a voice that he felt might not have emerged amid the various constraints of life back in the States. He later wrote about his new freedom for *Esquire* in 1961, in a piece called "The New Lost Generation" that seemed to capture the city's allure for many of the expats:

In my own case, I think exile saved my life, for it inexorably confirmed something which Americans have great difficulty accepting. Which is, simply, this: man is not a man until he's able and willing to accept his own vision of the world, no matter how radically this vision departs from that of others. . . . What Europe still gives an American—or gave us— is the sanction, if one can accept it, to become one-self.[19]

Why the Left Bank Was Cheap: Pressure from Below, Action from on High

The numbers are almost hard to believe. The real cost of housing in Paris dropped precipitously after the outbreak of World War I and remained low for decades, not bottoming out until 1950. According to publicly available data shared by the French government, the city's housing index (a measure of average home prices) fell in the 1920s to a level not seen since the days of Haussmann, a trend amplified by inflation that took hold after the end of the war.[20] A slight rebound followed the stock market crash in 1929—with investors desperately seeking stable assets—but housing prices continued to plunge thereafter as inflation exploded once again. By the end of World War II, France was left with some of the cheapest rents in all of Europe and North America: French residents were spending just around 3 percent of their income on rent immediately after the war, down from around 15 percent before World War I. In the U.S., Sweden, and the Netherlands, renters were all spending a quarter of their income on rent.[21] Another statistic is even more eye-popping: in 1948, according to French minister of reconstruction and urbanism Eugène Claudius-Petit, French households had spent seven times more on tobacco than on rent: 204 billion francs on the former, 25 to 30 billion on the latter.[22]

This reality was shaped by a mix of pressure from below—movements led by renters and political parties claiming to defend the interests of the country's working class—and public policies from on high, imposed to maintain the social equilibrium at an exceptionally turbulent time. At the center of it all was a system of nationwide rent control that was meant to be temporary, but was ultimately extended over and over again. In many ways, the story of how France got there begins just around the corner from the decrepit artist studios at The Beehive, at the southern edge of the city in a sleepy corner of the 15th arrondissement.

It was here, on a frigid afternoon in late January 1912, that anarchist-leaning agitator Georges Cochon, head of the recently renamed and increasingly active Tenants Union, pulled off his most successful coup yet. At this time, the housing market in Paris was a very different animal. Rents could be cripplingly high. They were eating into workers' paychecks. Tenants' rights were limited. On-the-ground conditions were forcing many left-wing radicals to reckon with the housing issue, but the mustachioed thirty-two-year-old with a fortuitously strange surname (his last name means "pig") was an especially savvy organizer who understood the growing influence of the press and how to grab its attention. In this case, he'd devised a spectacle to shine a light on the city's rising real estate costs: he'd planned his very own eviction and summoned as many people as possible to watch it happen live. This was agitprop *avant la lettre.*

By the turn of the century, Parisians were well accustomed with both evictions and a sneaky tactic used to avoid them known as the *déménagement à la cloche de bois,* the practice of renters discreetly abandoning their lodgings without alerting their landlords because they either couldn't afford the next rental payment or because they already owed money. The term *cloche de bois,* which literally means "wooden bell," was a play on words that referenced the loud metallic bells that professional movers rang to signal their presence to building concierges. By contrast, the down-and-out wanted to avoid detection—the whole point was to be as quiet as possible.

Although these secretive moves were often a source of embarrassment for the renters involved, Cochon and his fellow activists believed bringing more attention to them would help shine light on the city's burgeoning housing crisis. They felt the issue, together with the growing number of evictions, needed to be politicized—to be talked about openly rather than swept under the rug. As far as Cochon was concerned, even better if it could be done in a fun and lighthearted way.

With all this mind, Georges Cochon decided to stop paying rent on his own apartment, quickly earning the ire of his landlord, Madame Polycarpe Chazelles, who alerted the authorities. When police first arrived, at the start of the month, Cochon had hung a giant banner from his balcony: "Under the Third Republic, the Law Is Violated by the Police." He initially escaped eviction thanks to an administrative hiccup, but weeks later, his time had run out. On January 29, the newspaper of the tenants' union put out a call for a "great festival to celebrate the eviction of Comrade Cochon."[23] Inside what the press dubbed "Fort Cochon," the great organizer awaited his fate.

When the day finally arrived, officers broke down Cochon's front door and a couple of makeshift barricades to find him calmly sipping coffee with his family. The activist offered little resistance to a court official, but scuffles broke out between police and the crowd, angering journalists who filed a complaint against the Interior Ministry for violating the freedom of the press. This generated some sympathy for the cause. But the real victory came four days later when the Tenants Union organized a march to Cochon's new apartment on the nearby Rue Mademoiselle, a flat offered free of charge by a sympathizer.

The procession turned into a festival of its own. Accompanied by a brass band, a raucous crowd of over 150 union members and sympathizers belted out songs and banged on a variety of kitchen utensils as they carried Cochon's furniture and belongings through the streets of the Left Bank. The march was dubbed the "Racket of Saint-Polycarpe," a homage to Cochon's former landlord. It was so successful that the union replicated the model.

And the playbook worked: instead of undertaking physically and emotionally grueling moves by themselves, people risking eviction could call on the renters' union. The organization then either found sympathetic supporters willing to donate space or identified vacant buildings to move into. The day of the move, activists would show up en masse to the departure site, providing crucial strength in numbers in situations where leaving one's lodgings was legally dubious. (What right-minded landlord would want to scuffle with a bunch of menacing-looking radicals who had seemingly little respect for private property?)

At the end of the day, union supporters also acted as movers. All in all, they transformed what could be a private moment of shame into an expression of collective power, making clear that responsibility for housing problems lay not with individuals struggling to make ends meet, but with landlords and city officials.

Over time, the marches turned Georges Cochon into a minor celebrity. The mainstream press regularly covered his organization's demonstrations. Supporters wrote songs about him; the legendary painter and printmaker Théophile Steinlen drew him for a poster; postcards depicted his marches. But most importantly, the cost-of-living crisis in Paris eventually spurred the state to intervene.

By early 1912, Cochon's rabble-rousing had captured the attention of more powerful forces. That year, the question of housing appeared on the agenda of a labor union confederation congress for the first time, under the theme of "Expensive Living and Rent Increases," just as the Socialist Party began to pay closer attention, too.[24] Sometimes referred to as the French Section of the Workers' International (Section française de l'Internationale ouvrière, SFIO), the party affiliated with the inheritor of Karl Marx's original organization was rapidly gaining in influence. In the aftermath of the Commune, Paris had witnessed the rise of an influential anarchist movement, but the Socialists had gradually supplanted it to become the hegemonic force on the French Left. While members of the Tenants Union were outsiders—focused on direct action, not electoral politics[25]—the Socialists had begun to understand their cause was too important to ignore.

Since the 1890s, France had flirted with the notion of

affordable housing, ever since legislators aimed to spur the construction of homes for the least well off by giving tax breaks to private developers. But with municipal elections approaching in May, a pair of Socialists on the city council proposed a measure to bring more immediate relief. They called on the city to borrow some 200 million francs to build new apartments for low-income residents.[26] Remarkably, the city council gave its approval and kicked the issue over to the National Assembly, which, under France's hyper-centralized system of government, retained broad authority over local policies. In the meantime, Parisian Socialists went all out on housing during the local election campaign—railing against the misdeeds of greedy Monsieur Vautour (literally, "Mr. Vulture"), a common symbol for predatory landlords.

By this point, the issue had gone mainstream. After the elections, the French Parliament approved the request from Paris and passed a broader national housing law that greatly enhanced the ability of cities to intervene in the private market.[27] It was a quiet revolution in French housing policy. Under what was known as the Bonnevay Law, municipalities could now directly oversee affordable housing through new public entities known as Offices for Affordable Housing, *Offices publics d'habitations à bon marché*.[28] Although these institutions initially suffered from funding difficulties, the architecture for French social housing had been put into place. "The housing crisis and difficult incidents it created this winter in Paris have profoundly moved public opinion," the center-left legislator whose name was associated with the bill told Parliament. "The question of workers' housing has moved to the front of public preoccupations."[29]

* * *

More immediate relief for renters arrived just after the outbreak of World War I. Empowered by a series of wartime emergency laws approved by Parliament, the government published
a decree that temporarily froze rental payments and effectively
prohibited evictions nationwide, allowing almost all renters to
postpone their payments until the end of hostilities—renewing
the measures every few months as the conflict carried on.[30]
(In this respect, France was part of a broader European wave,
with the U.K. and Romania, among others, applying similar
measures.)[31] But while the moratorium officially came to an
end in 1918, it was followed by an even bolder intervention
into the private housing market. In 1919, the French government approved a new law against so-called illicit speculation
that required landlords to keep rental prices in line with their
1914 levels—in other words, imposing a form of nationwide
rent control.[32] While subsequent laws authorized further price
hikes for tenants in a limited number of circumstances, the
broader system of rent restrictions remained in place through
World War II.[33] It wasn't until after the war that the government began to unwind them and paved the way for landlords
to hike prices.

While hard to imagine today, the boldness of the measures
testifies to the sheer terror that officials felt about the prospects of inflaming the country's working masses—and indeed,
from their point of view, there was a good deal to worry about.
The tenants' movement continued even after Georges Cochon
left the spotlight, with a new organization leading marches,
recruiting members in Paris and the suburbs, and calling
on the state to maintain strict limits on prices.[34] During this
stretch, millions of French workers were regularly casting bal-
lots for either the Socialist Party or the Communist Party, mass

membership organizations that were committed—at least on paper—to the overthrow of capitalism. Founded in 1920, the latter was inspired by events in Russia that showed just how much things could spin out of control, while France's very own elections in 1936 showed that these parties were capable of conquering state power themselves. Although it was short-lived, the Popular Front alliance that united Socialists, Communists, and the center-left Radical Party formed a solid governing majority. The massive strike wave that accompanied their victory suggested even greater upheaval was within the realm of possibility.

For those committed to protecting liberal democracy and capitalist markets, the turmoil demanded prudency. As they weighed their options and balanced competing interests, state officials and legislators ultimately opted for a strategy of maintaining "public order," aiming to avoid a scenario in which angry workers might ask for hefty wage gains to cover the costs of rising rents or lash out in even more dangerous ways.[35] All things considered, it was better to upset landlords than run the risk of political instability.

This was the consensus that reigned until after World War II. Only then did rent controls come under enough scrutiny to be repealed. As they surveyed the country's badly damaged housing stock, policymakers pointed the finger at the restrictions for discouraging new investment—there was a sense that developers needed more incentives to commit to construction projects, and that landlords needed to be pushed to perform repairs and basic maintenance on their apartments. They weren't necessarily wrong about the shoddy state of housing. Even on the eve of the war, only just over a third of homes in France had running water,[36] while in Paris, it was still commonplace for residents to use shared water sources on each floor.[37]

This was the logic behind the landmark legislation of 1948, which, in many respects, remained fairly tenant-friendly. Under the new law, rent controls remained in effect in France on homes built before 1948, and renters benefited from strong protections against evictions. On the other hand, rental prices were freed up on any constructions made after 1948—a measure designed to encourage developers to build new housing. To soften the blow of the transition, the government created a low-income housing aid program to compensate renters in need of support.[38]

While the contours of a new real estate market took shape, actual housing prices in Paris continued to fall even after the new regulations took effect, not hitting their lowest point until 1950.[39] Although rents began to rise thereafter, it would still take several years before developers committed to major new construction projects. The great suburban housing complexes— the housing projects known as the *cités* or the *grands ensembles* (large complexes)—wouldn't come until the middle of the decade. For most people living in the city, the housing situation hadn't changed a great deal. Vacancies could be hard to find, but apartments themselves were inexpensive.

Depicting a Working-Class City

The artists themselves, sustained by the city's cheap rents, provided some of the best accounts that exist of the midcentury transformation of working-class Paris. Clearly, the city's blue-collar character wasn't of interest to the biggest names in the Parisian literary and art worlds during this period. For them, the capital was simply a place to live affordably, to find inspiration, and to enjoy oneself—not necessarily a subject to be depicted. Fortunately, another crop of writers, painters, filmmakers, and photographers were drawn to capturing the swarming metropolis around them, and with a predilection for its ordinary inhabitants and their living conditions. Their art is imbued with the spirit of working-class Paris and its quotidian rumblings: its cramped, inexpensive, and dilapidated housing stock, its rapid expansion, and its uncertain future.

Published in 1933, *Down and Out in Paris and London* was driven by George Orwell's interest in poverty and low-wage work. But it's also an illustration of how boarding houses enabled people on the margins of society to continue living in the center of Paris—a lower tranche of the working class that bounced around odd jobs as they looked for more stable gigs. The housing conditions of these people were unenviable, and many of them were in rough spots in their lives, but they were still in the heart of the city. In Orwell's account, "cobblers, bricklayers, stonemasons, navvies, students, prostitutes, rag-pickers," and others packed into the hotel where the author stayed, a five-story, forty-room building on the fictional Rue du Coq d'Or, based on the actual Rue Pot-de-Fer in the 5th arrondissement on the Left Bank.[40]

Marcel Carné's 1938 film *Hôtel du Nord* captured a similar tranche of society, albeit on the other side of the Seine. Revolving around a suicide pact that goes wrong, the drama takes place at a cheap hotel on the Canal Saint-Martin inhabited by low-paid workers and others on the margins of the labor market, including a locksmith operating the canal. The rooms are simple. But the prices allowed for the four main characters—a prostitute, a pimp, and two unemployed young people—to live in central Paris.

While the boarding houses epitomized a certain kind of rough and precarious city living, other working Parisians could afford to live in more stable conditions. This was the unglamorous swath of the city celebrated by the poet Léon-Paul Fargue in his 1932 *Le Piéton de Paris*, a survey following in the grand tradition of the flâneurs, the long line of detached observers of Parisian life going back at least to Louis-Sébastien Mercier.[41] The scorn Fargue reserves for the better-known quarters—Montmartre is depicted as being well past its prime, and Montparnasse is referred to as a "miniscule and swarming neighborhood without history or legends"—contrasts with his admiration for the northern zone of La Chapelle and its surrounding areas.[42]

At its core, this was a place where ordinary people could live and work a mix of modestly paid jobs. Fargue dispels the notion that the area was overridden with "crime" or "bedbugs," and shows that life didn't simply revolve around the railyards with which it was associated. While workers based at the nearby Gare de l'Est and Gare du Nord certainly made their presence known, Fargue paints a portrait of the small warehouses, dance halls, street markets, restaurants, and bars that gave these quarters a complex street life of their own—all of it accompanied by an undeniable seediness that emerged at night. "It's a charming place and a serious place," Fargue writes in his love letter to the north of the city. "Serious in the way the word applies to Burgundy wine, to cassoulet, or to brie from Melun. It's a serious dish."[43]

The writer and journalist Henri Calet was similarly drawn to working-class Paris—which, by the time the post–World War II recovery had set in, was benefiting from a steady improvement in living standards, though pay rates and housing conditions remained modest. In 1954, Calet published a collection of his reportage profiling the overlooked mix of blue-collar and service workers who made up a majority of city residents. "I'm thinking of another Paris," he wrote in the introduction to that book, *Les deux bouts*. "A Paris that is commercial, artisanal, industrial—in a word, useful—a Paris in work-clothes."[44]

One of the most striking things about Calet's work today is the ease with which these ordinary people could live and entertain themselves—on salaries and in places that are effectively impossible to imagine in twenty-first-century Paris. None of his interview subjects were living in luxury, but the income-to-rent ratios provided a certain sense of stability. One of his subjects, a fifty-two-year-old bus ticket collector, could reside with his family in a fairly central location, in the 11th arrondissement—he and his wife spent just a seventh of their combined monthly income on rent, a fact we know thanks to Calet's near-obsessive attention to detail.[45] A twenty-four-year-old department store saleswoman living with her typographer parents near the Luxembourg Gardens could imagine finding a flat with her twenty-three-year-old fiancé who was employed at the same department store. And a twenty-five-year-old refrigerator and vacuum cleaner salesman could afford to spend most of his extra cash pursuing his hobby of photography. (This particular character spent just an eleventh of his income on rent, at a hotel near the Sorbonne, which happened to be conveniently located near the Odéon Theatre, enabling him to regularly catch plays.)[46]

This is the working majority that looms in the background of many of the classic novels and films set in Paris at this time. It's a place that's far from rich but isn't exactly poor either, a city of hard-working people living in modest conditions.

Consider Raymond Queneau's iconic opening line from his 1959 novel *Zazie in the Metro*: the invented expression "Doukipudonktan" (translated alternatively into English as "Howcantheystinkso" or "Holifartwatastink"), which is inspired by the stench of metro passengers.[47] The main character's frustrations stem ultimately from the general absence of hygienic infrastructure. "Ts incredible," Gabriel laments in the book's opening paragraph, "they never clean themselves. It says in the paper that not eleven percent of the flats in Paris have bathrooms, doesn't surprise me, but you can wash without. They can't make much of an effort, all this lot around me."

In François Truffaut's *The 400 Blows*, the classic of New Wave cinema released in 1959, much of the action takes place around Pigalle, a neighborhood filled with the mix of manual laborers, service workers, and white-collar employees that was then emblematic of central Paris. The main character's apartment—in reality, filmed at a building on Rue Marcadet in the 18th arrondissement—is both overcrowded and in visibly shoddy condition. Heated by a coal-burning fireplace, the family's one shared living space is taken up almost exclusively by their dining table; the parents share a small bedroom; the star of the film, the rebellious thirteen-year-old Antoine, lives in the hallway on a pullout sofa, sleeping under coat hangers. When Antoine takes down the trash to the ground floor, the camera shows a dingy stairwell, with paint peeling from the walls. The family is not supposed to be facing any particular economic hardship: viewers aren't told what Antoine's father does for a living, but he does wear a suit and tie to work.

Albert Lamorisse's *The Red Balloon*, which came out in 1956 and takes place exclusively outside, captures the city streets and apartment exteriors in the more squarely working-class area of Belleville. The filthiness of the buildings is striking, with black soot suggesting that owners haven't bothered to clean them in decades. Meanwhile, the young boy who carries the balloon crosses a staggering number of empty lots—spaces where grass is growing freely in the middle of the city, surrounded in some cases by wooden sheds. Evidently, land was not particularly valued here at the time and the easing on rent regulations wasn't doing enough to encourage new construction.

Truffaut's classic *Jules and Jim* (1962) provides another glimpse into the open, relatively undeveloped space that once existed around Belleville. In the film, Jules lives in a stand-alone home in an area known as Villa Ottoz, demolished about a decade later to make way for the Parc de Belleville. At the time of the filming, this particular area was known for being a hub for artists. It was surrounded by something of a rough neighborhood, though perhaps an eccentric bohemian like Jules wouldn't have minded being here—where else could one find such a big home in Paris?

But for a depiction of the apartments inhabited by the neighborhood's working-class majority, the fiction of Belleville native Clément Lépidis is far more instructive. In *La main rouge*, published in the 1970s but set in the late 1920s, when the area was filled with Greeks and eastern European Jews, Lépidis describes a flat sitting on a narrow passageway that once connected Rue de Belleville and Rue Rébeval: "a house that resembled many in Belleville." The character lives in a single room on the fourth floor—a worn-down, brown doormat lies in front of the door—which can be accessed by turning a "broken, white porcelain" knob:

The room was not very big and the furniture was basic: a table with a flap, a mirrored armoire with little space, an iron bedstead. The parquet floor cracked with each step. On a wooden dresser stood a basin and a portable gas stove. On a string stretched across the wall by hooks hung three saucepans, a ladle and a skimming spoon with blue enamel.[48]

Given the general lack of upkeep and landlords' broad indifference for the neighborhood, the room probably wouldn't have looked very different just a few decades later.

The Aura of the Outskirts

While Paris was a familiar subject, the gaze of artists increasingly extended to the action outside the city limits, too. From the disappearing agricultural landscapes to the shifting demographics of the population, the transformations here were massive in scope and—compared to the capital—taking place at a frenetic pace. Once a sleepy ensemble of farmlands and small villages, the Paris suburbs were now being urbanized themselves. The *banlieue*, as it's known in French, was evolving into a new home for the region's working population, deeply dependent on Paris—but also, critically, regarded as a distinct world of its own.

The impetus for the changes was industrialization. While Paris retained the limits of its last expansion in 1860, large employers in search of space increasingly set up shop just outside the city. Snaking upward after flowing through Paris, the Seine made for the convenient shipping of goods, which meant its banks, canals, and the northern outskirts of the capital were particularly busy. Development picked up in the early decades of the twentieth century, with new factories opening up and nearby areas expanding to house a workforce churning out everything from automobiles and chemicals to cigarettes and electric power. Not unlike the old faubourgs, the industrial zones and the neighborhoods that sprung up nearby developed identities of their own. Early on, it was the subpar housing conditions that drew in filmmakers and photographers—the contrasts with life inside city limits fueled a more enduring fascination.

Up until the 1950s, even before arriving in the banlieue from Paris, one had to cross a shantytown known simply as "la Zone." Filling what was initially unoccupied military land that lay between the city's fortifications and the start of the suburbs, thousands lived in ramshackle huts and sheds, their population peaking around World War I. While the Zone's poverty and association with crime grabbed the attention of various painters and songwriters from its inception, one of the area's only cinematic depictions comes from Georges Lacombe, a short film entitled *La Zone* (1928).[49] It shines a light on the miserable state of affairs: the roads are unpaved; residents live in carriages; the Zone's major income-earners, the ragpickers, start their days at five in the morning, when they commute to Paris to collect trash and other unwanted items.

It's remarkable how similar to Lacombe's depiction the housing conditions can appear at times in Eli Lotar's 1946 documentary *Aubervilliers*, which, as the film's introduction explains, was aimed at raising awareness of the grim living standards in this northeastern industrial suburb of Paris. Things could be rough in the capital, but the squalor was on another level here. As Lotar's film shows, a whole swath of Aubervilliers

lived under tin roofs and among crumbling apartment buildings that had sprung up around the docks and factories. In one
sequence, a woman leaves her home to find a water source. In
another, an elderly man shows off his shed where he hangs
bread from the ceiling to avoid rats. The last remaining farm-
ers transport their produce via a horse and buggy.

A then relatively unknown Robert Doisneau depicted a similar sense of material deprivation in *La Banlieue de Paris*, a 1949
series of photos accompanying a text by Blaise Cendrars.[50] His
shots raised questions about just what kind of neighborhoods
were being created. The mix of development was chaotic: a
hodgepodge of Haussmann-style flats, single-family homes,
smokestacks, industrial yards, and plenty of fields with dirt
and overgrown grass. Looking at the album now can serve
as a reminder that the development of the banlieue was once
very much up for grabs—though, in a few shots, one can make
out the giant housing projects that would soon come to define
these towns' skylines. The high-rises became known as *grands
ensembles* or *cités*, with the biggest clusters meant to form
effectively self-sufficient neighborhoods where residents could
access most of the services they needed. These massive projects
were the French state's solution to the postwar housing crisis,
but they came with problems of their own.

The masterful 1963 documentary *Le Joli Mai*, from the New
Wave–adjacent Chris Marker and Pierre Lhomme, shines a
light on the complexity of the debate about the *cités*, which was
already emerging at the time. On one level, it suggests the aesthetic critiques were something of a bourgeois privilege: the
film includes interviews with former residents of dilapidated
old flats in the suburbs, who are thrilled to trade their slums
for newer, cleaner buildings. At one point, viewers hear from

a resident of one of the shantytowns inhabited by the most disadvantaged immigrant workers who'd flocked to Paris for work in the decades following the war. A symbol of the hostility faced by low-paid, foreign-born laborers and their families, the last of the major *bidonvilles* wouldn't be demolished until the 1970s.[51] But Marker and Lhomme also convey the monotonous and alienating nature of the new projects, tying their lack of imagination to developers' desires to control costs.

The filmmakers were onto important insights about the ways that ill-conceived architecture and poor city planning can negatively affect people's day-to-day lives—and in retrospect, these misgivings proved to be fairly well grounded. By putting people in giant high-rises, the state was effectively cutting them off from one another and from the rest of the city, reducing their ability to interact with neighbors and to benefit from the simple pleasures of street life. The most far-flung housing projects in the banlieue were never meant to be easy to reach from Paris without a car—not to mention from other suburbs. Residents of the *cités* face many different challenges today, from a lack of jobs to the absence of public services, but the isolating effects of their residences have a way of amplifying the problems.

Jean-Luc Godard's 1967 film, *Two or Three Things I Know About Her*, offers a negative take of a different flavor. Filmed at what was then the brand-new Cité des 4000 in the northern suburb of La Courneuve, the film is critical of the modernity promised by the new developments, which are portrayed as entities ready-made for high-capitalist consumption. In one of Godard's most enduring shots, an array of consumer goods is organized like the housing projects themselves: dishwashing detergent, toothpaste, instant soup, and so on all representing high-rises. Fifty years later, this vision of the *cités* as mini capitalist utopias can feel somewhat surreal, given how much it contrasts with the negative attributes associated with them now. When the projects were going up, problems like segregation, crime, and unemployment were all supposed to be part of a bygone era of economic development; today, the *cites* have come to embody these very problems.

Gone for Good

In many respects, Paris is a radically different place than it was midcentury. Housing conditions are much better, and the costs much higher. It's far less blue-collar than it once was. What were once defining pieces of the cityscape have either vanished or been irrevocably transformed. To put it bluntly, there are parts of the city that are lost and they are never coming back.

One of the most effective tools for surveying the wreckage is the work of the "humanist photographers," a group that carried out the tradition of capturing Paris via camera, though with an increased focus on how ordinary people were using the space around them. These shots still resonate so much today, in part, because of their universality: there is an obvious timelessness to the subjects and emotions in the foreground. And yet, they're also rooted in a very particular postwar version of Paris, that unpretentious city dominated by working people that has been erased by successive waves of gentrification.

Extremely rare in today's Paris, empty lots were a feature of the city well into the 1950s. The photographer Willy Ronis's explorations of Belleville and Ménilmontant show how residents used them to play the slow-paced game of boules known as *pétanque*, walk their dogs, and lay around idly. Among the work of Henri Cartier-Bresson, the most commercially successful of the photographers, is a remarkable shot of young kids playing in one in the Marais, perched upon cobblestones.[52] Izis Bidermanas, a Lithuanian Jew who immigrated to Paris in the 1930s, took a photo of an empty carriage sitting in an empty lot on the edge of the 14th arrondissement.[53] It can be jarring and even somewhat enchanting to think that there was, once, actually unused space in this city—that there were things left to be built and to be created. There were parts of Paris that had no purpose, no defined objective. Since then, this abnormally small city has, more or less, reached its completion. Unless the limits expand, we've witnessed the end of its development.

This Paris was a much dirtier city, too, in just about every way. Many buildings seemed to be enveloped in a fine layer of soot. The grime and the dust settled between the cobblestones, accumulated in the courtyards, blew into the bars and bistros, and sat unattended on the gray zinc roofs. The latter have since become yet another part of the city's marketable lore—government officials are now pushing for the "roofs of Paris" to be featured as a UNESCO world heritage site—but Cartier-Bresson's 1953 aerial shot shows when they were scruffier. Before they entered the radar of the forces who understood they could benefit from the city turning into a playground and a museum, the rooftops were just an afterthought.

There are also certain neighborhoods that no longer exist—in some cases, buildings and streets have been literally wiped from the map. A large part of that was due to the process of *rénovation urbaine*, "urban renewal," imposed around the same time as it was in the U.S.[54] Starting in 1958, the French government began subsidizing private developers in Paris to improve the housing stock in certain neighborhoods and increase their attractiveness for business. In the 1960s, several peripheral parts of the city underwent publicly financed face-lifts: giant new towers transformed a pocket of the 13th arrondissement just south of the Place d'Italie; the controversial Tour Montparnasse in the 14th arrondissement became France's tallest building; a string of new high-rises sprung up along the Seine in the 15th arrondissement. Many of these developments did fill a real demand for housing—though, in addition to being clean, spacious, and modern, they had the crucial benefit of being freed from the pre-1948 rent controls.

Some of the most consequential renovations were directed at the 19th arrondissement around Belleville, where dozens of buildings were razed. Perhaps nowhere was the damage greater than at the Place des Fêtes, with this bustling square transformed into a plaza of nondescript high-rise housing towers.[55] A photo by Willy Ronis gives a sense of what the street life used to be like: in keeping with the French tradition, a crowd on the first of May eagerly awaits their turn to buy lilies of the valley, flowers gifted to celebrate the arrival of spring.[56]

The greatest casualty from this period was the market at Les Halles, the sprawling bazaar in the center of the city that was demolished in the early 1970s. Its ancient characters were naturally photogenic, no-nonsense cleaver-welding men and women whose jobs hadn't fundamentally changed since Émile Zola wrote about them in *The Belly of Paris*. A particularly striking photo by Robert Doisneau, who was drawn to the vendors, captures the ordered chaos of the operation in motion: mountains of crates are stacked up; men are peeing in urinals, their heads and feet visible to the crowd around them, as nearby shoppers shuffle by undeterred. Officially, policymakers argued that the activity of the marketplace was fueling congestion in the heart of the city. But the destruction of Les Halles can also be

Robert Doisneau, *Vespasienne et cageots Les Halles 1953* (Urinal and Crates), 1953. © *Robert Doisneau/Gamma Rapho.*

viewed as a textbook case of gentrification's worst dynamics: its removal enabled developers, landlords, and businesses to unlock highly valued land in central Paris, tapping into gains that were being blocked by the presence of less lucrative affairs. Under the ground where these markets once defined the guts of working-class Paris, the government built a massive new transit hub connecting metro lines to the new suburban rail network—aboveground, new apartment buildings and a shopping mall completed the disfigurement.

While the buildings are mostly all still standing, it can be painful in a different way to look at the shots of the bars, night-clubs, and underground lairs of bohemian Saint-Germain—the *caves*, as the latter were called—knowing what the neighborhood has become. In the photos of the late 1940s and early '50s, young people are hulking around café tables and dancing in smoke-filled rooms where saxophonists and trumpet players entertain crowds aware they are in (at that time) one of the world's jazz hubs. Today, Saint-Germain-des-Prés has become one of the more odious places in all of the city, hitting that sweet spot where bourgeois ostentation, luxury fashion, and mass tourism manage to collide.

One of the most arresting aspects from that era of Parisian street photography is, indeed, the presence of certain categories of people in neighborhoods they're no longer welcome to live in today: a group casually taking wedding photos in the Marais; a mix of elderly people and middle-aged men playing chess at a café in Montparnasse; a grungy-looking flutist at the Rue Mouffetard. But even more striking is the overall class composition of the crowds: the people whose eyes are lighting up as they watch fire-blowers at the Place de la Bastille; others gazing at performers at a funfair in the park; the people lounging around smoking and drinking inside the no-frills bistros or shuffling through the markets. Many are in work clothes or sporting caps, which remained a strong class signifier. In the mid-1950s, Paris was a city where two-thirds of workers were either *ouvriers* or *employés*, wage-earners without managerial responsibilities—and it showed in the way they dressed.

This is the Paris of Léon-Paul Fargue and Henri Calet: a city that was far from destitute but could've used a pay raise—a place where most inhabitants got by frugally but also had breathing room for existence outside of work; where intricate and busy street life flowed in just about every direction. This is the Paris that writers and visual artists once flocked to in droves—and, like the city's reputation as an artistic mecca, it has vanished over time.

The Old City Resists

Today's wave of hypergentrification is a fairly recent phenomenon, with the stratospheric price hike taking off around the year 2000. This is, of course, a global story, with shifts in international capitalism driving similar processes across Europe and North America. Still, certain public policies helped lay the foundation for the boom in Paris, and the 1980s marked a crucial turning point on both the national and local fronts.

Socialist François Mitterrand won the presidency in 1981, and his legislative majority passed new nationwide rent controls the following year. Part of a broader wave of ambitious progressive reforms, the Quillot Law extended price caps to apartments built after 1948, applying across the nation's privately owned housing stock.[57] But the Socialists, backtracking on their initial economic stimulus agenda, lost control of the National Assembly in 1986. That year, a rival right-wing majority repealed the rent regulations and paved the way for landlords to set prices as they chose. Three years later, another law capped increases during lease periods and before the renewal of leases, but property owners remained otherwise free to set rent levels. This is the regime that shaped the Parisian housing market in the decades that followed, gradually replacing the generous tenant protections enshrined in the original postwar system. A dwindling share of Parisian tenants are still protected by the 1948 law, but only because they've continuously occupied their flats since before the reforms of 1986. They are, quite literally, a dying breed.

Just as national lawmakers were taking a hammer to the underlying regulatory regime, the municipal government of Paris implemented another wave of urban renewal, specifically in the east of Paris. Ironically, it was a major Socialist reform that helped pave the way. Under a series of "decentralization" laws in 1982 and 1983, the city of Paris was granted sweeping new authorities, including the right to impose urban development policies on its own. Just a few months later, that great responsibility fell to an alliance of right-wing forces who triumphed in the first-ever direct election of the city's mayor.

Launched by Mayor Jacques Chirac in 1983, the urban renewal program sought to improve housing conditions and to create "new neighborhoods" around the Seine and in the northeast, but also to "open" eastern Paris to "high-level service" jobs.[58] As before, development went hand in hand with displacement: subsidies encouraged white-collar sectors like media and tech to set down roots in the area, while much of the new social housing the program created was reserved for residents earning well above the lowest qualifying amounts. It can sound odd to American ears, but in France, publicly managed flats are not reserved for the poor.

Paired together, these policy shifts helped encourage the exodus of low-income residents from Paris proper. As low-wage workers left, white-collar professionals took their place, early flickers in the gentrification inferno raging across the city today. In 1982, manual laborers and service workers still made up just over half the Parisian working population. By 1999, that rate had fallen to 35 percent, well below the national rate of 53 percent.[59]

In the face of all this damage, it can be tempting to surrender to the wistfulness, to lose oneself in the long list of things that are lost and never coming back. And yet, while the transformation of the Parisian population and street life is especially noteworthy, the very same black-and-white street photography that invites nostalgia also contains reminders of what's constant— the traces and spirits of a city that's still there.

For one, the bones of Paris remain basically intact, a testament to the backlash the urban renewal projects generated. Other major cities around the world haven't been as fortunate, especially in the U.S.[60]

The core architecture of Paris is still standing, as are the vast majority of its streets, including in the north and east of the city. Some of Belleville has been lost, but many of the passages, alleyways, and narrow lanes photographed by Willy Ronis are still there, climbing the slopes and traversing the abandoned rails of a former train line, La Petite Ceinture, that have recently opened to foot traffic. If the dirtiness sticks out in so many of the images from the 1950s and '60s, it's in large part because the rest of it looks so similar to what exists now.

Willy Ronis's night shots of the nearby Buttes Chaumont Park don't feel terribly dated either. The park is still a destination for the people of eastern Paris. On those lazy summer days where the sun doesn't set until 10 p.m., it's filled with them: the couples walking their dogs; the joggers, the boxers, the tai chi practitioners; the gay men who set up on the same spot on the hill and eye each other from the security of sunglasses; the women in headscarves, the men in yarmulkes; the families taking wedding photos and friends celebrating marriages at the nearby city hall; the crew of twenty-somethings nodding along to repetitive electronic music for as long as they want because, for a few weeks in the summer, the gates never close.

Hints of the picturesque Parisian street life—the one that can border on cliché but inherits a deeper tradition—are still around. While the fortress of Les Halles is long gone, its fragments are scattered across other open-air markets throughout the northeast. There are still plenty of street musicians—accordion players and guitarists with varying degrees of talent; pop-up brass bands; an older American guy has been playing folk and country songs on the metro for years. There are still the outdoor booksellers on the Seine, the *bouquinistes*, some of whom carry valuable stuff in their padlocked evergreen safes.

A certain popular left-wing political culture is alive and well, too. The crowd may be more elegantly dressed in Willy Ronis's photo of the annual commemorations of the Commune at Père Lachaise cemetery, but today the ritual march is just as well attended. The Fête de l'Humanité, a late summer festival organized by the former official daily newspaper of the Communist Party, is still going strong. Once photographed by Robert Doisneau in 1945, the festival and its mix of music, hearty food, and political debate continue to draw in tens of thousands every year.

Of course, the left-wing sympathies of eastern Paris extend beyond vague cultural affinities. If you look at maps of how the city voted in the 2022 presidential and legislative elections—including the tallies of the main left-wing candidate Jean-Luc Mélenchon and the left legislative alliance—it is striking how much they overlap with the old revolutionary heartlands: the hubs of support for the Commune and the once-mighty Communist Party in Paris proper, those parts of the city to which workers and the poor were exiled under Haussmann. Major demonstrations of left-wing parties and trade unions all still tend to start and end in eastern Paris, too, revolving around the nexus of the Places de la République, Bastille, and Nation.

In some of these photos, one can get the sense that a certain kind of edginess has been sanded down—that the splinters, blemishes, and cracks of old Paris have been removed at the behest of occupants who have little tolerance for them. Perhaps much of what the writer Lucy Santé so memorably deemed "the other Paris" is gone for good—that city of slackers, ruffians, gangsters, sex workers, barflies, and people close to the brink by force or by choice. But bits of it still exist. Like the reduced ranks of the working class, it's been compressed, with remnants lingering around the peripheries and eastern quarters of the city.

Homelessness is very much present in Paris, much of it far from the center. Recurring encampments of heavy drug users, mostly people smoking crack cocaine, have shifted around the less desirable edges of the city. Camps of migrants have been similarly tolerated in the upper parts of Paris, but not elsewhere. Famously captured by photographer Georges Brassaï in *Paris by Night* (1933)—a book that influenced many photographers working a couple decades later—sex workers still openly await clients in the street, especially around Belleville and the Porte de Clignancourt. Run-down hotels that thrive from the sector dot this part of the 18th arrondissement, in particular.

A certain kind of decrepit, bare-bones bistro still exists, too—the kind of place where the bartender could theoretically make a ham-and-butter sandwich on a baguette, but is focused mostly on serving espresso and pouring mediocre beer and wine; where the middle-aged male regulars are hammered by the early afternoon; where the ban on smoking indoors is interpreted loosely; where some light gambling might be going on in the back. Spots like these are captured by Doisneau and Ronis, but their spirit shines through even more brilliantly in a couple of underappreciated literary works from the same era. In Jacques Yonnet's *Rue des Maléfices* (1954), which blurs the lines between fiction and nonfiction, the author takes readers through hole-in-the-wall drinking establishments around the Rue Mouffetard, where various interlocutors offer up a series of haunting anecdotes. The same sort of spot caught the eye of Jean-Paul Clébert in *Paris Insolite* (1952), a deeper chronicle of the Parisian underbelly that featured reportage from bars filled with lonely single men playing dominos and cards. Blending into these dilapidated establishments they spend their days in, these characters are transmitters of a kind of dark medieval energy—a theme especially prominent in Yonnet's book.

It can be hard to find their kind in the more central parts of the Left Bank today. And perhaps the sharing of secrets and mysteries hinged on the proximity of these establishments to certain parts of the city—once you remove the link between bar and neighborhood, the transmission is cut off. But the sketchy and somewhat tragic dive lives on in the northeast—where the regulars talk each other's ears off, complaining about how the city's becoming too expensive and losing some intangible, hard-to-describe part of its character, as Parisians have been doing since the days of Haussmann and probably even before then.

What's left today is, without a doubt, a reduced slice of what there once was. Young artists have long since moved on to other, more affordable cities. Residents' jobs no longer provide the security they once did. Public officials feel less pressure to make concessions to those earning modest incomes. Still, these condensed traces of a city that used to belong to working people are hanging around and worth fighting for.

5

STORMING THE GATES OF DISNEYLAND PARIS

When the twenty-seven permanent residents of the Hôtel du Marché, a dark and dingy furnished hotel in the 19th arrondissement, woke up on the morning of June 30, they weren't sure where they'd be spending the night. Three months earlier, they'd received a letter from hotel management demanding they clear out their belongings by this date. A new owner was taking control of the property and they were told they needed to go. In case things weren't clear, a sign posted in the lobby carried a menacing message: "As you know, the hotel will cease activity shortly. . . . We have the obligation to empty the hotel's furniture and free up the space."

Just before noon on that pivotal day, about a dozen residents milled around anxiously outside the building, waiting for a protest to begin. One of them had been in touch with a prominent housing rights organization, Droit Au Logement (DAL), which, in turn, had alerted city government and informed residents they could not be forcibly removed from their homes without a court ruling. DAL activists had promised that that afternoon, they would show up for a rally calling on residents to be protected from eviction and provided decent housing, but they hadn't arrived yet. It was an abnormally brisk summer day: a light drizzle quickly gave way to pouring rain.

As the rain picked up and the umbrellas opened up, I chatted up a handful of the residents, a disproportionally elderly bunch. Rents were low—varying from €400 to €600 a month—but the living conditions were straight out of the last century. Each of the five floors shared a single toilet, and residents on the first four floors shared a single shower. It quickly became clear these people weren't really here by choice. They were out of options in a city that had grown hostile to their kind.

Nearly all of them were single, living alone.

"I don't know where I'm going to go," Gérard, a paunchy seventy-three-year-old retired newspaper vendor who'd been living for eleven years in a nine-square-meter apartment, told me. He said he got by on retirement benefits at the "minimum" level, between €600 and €700 a month.

Gérard had worked twenty-five years at a stand at the Laumière metro stop, just around the corner from the hotel, before finishing his career in a succession of jobs at three kiosks around the city and suburbs: in the 11th arrondissement; in Barbès in the 18th; and finally, in the posh suburb of Levallois-Perret.

He insisted he'd rather not live at the hotel, but at a certain point, it just became easier to stay. "It's a part of life, it's a part of the suffering of life," he said matter-of-factly, his expression not budging from when he was recounting his career. "At first, you think it's just going to be a few months, and then, well . . ."

A similar feeling of inertia hung over Mouloud Daho, a

sixty-four-year-old retiree living in a first-floor studio. Daho had spent the last fifteen years of his professional career as a baggage handler at the Charles de Gaulle International Airport in the northeastern suburbs, hauling suitcases for low pay at ungodly hours of the day and night. Now he was living in a thirteen-square-meter apartment. Daho cooked with a pair of hot plates, mold was growing around his washbasin, and his windows looking onto the street were cracked, held together by Scotch tape. He told me he'd dealt with multiple bedbug infestations and regularly encountered cockroaches.

Daho said he'd use the shower only about three times a week. It was a whole process, he explained: residents needed to go to the ground floor, request the key from the building's concierge, and then occasionally wait in line. Sometimes down there he'd run into a disabled elderly resident and another tenant who graciously helped the former wash himself. But he'd never run into Marcel, an eighty-six-year-old veteran of the Algerian War who'd been living here for twenty-six years. Due to crippling arthritis, Marcel was physically incapable of venturing downstairs and spent every day confined to his apartment.

Then there was Rabia, a sixty-three-year-old who'd been living in a nine-square-meter apartment for the last eight years. He'd worked in moving and construction, floating among a series of odd jobs. "It feels like we're not in France," he told me. "Let's stop kidding around here."

All of it was especially unfortunate, Rabia said, because their neighborhood had just been getting nicer. Indeed, just around the corner from the hotel at 48 Rue de Meaux sits the newly renovated Secrétan Market, a former municipal food market converted into a series of upscale private businesses: a gym, a wine bar, a women's clothing retailer, a bike store, an organic supermarket. There's an indoor rock-climbing gym next door.

"It's a shame," Rabia said. "The moment where the neighborhood starts to get nicer is the moment we have to leave."

I nod silently, but I thought to myself, *That's exactly the point. You're not supposed to be here anymore. This neighborhood is not meant for people like you.*

Fortunately, the activists from DAL came bearing good news. Speaking into a megaphone, an activist announced the city of Paris was sending officers to ensure no residents would be kicked out. He reminded everyone that the hotel owners and the police had no right to forcibly remove anyone from their homes without a court decision. But he stressed that residents needed to stay vigilant and continue holding rallies like this one, maintaining pressure on the city to find a solution for them.

Afterward, the crowd of a couple dozen fired off a familiar chant that's hard to translate into English, in part because it implies a type of state action that's rarely practiced in the United States or the United Kingdom: *Pas d'expulsions! Relogement!* "No evictions! Rehousing!" Draped over a café terrace, DAL banners proclaimed the group's deeper ambitions: "Stop Speculation!" "Lower Rents. Stop Evictions."

As the following months proved, these weren't just empty slogans. They were the rhetoric of an experienced organization that has the connections and the muscle to back it up. Over that stretch, DAL organized a couple of follow-up rallies at the hotel, drawing in members of Parliament and city councillors. In the face of pressure and public outcry, the city government promised residents they would be relodged elsewhere.

All in all, the organization had helped ensure that at least twenty-seven people still have to a place to stay.

The battle to preserve what's left of working-class Paris is going to be uphill. But if at least part of the city is to remain livable for ordinary people, then that will almost certainly be the product of dogged activists like DAL—the consequence of pressure from below that sways the decision-makers on high. In France, local and national policymakers have broad authority and powerful tools at their disposal to intervene into housing markets—which they've used to varying degrees. But as with just about any improvement of living standards, the critical question is as follows: How scared are the elites of what might happen if they don't act?

After that first rally in late June, I headed to a nearby brasserie with the founder and head of DAL, Jean-Baptiste Eyraud, a man who's devoted much of his life to the struggle for affordable housing in Paris. The tall and slender sixty-eight-year-old is a tireless advocate for people in need of immediate fixes and a relentless critic of public housing policy, with an organizing approach grounded in direct action. On our way over, he cracked a joke about the "bobo climbing gym," shaking his head in mock disgust.

Like many activists with a certain level of influence, Eyraud is extraordinarily in demand, but he seems to relish the work. In our long conversation, his phone went off every ten minutes or so—he took long pauses, firing off texts and giving instructions—but he picked up immediately where he left off each time.

"We're not omnipotent!" he told me over coffee as the last

of the lunch crowd filtered out. "But we intervene when we're called upon, when tenants come and see us."

"We get concrete results," he continued. "People have trust and they get involved in mobilizations because they have the hope, with good reason, that they're going to be able to find housing. It's also about lifting one's head up, it's about pride.... People are keeping their heads down with their bosses, the police, their landlords. There's all this too—there's a fear of being alone and then realizing you're not alone."

Since it was founded in 1990, DAL has helped find housing for 33,000 people, according to Eyraud, the product of near-constant street protests and individual assistance for tenants so they can better exercise their rights within France's complex housing bureaucracy.[1] It counts around four thousand dues-paying members, as well as a broad network of allies and supporters, from friendly politicians and labor unions to immigrant rights' groups and human rights NGOs.

Much of DAL's work involves helping tenants take advantage of a renter-friendly law that the organization itself helped win back in 2007. Since then, low-income people who either meet one of a set of criteria (among them, homelessness or unsanitary living conditions) or who've waited for an "abnormally long" period on the waiting list for social housing can trigger what's known as their "enforceable right to housing." In response to qualifying applicants, the French state must present housing options that fit candidates' needs. The definition of an "abnormally long" period varies nationally, but it's set at six years minimum in Paris, and three years for most of the city's suburbs. As with many of France's progressive laws, the measures sound great on paper, but they can be tricky to enforce.

Many tenants don't know their rights, the applications require a lot of paperwork, and it can take time for the different pieces of the state machinery to kick into motion.

DAL's other work entails organizing rallies calling on the state to enhance tenants' rights or seize vacant homes. But the group is often playing defense, like at the Hôtel du Marché. In many ways, the story of the hotel is emblematic of what's happening to Paris: in a context of rampant gentrification, landlords and developers are feeling empowered and tenants are being squeezed out.

As Eyraud explained, until early 2021 the same family had owned the hotel since the 1920s. But they decided to sell the property to Genestone, a small commercial real estate developer based in the western 16th arrondissement of Paris.[2] The firm was apparently planning to flip it—a common occurrence in a sizzling-hot real estate market like Paris. Just a few months later, Genestone signed a sales promise with another developer called Osmose. While neither company responded to my interview requests, Eyraud believes the plan was to turn the derelict building into a more traditional hotel geared for short-term stays.

"Furnished hotels are often transformed into tourist hotels because they're all of a sudden much more profitable," he told me. "It's like magic. You're going from [collecting] €450 in rent a month to maybe €140 a night."

But the sales promise included one critical condition: the building needed to be emptied of residents by the end of June 2022. Here, Genestone didn't do the proper legwork. If the owner of a furnished hotel plans to shut down operations, they don't only need to notify tenants—they need to obtain a court order authorizing evictions. In this case, there was never any such order. Instead, building managers were apparently count-ing on people feeling pressured to leave—a strategy that was sloppy and unlawful, and in Eyraud's estimation, symptomatic of the kind of brazenness on the part of the forces conspiring against tenants in the city today. "It's general impunity," he said. "We have laws that aren't being respected."

"These little real estate sharks, these little piranhas," Eyraud said with a frown, pausing and pressing his tongue against his front teeth to mimic the sound of fish swimming rapidly, "they're looking for opportunities to turn short-term profits."

The good news is the mobilization worked. By failing to vacate the premises, residents of the building at 48 Rue de Meaux had effectively blown the sale to smithereens. Shortly after the June 30 deadline, Osmose dropped its plans to pur-chase the property, leaving Genestone to handle the PR night-mare it had helped create.[3] But one can't help but think, what would've happened if none of the tenants had contacted DAL?

In contrast to other housing groups that view street protests as a tool to be used sparingly, DAL places direct action at the very core of its model. Not only does the organization regularly call for demonstrations, but it offers dues-paying members what's dubbed the *prime à la lutte*, or the "struggle bonus." Organiz-ers take note of members who show up to various actions—and their presence is used to allocate housing opportunities that come their way. The idea is simple: if you're eligible for state aid and if you show up to protests, you'll eventually get a spot.

"Sometimes social housing providers will tell us they have space for a hundred people who've exercised their enforceable right to housing," Eyraud explained. "Who are the hundred people going to be? It'll be the hundred who are most mobi-lized. . . . The more present they are, the better placed they'll be on the lists of relodging that we obtain."

Eyraud pointed to the group's victorious campaign earlier in the year at the Place de la Bastille, "The Forgotten of the Enforceable Right to Housing," a two-month-long occupation of a portion of the square, launched to mark the fifteen-year anniversary of the renter-friendly law and to bring attention to its shortcomings.[4] Eyraud said about 250 households took part overall, including some who showed up for just a day or two— but ultimately, regional authorities made renewed promises to find housing for only 152 families. Those spots went to those most mobilized: the people who slept there regularly and took part in the various demonstrations.

Ultimately, Eyraud says the "struggle bonus" both discour-ages favoritism and reinforces the group's primary strength, which is its use of collective action. The leadership lives out its commitment to rank-and-file action power, too. Despite the group's significant national influence, DAL counts only four permanent staffers who each earn 1.2 times the minimum wage. Eyraud himself lives in social housing, in the La Réunion neighborhood of the 20th arrondissement. And he maintains a fierce commitment to political independence, telling me with some amount of pride that he's refused to join electoral cam-paigns that have asked him to run alongside them. "We don't give gifts to anybody," he said. "We maintain our autonomy from political, religious, and institutional organizations."

When I ask if he considered Georges Cochon to be a source of inspiration, Eyraud acknowledged Cochon's one of many. "He's a source of inspiration, but at the same time, the modes of action, the demands, the struggle of working people without

housing or with poor housing are a bit eternal," he said, pointing to various struggles of the nineteenth century.

While he works regularly with far-left groups and anti-
capitalists of different stripes, Eyraud isn't terribly attached to
the Marxist tradition himself. "The housing question has been
somewhat hidden by the political Left," he told me. "Engels's
line is that real estate speculation is inherent to the capitalist
system, so we need to destroy the capitalist system. And then
there's the idea that the forces of revolution and social change
are at the workplace, not in the neighborhood."

He's also more or less made his peace about what the French
call "Le Grand Soir," or the "Great Evening," the moment of
the great revolutionary triumph over capitalism that has never
really materialized—at least not in this country. Whether it
arrives or not, he believes low-income neighborhoods are the
site of high-stakes political struggle: places that deserve to be
defended against the predatory forces that have a financial
interest in their destruction.

Still, he told me he's disappointed that housing movements in
his hometown aren't as powerful as their counterparts in Berlin. Activists in the German capital have helped put forward a
couple of bold initiatives: in 2020, the city council passed a law
freezing the overwhelming majority of rents at the prior year's
levels.[5] It was overturned in court in 2021, but later that year,
Berlin voters approved by referendum a plan to expropriate
properties owned by large corporate landlords.[6] "Over there,
they organize building by building, neighborhood by neighborhood," he said. "And when they take to the streets, there
are tens of thousands of them. . . . That's what we're missing
in Paris."

Despite the minor victory, he said there was something discouraging about the way the defense of the Hôtel du Marché went down. "The residents of the neighborhood should be leading this!" Eyraud said. "We show up, we have people from around the city, but it's not the neighborhood. They should be the ones leading this."

Maybe the fabric of this part of the 19th arrondissement has already been altered beyond recognition, cleansed of its stains and repurposed for the new Paris. After chatting with Eyraud, I thought back to the rally, which—it is true—did feel like it had concerned a specific building rather than the neighborhood as a whole, as if the Hôtel du Marché had specific issues that had no relation to its surroundings. While some pedestrians did stop by to watch, most continued going about their days, heading into the café next door, popping into the rock-climbing gym, picking up organic apples and pears. To many of them, the building must've seemed like an outlier—that sketchy-looking place where the old, poor people lived.

When I asked a fellow journalist friend whose flat is located near the Hôtel du Marché, he responded the way many neighbors might have if asked that same question: "I've actually always wondered about that place, it's almost right next door to me."

In recent years, Paris has become something of a model for progressive urbanists interested in the idea of walkable, environmentally sustainable cities. Much of that admiration is due to a series of measures adopted by the governing Socialist Party, which has led a coalition running the city since 2001—and in particular, the actions of Anne Hidalgo, the mayor since 2014 who was re-elected in 2020. Under her watch, the city has opened up new bike lanes, banished cars from the banks of the Seine, expanded a popular and affordable bike-sharing program, and pedestrianized much of the city center. She's a firm believer in the notion of the "fifteen-minute city"—a place where residents can accomplish their regular daily tasks by walking or biking short distances.

When it comes to housing policy, the city's record is far more complicated. It's true that certain free market doctrinaires will tell you the city's various attempts to regulate the housing market are aggressive and disastrous—that the alliance of Socialists, Greens, and Communists running the city are proto-Marxists who've all but declared war on landlords and private enterprise. And yet, their record speaks for itself: it's this coalition of left-wing parties that has presided over the steepest acceleration in housing prices in the modern history of Paris and the continued exodus of working-class people from within city limits.

It's a legacy that needs to be grappled with if the city is to properly stave off further gentrification—and one that likely contains lessons that apply beyond the French capital. Which public policies have worked? Which ones haven't? And how can pressure from below bend the power of the state in the direction of working-class and low-income people?

The Power of Social Housing

In the vast toolbox available to policymakers to regulate housing markets, there's one instrument historically proven to be more effective than the others. The best way to keep housing affordable is to remove it from the private marketplace entirely—taking what's otherwise a commodity prone to speculation and transferring it into public hands. If developers and landlords are constantly hunting for new opportunities to exploit, why not close the gates and cut off access entirely? It's an even more pressing question in a place like Paris, with the very limited space it has available for new construction projects.

Since 2001, the year the Socialists won control of municipal government, the share of social housing within city limits has risen from 13 to 22 percent.[7] That rate is just slightly above London, which still counts a non-negligible share of council housing, and far ahead of New York City, which has, by far, the highest such level of any major American city.[8] But Paris also has a higher share of social housing than many other European cities, ahead of Antwerp, Barcelona, Rome, Madrid, and even Berlin.[9]

All of this is a source of pride for the city's deputy mayor for housing, forty-two-year-old Ian Brossat. One of the leading figures in the French Communist Party, a small force on the national level that nevertheless maintains a foothold in municipal governments across the country, Brossat is one of the most prominent critics of the cost-of-living crisis in Paris. He's a talented politician who mixes a sharp focus on policy with the sort of fiery, grand rhetoric his party is known for—as comfortable in granular policy debates as he is in big-picture discussions.

"The presence of social housing is keeping us from having a generalized gentrification of Paris," Brossat told me over the phone in the summer, a time in which many offices operate on reduced schedules or simply close down. "Social housing allows in the long run to maintain a population within Paris that would otherwise have been kicked out," he added. "It's an advantage that we have compared to other large cities around the world."

The figures back up Brossat's case. If affordable housing is the lifeblood of working-class Paris, then social housing is something like the bones or the marrow. It makes up a whopping 43 percent of the housing stock in the 19th arrondissement and 36 percent in the 20th. There's a lot of it to be found in the 13th arrondissement and in the eastern half of the 18th arrondissement, too. Whatever happens in the open market, publicly financed flats are keeping tens of thousands of low-income Parisians in these neighborhoods. It's what keeps the West African fish markets alive in the Goutte d'Or. It's what sustains the Kabyle cafés and the Chinese restaurants of Belleville.

The system has its particularities. Unlike in the U.K. or Austria, French cities usually don't directly own social housing. France's multiple levels of government subsidize a series of social housing providers that manage properties (*bailleurs sociaux*). Some of these are fully publicly owned, others are semi-public, while the rest operate as private companies but are still required to follow strict public guidelines. About half of the social housing built in Paris since 2001 has come from new construction projects; the other half has come from the city acquiring properties, including deals that involve the public rehabilitation of dilapidated buildings.[10]

For what it's worth, the expansion of social housing isn't the exclusive product of municipal political will—it's mandated by national law. Since 2000, French municipalities with more than 3,500 residents in urban areas are required to hit social housing investment targets, with a goal of reaching 25 percent social housing by 2025. Qualifying towns that fail to hit these goals are required to pay financial penalties to the national government, a scenario that applies to about a third of the towns concerned.[11] (Conservative-run Nice, for instance, had to pay a €1.8 million fine in 2022, and many of the wealthy suburbs to the west of Paris have similarly opted to bite the bullet and take the sanctions.) Still, as Brossat points out, the city of Paris is going above and beyond the national law, aiming to hit a 30 percent target by 2030.

Given all this investment, Brossat has a different take on the exodus of working-class Parisians and the real estate boom. While he finds both trends discouraging, he said they'd be even worse absent city intervention. "Where would Paris be if we didn't have this significant share of social housing? Where would it be if we hadn't doubled our share of social housing over the last twenty years?"

Still, some affordable housing advocates bristle at the way the social housing expansion has been carried out.

For one, they argue authorities should be creating even more of it. That may be hard to imagine in today's political landscape, where the municipal budget is the product of tense negotiations dominated by a centrist coalition leader, and where voters themselves are increasingly moneyed and may not even favor such a program. One of the many nefarious effects of gentrification is its ability to erase hostile constituencies—unreceptive electors can literally be priced out of the political equation. Still, other cities show such a program is possible: in Vienna, more than 60 percent of residents live in publicly subsidized apartments,[12] and municipally owned or financed apartments make up nearly half the housing stock.[13] It's not as if there isn't demand in the French capital: of the 234,000 people who requested social housing in the most recent annual data, just 12,000 were given spots.[14]

A more immediate point of contention is the type of social housing being created. In France, publicly managed housing isn't reserved for the least well off, and critics say those most in need are being overlooked in favor of more solidly middle-income residents.

Danielle Simonnet, a freshly elected MP in the National Assembly who represents part of the 20th arrondissement with Jean-Luc Mélenchon's left-populist party La France Insoumise, has long made this critique. She served on city council from 2008 to 2022, often butting heads with Hidalgo and Brossat's coalition.

When we spoke at the Café Bourbon, a longtime haunt for MPs and their staff just next to the National Assembly, Simonnet pointed to publicly available figures: nine in ten of those who requested social housing in Paris in the most recent year of data belonged to the two lowest-income categories. Nevertheless, 30 percent of the social housing put onto the market in Paris is reserved for middle-income people.[15] For a family of four in Paris in 2022, that tranche is set between €56,000 and €74,000 in annual household income—a sum that's well above what low-wage workers earn in France.

"You have a housing policy that is discriminatory toward working-class people," Simonnet said. "In the name of mixing populations in social housing, and in the name of preserving the middle class, working-class people are being run out of the city."

According to Simonnet, even projects that appear worthy at first glance, such as those improving housing stock in disrepair, can exert the same effect. "If, in a neighborhood you're building 30 percent [social housing for middle-income categories], at the end of the operation, maybe you've built social housing where there wasn't any, you've rehabilitated a neighborhood, you've fought against dilapidated buildings, but at the same time, you've removed a share of what was accessible to working-class people," she said.

This point of view marks a full-fledged ideological disagreement with City Hall. The current government believes it's important to reserve a considerable share of the growing social housing stock for middle-income residents. It's part of what Mayor Hidalgo often refers to as *mixité sociale*, or "social mixing," the intermingling of people of different socioeconomic backgrounds that's presented as a kind of value in and of itself—not unlike the way American progressives talk about ethnic or religious diversity.

"Middle-class people are also having difficulties finding housing in Paris," Brossat told me in response to the criticism. "Housing policy needs to be directed at everybody struggling to find housing in the private housing market, so of course, the most modest categories, but also the middle class. . . . I refuse to condemn middle-class people to the private sector."

For Brossat, the current municipal housing policy isn't discriminatory, but rather in line with the broader aims of social housing.

"Social housing, as it was conceived in France, is addressed at a very broad swath of the population and not only the most precarious categories," he said. "Nothing would be worse than a housing policy that's completely ghettoized in which we're only packing in families that are in extremely difficult situations."

He argued that left-wing critics who think the city should reserve more flats for low-income residents are effectively advancing the aims of conservative critics who want to wind down social housing altogether. "While [the critique] is presented in leftist language, it's a very right-wing conception [of housing]," he said. "In reality, this is a right-wing discourse and it's historically the right that has aimed to reserve social housing for the poorest categories of the population. . . . If social housing is only for the poorest people, then nobody's going to want social housing, including the poorest who don't want to live in ghettos. And understandably so."

There's another dispute, closely related to the one about *mixité sociale*, regarding where publicly financed new homes should be placed. Under Hidalgo's watch, the city has deliberately sought to prioritize social housing in neighborhoods that have previously resisted it—namely, the historically bourgeois arrondissements in the west where existing rates run well below the overall municipal level. Policymakers justify this strategy in terms of "social mixing," but also say it's about making wealthy neighborhoods take their share of responsibilities in running the city.

It's another point of friction between authorities and housing activists. For his part, Jean-Baptiste Eyraud has stressed he has no qualms about the city investing in new projects in the west, but he also believes that social housing needs to accommodate existing demand. Fundamentally, he thinks the city needs to reserve more of its limited supply for low-income residents. Under that logic, he argues authorities shouldn't hesitate to invest in new projects in the eastern arrondissements where most working-class Parisians actually live, even if these parts of the city already have large shares of publicly managed housing stock.

"The line from the city is, 'There's already a lot of social housing in the east of Paris,'" said Eyraud as he scouted a new text on his phone. "We've been telling them for years, 'Yes, because the working class used to represent 60, 70 percent of residents there, twenty years ago. Now there's less of them!'"

The city's commitment to create more social housing in wealthy neighborhoods is not without tension. At a point during our communications, Ian Brossat's top staffer invited me to an inauguration ceremony of a new social housing complex in the famously bourgeois 16th arrondissement, on the Rue Jasmin in the southwestern corner of the capital. It was supposed to be a festive moment, but the sense of unease was palpable.

The building has an unusual origin story. It was constructed on a lot expropriated from an older uncle of Syrian dictator Bashar al-Assad, a man found guilty of corruption and money laundering by a French court.[16] But other than that, it's like many of the newer projects in the west of Paris. It's in pristine condition and blends seamlessly into a sleepy residential cityscape. It features a childcare center downstairs and boasts climate-friendly design, with high-grade energy efficiency standards, solar thermal panels, and a pretty little shared exterior green space on the ground floor. Most importantly, it's home to residents who almost certainly couldn't afford to live here otherwise: all thirty-four units are reserved for tenants from the two lowest-income categories, known as PLAI and PLUS.

At the opening of the inauguration ceremony—in front of

journalists and residents themselves—the head of housing policy for the 16th arrondissement, an older right-winger at odds
with the left alliance running City Hall, openly criticized the
income levels of the new tenants, referring to them by their
bureaucratic acronyms. "The only regret we have, Mr. Mayor,
is that you didn't want to have a mix of PLAI, PLUS, and PLS
[the middle-income category]," said Jacques-Frédéric Sauvage,
turning to Brossat. "We would've preferred PLS because when
you mix, it's easier to integrate people."

Officially color-blind, French political discourse is full of
euphemisms for talking about immigrants and ethnic minorities, and it's hard not to see this as a near-perfect illustration
of the nation's dog-whistle language around race. Sauvage's
comments weren't just an explicit criticism of the presence of
poor people in his district; they also alluded to their immigrant
backgrounds. On my way out, I checked out the mailboxes on
the ground floor—the alphabetical list of names was dominated
by common surnames of non-French origin, mostly from the
Maghreb and West Africa.

After the ceremony, residents helped themselves to cocktails
and a variety of petits fours. That's when I met Nouria, a fifty-
two-year-old who since 1995 had been on the waiting list for
social housing in Paris before receiving an offer to relocate here
in May 2022.

The move should've been nothing but a source of relief. Before
this, she'd been living in a two-room, thirty-three-square-
meter flat with her husband and four children in the 18th
arrondissement in La Chapelle, on the Rue Ordener, near the
Marx Dormoy metro station. While the new apartment costs
more (€1,076 a month, compared to €780), they can afford it
because of her job at a government ministry—and the living

conditions are an unambiguous upgrade. It's a seventy-two-square meter apartment with three bedrooms and a living room, which means they're not living on top of one another like before.

Still, Nouria told me she cried when they decided to accept the offer—and they were not tears of joy.

"I was wondering if I made the right move accepting this," she said as she sipped from a glass of red wine. "It's a big change. We spent practically our entire lives in the 18th. Remaking a whole life in another neighborhood that's totally different is difficult, especially if the people in the neighborhood don't help very much."

Like much of the largely residential 16th, there's a stuffiness to the air around Jasmin. Social activity is largely limited to a single avenue that runs north-south, laid out by the Baron de Haussmann to provide a sanctuary for wealthy residents. A century and a half later, the Avenue Mozart is lined with expensive restaurants, real estate agencies, and luxury hair salons. There are noticeably fewer immigrants around, and fewer languages being spoken outside of French.

While the 16th arrondissement has long been a bastion for conservatives, it's lurched even further to the right in recent years. Nowhere in Paris did the identitarian far-right polemicist Éric Zemmour score better in the 2022 presidential election than in this district. His calls to fight the Great Replacement, a conspiracy theory alleging that European elites want non-white immigrants to take over the continent, won over nearly a fifth of first-round voters.[17]

In many ways, this neighborhood is the diametrical opposite of Nouria's old one.

"The 18th was more working-class, more family-friendly.

Here it's less family-friendly, but I hope that in this building, we'll have this sort of ambiance and that we'll be able to have friendly relations with our neighbors," Nouria told me. "We're ready to adapt, but it might be a bit harder for the people in the neighborhood."

Rent Controls

Whether in Paris or elsewhere, another immensely powerful tool for regulating the housing market is rent control: imposing ceilings on how much landlords can charge for rent as well as caps on rent increases. In a capitalist market, such restrictions aren't a panacea: without other initiatives to create more housing or to transfer more of it into public hands, they can have a tightening effect on supply. Still, most affordable housing advocates agree that rent controls are a valuable instrument to be deployed as part of a broader strategy. In the case of Paris, supporters view them as complementary to a robust program of social housing and other pro-tenant policies.

And yet, until recently, rent restrictions weren't even on the table. After a conservative parliamentary majority successfully repealed France's rent controls in the mid-1980s, the issue was largely set aside by the Socialist Party, abandoned alongside other ambitious pledges. Under President François Hollande, a new law finally authorized cities to impose rent controls, but it was challenged in court. And while Paris did impose restrictions from 2015 to 2017, a judge tossed them out the following year. It wasn't until 2019 that the National Assembly paved the way for the city to once again impose rent caps—which Paris officials signed off on almost immediately.

Still, the existing policy has major defects.

For one, price ceilings aren't set by elected city representatives, but by national authorities—more precisely, the regional prefecture of Île-de-France, whose chief is appointed directly by the president. Thus far, housing advocates say the ceilings have been set too high. At the same time, enforcement from regional authorities has been extremely limited. Over the first two years of the policy, just nine landlords were fined for breaking the law, with none of them paying more than €1,500.[18]

The laxness appears to have encouraged many landlords to simply flout the law. According to a 2021 study by a prominent housing rights organization, about a third of the rental listings in Paris did not respect rent control restrictions, exceeding the limits by almost €200 a month on average.[19] Tenants of small flats made for frequent victims: a whopping 47 percent of apartments measuring less than thirty square meters were advertised at prices that did not respect the official ceilings.

After a wave of criticism, the city of Paris successfully requested a transfer of enforcement powers from the prefecture to the municipal government, a small victory that took effect in 2023. Instead of simply begging the regional prefecture to administer the law, the city by itself can now crack down on disobedient landlords—and it plans to significantly ramp up controls. But it was only a partial victory. The city still doesn't have the ability to set price ceilings on its own, and that touches on a bigger challenge that runs to the very core of the French mode of government.

"The problem we have is that the majority of regulatory tools for the private market are in the hands of the state," Brossat told me. "There are two possibilities. Either the state takes responsibility and takes more of an active approach in housing policy—even if, at the moment, I don't see many opportunities there. Or, at the very least, it gives more power to cities and, in this case, lets us do more than what we're doing today."

The country's Jacobin heritage is a double-edged sword. France's national government has the authority to impose redistributive policies on a broad range of issues—healthcare, transit, energy, and housing can all be transformed overnight. But when the political will is lacking or is moving in an opposite direction—as is often the case in the era of President Emmanuel Macron, elected in 2017—it can make things very difficult for local officials to achieve even modest progressive reforms. How to address this problem is a long-standing source of debate, including within left-wing circles. But on the issue of housing, there is an emerging consensus that local authorities need more power to act.

Although elected on the national level, MP Danielle Simonnet believes the city of Paris needs to have more authority in the housing field. She said it should be able to fix prices on its own.

"If the population wants rent controls to be lower, then the town's elected officials need to be able to do that," she told me. "But the state also needs to be able to impose rent decreases in cities, to ensure that ghettos for the rich don't protect themselves under the pretense that they alone should have that authority."

Beefing Up Supply: Preemptions, Requisitions, Taxes, and Taking on Airbnb

While social housing and price controls account for the two biggest levers of pressure, French authorities do have other tools at their disposal in the struggle for affordable housing: a variety of instruments that can be used to beef up supply and keep apartments out of the hands of speculators.

Despite its relative lack of power, the city of Paris has one fairly distinctive weapon in its arsenal, which is its "right of pre-emption." Property sales must be reported in advance to the city, which, under French law, has the ability to preempt and acquire ownership of the property in question. It can then either purchase at the price that's already been agreed to—or try to negotiate a lower price in a lengthier process overseen by a judge. Local authorities have increasingly exercised this right in recent years, using it as a tool to shore up new social housing stock. Since Anne Hidalgo arrived in 2014, the budget devoted to preemption has nearly doubled, reaching over €140 million a year.[20]

Given the inflated state of the market, however, the sales themselves can be quite costly—and a limited city budget complicates the task. When complemented with an attachment to the principle of social mixing and a reluctance to saturate northeastern Paris with low-income housing, it means plenty of sales go untouched in neighborhoods that could stand to benefit. For instance, Jean-Baptiste Eyraud argued the city should've stepped in and bought the furnished Hôtel du Marché. Brossat told me it was too expensive given the limited number of flats available in the area.

Other tools are aimed at reducing the number of vacant or underutilized homes in Paris. According to the statistics agency INSEE, there are about 126,000 secondary homes in the French capital, making up 9 percent of the city's housing stock.[21] (Of the nation's big cities, only the Riviera tourist hub of Nice has a higher rate.) These secondary residences are concentrated heavily in the central parts of Paris frequented by short-term visitors, essentially the postcard version of the city: the first four arrondissements on the Right Bank and the three northern arrondissements of the Left Bank, stretching together from the Champs-Elysées and the Eiffel Tower to Notre Dame and the Luxembourg Gardens.

According to a separate set of government figures, there are roughly one hundred thousand "frictionally vacant" apartments in Paris—flats that, in theory, are being prepared for sale or are already in the process of being sold. Then there's an additional group of nearly nineteen thousand homes that have been unoccupied for more than two years, most of them located in the central business part of the city, with the highest rate found in the chic 8th arrondissement.[22]

When it comes to the latter group in particular, housing activists have called on the authorities to deploy their powerful right to requisition, a legally viable maneuver in France. Under a law that dates back to 1945—just after the end of World War II—the state can temporarily seize homes and apartments to lodge people for up to a year, so long as it compensates property owners in exchange. Once again, however, the city of Paris doesn't have the authority to act alone. It requires sign-off from the national government, which has declined to take this route in recent years.

Brossat has urged the state to exercise this right. But he also wants to drive up the tax rate on secondary residences—a levy approved under Socialist president François Hollande. As it stands, the charge is added to the standard housing tax, but it's restricted from exceeding 60 percent of the latter, and any increase requires national parliamentary approval. In practical terms, it means the owner of a secondary residence in the

French capital today isn't paying more than 21 percent of the home's value in taxes every year.[23] "We should be able to tax secondary residences more heavily," he told me. "Either to bring in revenue because we always need extra revenue and it's not absurd to put that on the shoulders of people who have enough money to have a secondary residence in Paris. Or to encourage property owners to sell or lease."

Finally, the municipal government has overseen an effort to clamp down on Airbnb, a company it views as contributing to the high rate of vacant homes and fueling real estate speculation more broadly—both driving up prices and taking otherwise viable apartments off the market. Under current laws, landlords seeking to use the platform need to register their flats with the city of Paris. They're also barred from renting out their homes for more than 120 days a year. Under Brossat, the city has sought to crack down on landlords who don't respect these rules. In 2021, Airbnb was forced to pay an €8 million fine to the city of Paris for failing to register about a thousand properties with the city.[24]

Brossat argued that the city, all in all, is essentially doing the best it can do: it's building social housing and using the limited set of tools it has to try and calm the open market. "The gentrification of Paris isn't coming from social housing, it's coming from the private market," he said. "And so if we want to avoid it, we need additional maneuvering power to intervene in the market. That's the reality."

Simonnet agrees that the national government bears a hefty share of responsibility, but she also believes municipal authorities need to think more creatively about what powers they do have.

"They've never wanted to publish the list of vacant buildings," she told me. "They could have a more combative action and put posters on public space that say, 'This building is empty, the city should have the right to requisition it.' They're not doing that. If we did that, there would be a battle in public opinion to create a more favorable balance of forces."

"Maybe it would encourage collectives to move in and squat—and it'd be for the better!" Simonnet continued. "Each time there've been squats of empty buildings, the city was able to have a showdown with the police prefecture, with the state, with the government, to then use its right of preemption, or acquire it. Anyways, they're not doing this, and they should."

For a glimpse of the nightmarish scenario that could await Paris without effective state intervention into the housing market, it's worth taking a stroll around the Marais. The illustrious old bastion of the urban aristocracy is on the tail end of a gentrification cycle spanning nearly four centuries. After the middle classes fled during the nineteenth century, it descended into a dilapidated slum before gradually becoming trendy in the 1970s and 1980s. In the last decade or so, the Marais has ascended to another level entirely. The price per square meter is more than four times the average French monthly salary. It might be a stretch to call it a neighborhood—it's more of a theme park.

The Marais is packed to the hilt with secondary residences and attracts more Airbnb rentals than anywhere else in the city. The firm no longer publicly shares such data, but in the summer of 2014, the Marais had slightly more Airbnb guests than actual residents.[25] Streets are clogged regularly with tourists gawking at the area's gorgeous pre-Haussmann buildings, cute windy streets, and enchanting *hôtels particuliers*. But other than the art galleries and museums, most of the businesses are luxury brands and middle-brow clothing retailers that can be found in just about any other European or North American city. There are few primary schools and kindergartens still around, since so few people live here anymore.[26]

The area clings to its reputation as a gay neighborhood, with rainbow-colored crosswalks lining some of the central avenues, but even this heritage looks to be on the way out. The Marais has been without an LGBT bookstore since 2020, when the owners of the iconic Les Mots à la Bouche were forced to relocate to the northeast due to rising rents. Their old space was turned into a Dr. Martens retailer.[27] Meanwhile, L'Open Café wound down operations in 2022, with the owner selling the property to an investment fund for an undisclosed amount, becoming the latest to join an increasingly crowded graveyard of Marais gay bars.[28]

Likewise, the neighborhood's Jewish character has long since faded. There are a few older Jewish-run businesses left—restaurants serving a mix of Mediterranean and eastern European food and a couple of bakeries featuring traditional Ashkenazi specialties like babka, challah bread, and gefilte fish—but they largely serve tourists and are limited to a couple of blocks. The Jewish identity exists mainly as a thing of the past, like it could be on exhibition next to the Picasso Museum or the National Archives.

The Marais has its own unique history, but its streets offer a preview of what a hypergentrified Paris of the future could resemble. It's a place where most of the shops are internationally recognized brands catering to tourists; where life amid beautiful architecture built before the twentieth century is out of reach for low-to-middle-income residents; where diversity exists as an interesting historical reality—perhaps even as a value to be celebrated—but not as a meaningful part of day-to-day life. Ironically, the Marais actually fits much of Mayor Anne Hidalgo's criteria for the fifteen-minute city: it's extremely walkable; there are few cars and bike lanes galore. The only people taking advantage of it, however, are tourists and the super-rich.

In this Disneyland version of Paris, low-income people have no place living in apartments, let alone the fancy cocktail bars or swanky restaurants filled with tourists. But the hypergentrified parts of the city have even less patience for those living on the farthest margins of society: the homeless, migrants, and people with drug problems—anybody who tends to spend time sleeping in the streets. Blight and human suffering aren't supposed to ruin the ambiance, and intruders are often greeted with hostility.

This reality was illustrated in chilling fashion in January 2022. On a cold night in the Marais, a renowned eighty-four-year-old Franco-Swiss photographer lost consciousness and stumbled to the sidewalk of the Rue Turbigo, not far from his flat. He ultimately laid there, on the ground, for nine hours. It wasn't until a homeless person alerted authorities that firefighters arrived on the scene in the early morning—but by then, it was too late and the photographer was pronounced dead from hypothermia shortly thereafter.[29] More than a hundred homeless people die in Paris every year, but the conditions of this tragedy were of an unusual brutality and hard to dissociate from the setting: Where were the concerned neighbors? Why didn't pedestrians do anything? What went through their minds when they saw a motionless, elderly person lying on the street in the middle of winter?

It's impossible to get direct answers to these questions, but it seems fair to pin at least part of the blame on the geography of twenty-first-century Paris. The hypergentrified city keeps the most marginalized out of its territory.

As public survey data shows, Paris does count a significant homeless population in the immediate city center, but many live around large train stations, and not in residential neighborhoods. Far more have sought refuge in the outer arrondissements in the eastern half of the city. They're situated at the intersections dotting the northeastern and southern edges of Paris—sleeping under bridges and highway overpasses—or living in the two big parks on opposite sides of the city. In 2022, only a few dozen were living in the chic 16th arrondissement. More than three hundred were living in the 19th.[30]

An itinerant, crack-using population has been similarly kept away from the more desirable quarters. Ever since a group first emerged around the Place de Stalingrad in the 1990s, police have been shuffling them around the northeast. They've been back and forth to Stalingrad, to a nearby park overlooking the railyards, and more recently, to an industrial lot in the southeastern 13th arrondissement. The city recently created a supervised injection site inside a hospital near the Gare du Nord train station, but a proposal to create an addiction treatment facility in the 16th arrondissement was nixed by the national government—a decision celebrated by the district's elected officials.[31]

Nowhere have these unmarked boundaries been more exposed, however, than through the state's treatment of migrants. While thousands have flocked to the capital in recent years—many of them sleeping outside for a lack of housing options—encampments have been tolerated almost exclusively in the northeastern peripheries of the city. And despite the obvious differences, these young men do share some things in common with the elderly residents of the Hôtel du Marché. Both groups are scraping by in a city hostile to their kind. And with the help of activist groups, they've been fighting back—going up against the odds and taking on forces that would rather see them leave the city altogether.

The scene has repeated itself countless times, ever since migrants started arriving in greater numbers after 2015. They put up tents, they stick around for a few weeks or a few months. Activists provide food, water, and legal assistance on the ground. Eventually, the police intervene, dismantling tents and forcing people onto buses that take them to short-term emergency housing facilities. The images circulate on social media and television. Pundits debate the failures of French and European migration policy. Before too long, a new encampment goes up and the cycle repeats itself.

At first, many of the people sleeping in tents were from Syria, though, for cultural and linguistic reasons, France has always drawn in a significant share of migrants from West African countries like Guinea and Côte d'Ivoire. These days, more and more migrants are from Afghanistan.[32] One of the remarkable constants is where their sleeping bags go down, far from the center of Paris, almost always in the northeastern edges of the city.

"The state is doing everything to make sure Paris remains this inaccessible city that's very beautiful, very pretty," Marie-Laure Richter, a young activist who works with the migrant aid group Utopia 56, told me over Zoom, sitting alongside her colleague Elsa Descope. "There's a system of invisibilization of migrants, and that's what we see on a daily basis."

Of course, the tents themselves are the sign of far-reaching policy failures. As Richter and Descope pointed out, many of the migrants sleeping in the streets have either already applied for asylum or even already obtained refugee status. The French state is supposed to help direct both of these groups toward housing if they need it, but the main national network devoted to lodging asylum seekers is stretched woefully beyond capacity. As such, it's extremely common for migrants in Paris to spend at least one night on the street.[33]

The spaces they're allowed in are policed, quite literally.

Camps near the peripheral Porte de la Chapelle and the Porte d'Aubervilliers, the most popular spots, have been tolerated for several months at a time. On the other hand, attempts from Utopia 56 to install tents at the centrally located Place de la République, not far from the Marais, have been rebuffed. The repression was especially violent on an evening in November 2020, with media images of riot cops tearing up tents and beating back activists leading to a rare public reprimand of the police from the interior minister.[34] Several months later, housing and immigrant rights groups attempted another occupation of the square, resulting in a quick promise from the police to relodge those involved.[35]

"It's something that Utopia 56 believes strongly in—occupying these central spaces to put these people front and center. We try and do this pretty regularly, either through occasional protests or more long-term actions," Richter told me. "You see to what extent people don't want to see [the migrants]—the police, the prefecture, they're doing everything so that these people aren't seen. It's interesting to see the reactions of residents, too, who are sometimes startled when they discover a sort of refugee camp in the center of the city."

The group has faced criticism from some who accuse them of politicizing tragedy and being overly confrontational with the state, but that's precisely the goal. Utopia 56 seeks to prompt the broader public to think of people they'd rather not have to think about—and that includes pointing out double standards in the treatment of migrants.[36]

While the 2022 Russian invasion of Ukraine led the French state to grant temporary refugee status to tens of thousands of Ukrainians and drove authorities to find housing solutions for them, Richter and Descope lament that the same sense of solidarity has not been extended elsewhere.

"With all the initiatives that have been put into place for the Ukrainians, you realize there is space for emergency housing but that a welcome reception isn't unconditional. Certain people just can't benefit from it," Descope told me as Richter shook her head in disgust. "It's very upsetting."

When we spoke, Utopia 56 had just lent its support to an encampment in the upper 19th arrondissement for single men, most of them from Afghanistan. Many had been living in tents in the nearby suburb of Bobigny, but had decided—with the help of the group—to install a camp within the limits of Paris. For Utopia 56, the goal was also to increase visibility: to remind the government and the public that the problems of migrants, asylum seekers, and refugees can't be hidden on the other side of the Boulevard Périphérique.[37] Here, in one of the wealthiest cities on the planet, thousands of people are forced to sleep outside.

On a weekday afternoon, Richter accompanied me out to the

camp, near a tram station next to the Canal de l'Ourcq. About sixty tents were organized neatly under a bridge that seemed to tremble each time the tram passed overhead. Many residents were gone—they often leave during the day to find food or spots to shower—but about a dozen were still hanging around. They sat on steps overlooking the tents, scrolling on their phones and showing each other videos. A few joggers passed by without making eye contact.

After Marie-Laure Richter introduced me, one of the men asked if I'd be filming for TV, his eyes betraying a sense of disappointment once I said was just writing a book: "You need to show this on video! People need to see!"

I still managed to chat with Arif, a twenty-six-year-old from Afghanistan's Laghman Province, a district in the far east near the border with Pakistan. He told me he'd spent much of the last two years in the streets. He said he's been confused for a crack user.

"When I see some people look at me, they think maybe this man's crazy because I have nothing and I live in the street," he said in basic English. "They think maybe he's crazy, maybe he's a smoker or something. In France, there are too many people not living in homes."

Sleeping in the street is immensely stressful. Arif said he's been held up at knifepoint. He doesn't get a lot of sleep, just one or two hours at a time. When we spoke, he was agitated because he'd just lost some critical documents, having left them behind at another camp in Porte de la Villette.

He recently obtained his refugee status, but is having trouble navigating the system to receive financial aid and anything beyond short-term emergency housing. "When I came here, I thought it was such a beautiful country, but here there are too many people who don't know my problems," he said. "For example, you don't know what my problems are."

Arif's sister lives in Pakistan and his brother resides in Turkey, but he said he wanted to stay in France. "The dream for me is I stay here," he told me. "I get good sleep, I have work and that is my life. Good home, good work. But now that life is nothing."

Unlike the camps in Calais, where most of the residents are preparing to venture across the Channel into the U.K., many of the migrants here want to build their future in France.

Twenty-year-old Matiullah told me he's been in Paris for four years, mixing short-term emergency stays with time in the street. He was in a tough spot, as his first asylum request was denied, but he said he was hoping to win on appeal. He doesn't have the right to work yet, but speaks French well. Like Arif, he wants to stay. "It's a good country and I like the language," he said.

At a certain point, any serious plan to conserve what's left of working-class Paris is going to have to acknowledge the fact that the majority of low-income people in the region no longer live within the city limits. They now reside in the suburbs and, in general, to the north and east of Paris. While the capital's population of about 2 million holds steady, nearly 9 million live in the suburbs. Under such circumstances, it can even feel somewhat silly to keep using the term *banlieue*, which reduces a vast and complex urban environment to its position vis-à-vis Paris. There are echoes here of the term *province*, a much-maligned term used to describe everything outside of the capital whose use has thankfully begun to fall out of fashion.

The banlieue has a tremendous amount of diversity—and, of

course, how could there not be in an area inhabited by so many? There are giant housing towers; American-style single-family homes; brick and stone apartment blocks that look like the ones in Paris. There are wealthy enclaves, middle-class neighborhoods, and low-income housing projects cut off from their surroundings. What's clear, at any rate, is that the struggle for affordable living in Paris will be shaped by whatever happens in this vast, complicated, and divided expanse. If the battle is to be resolved in an equitable fashion, it's going to have to acknowledge the fact that, ultimately, the city of Paris belongs to these people too.

6

THE WORLDS OF
THE BANLIEUE

Alain Tsamas is an early riser. The forty-three-year-old usually sets the alarm for 3:45 a.m., leaving just enough time to make his 6 a.m. shift in the butchery department at grocery chain Monoprix. He's usually out of his flat in the northeastern suburb of Aubervilliers by 4. Since the metros and suburban rail lines aren't open yet, Tsamas starts his commute on the reduced-hours night bus to the Gare de l'Est train station in the north of Paris. That's where he hops on another night bus that crisscrosses the city, descends the banks of the Seine, and shuffles through the quiet streets of the Left Bank until it arrives in the well-to-do suburb of Issy-les-Moulineaux, a town just outside the southwestern limits of Paris where he's been working for more than a decade.

"At that time, you know, it's not the sort of people you're used to seeing during the day," Tsamas told me. "It's a lot of people who are living on the edge. A lot of junkies, too."

Tsamas is in the very first wave, but the people on those buses are part of a daily commuting pattern that's one of the biggest in Europe, if not the world.[1] Nearly two in three of those working in the French capital—just over a million people—reside outside the city limits.[2] Most of them cannot afford to live within Paris, but are effectively responsible for keeping the city running: construction workers, transit workers, sanitation workers, janitors, housekeepers, cooks, waiters, cashiers, nurses, secretaries, and administrative staff helping to keep businesses afloat.

Their homes are dispersed across a broad zone that surrounds the city, particularly the eastern half of the Île-de-France region. And for most of the week, they're separated from one another at thousands of individual workplaces. But the early morning commute offers a fleeting moment of congregation. This hidden cohort of essential workers can be spotted waiting on train platforms in the suburbs and flowing out of the major rail hubs—the Gare du Nord and the Gare de l'Est, especially—though they're concealed again shortly thereafter, even in the metro. By the time suburban workers are packed into these trains, designed for and still overwhelmingly favoring Parisians living in Paris, they blend in with residents of the city proper.

When Tsamas punches in at Monoprix, he follows a familiar routine. Because the chain ditched fresh meat cuts in favor of pre-packaged products about a decade ago, his job is essentially managing the stock. He surveys products that are ready to be sold and sets aside those nearing their expiration dates, which are then discounted or donated. He handles incoming stock and places orders for new products. But these days, he's also required to help out other departments in need of aid, which means he often hauls around fruit and vegetables, packs of water, and bottles of wine and liquor. He gets one twenty-minute break and finishes by 12:30 p.m.

Tsamas has worked most of his adult life at Monoprix—twenty-two years, including sixteen of them at this same store in Issy-les-Moulineaux. He's full-time, thirty-five hours a week. And yet, he earns just €1,900 a month before Social Security contributions, which comes to about €1,600 in take-home pay. It's just above the rate for new hires and the national minimum wage. The limited income stream makes living in Paris—or closer to work, for that matter—all but impossible.

"It's not really a choice," he said of living in Aubervilliers. "It's a constraint tied to income. We've got precarious salaries, so we live in the places where it's financially possible in terms of rent. . . . Rent prices are going up, energy prices are going up, everything's going up except our salaries."

Few of Tsamas's colleagues actually live within the limits of Paris. Nearly all live in the seven suburban *départements* surrounding the city. "I'm lucky actually," he told me. "I'm not that far away, I'm in the north, but I have night buses near me. We had a colleague who lived in Normandy [the northeastern coastal region that begins some seventy-five kilometers away] who started at seven in the morning. We have another colleague who starts at noon who lives in Rouen [the capital of Normandy, about two hours from Paris by train]."

As a union delegate who knows the employer well, Tsamas has plenty of gripes over wage levels, working conditions, and the increasingly hard-nosed management culture, but he said all the issues are amplified by the grueling commute.

"You know, a lot of colleagues are only sleeping three, four hours a night," he told me. "A lot of people have sleep problems. It's even harder in the summer when you get the heat waves.

You might fall asleep at around midnight or 1, but then you have to wake up at 3 or 4. A lot of colleagues feel the fatigue in the break room. . . . You're doing low-paid work that's very demanding with difficult conditions, and then on top of that, you live far away and you're tired."

The banlieue is made up of multiple worlds, all of them bearing traces of the city they're built around. Eleven million people live in the extended metropolitan area, according to INSEE, and more Parisians themselves are moving to the cities and towns of the banlieue: about 70,000 of the 120,000 who leave the capital every year on average resettle within the broader metropolitan area; of this group, nearly 60,000 resettled within twenty kilometers.[3] It's an extraordinarily diverse zone that defies easy categorization, made up of everything from housing towers and dusty apartment blocks to family homes and sparse tracts of farmland. The internal social borders may not be as sharp or as well-defined as they are in Paris proper, but the wealth and income divides extend out here, too.

To the immediate west of the city lie a string of wealthy towns connected to the tissue of bourgeois Paris, conveniently located near the towers and office buildings of La Défense. That includes places like the famously posh Neuilly-sur-Seine, a dense refuge for the ultra-rich known for its conservative politics (polemicist Éric Zemmour won nearly a fifth of the vote here in the first round of the 2022 presidential elections), and the more verdant Saint-Cloud, famed for its royal gardens. To the east of the city lie a web of municipalities filled with large shares of low-income residents that can point to a plethora of different ethnic backgrounds and national origins. There's an immense amount of socioeconomic diversity within many of these cities, but collectively all three *départements* immediately surrounding Paris are known as the *petite couronne*, or the "little crown."

As one moves further away from the capital, deeper into the *grande couronne*, "the big crown," the sense of urban living slowly starts to fade. There are less public transit options and more cars. The towns more closely resemble suburbs in the American sense, albeit with clusters of housing projects in all directions. The west does feature some pockets of lower-income residents, typically around the social housing developments.

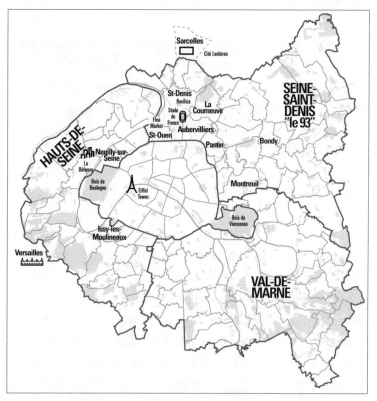

Paris and the "little crown."

And solidly middle-class communities can be found throughout the eastern suburbs of Paris, scattered within pockets of unextragavant single-family homes. But all in all, like Paris, the east-west divide looms large.

If there is a successful struggle to build a more livable and equitable urban area, then it will almost certainly be thanks to what plays out in the east of Paris. This is where much of the city's low-wage workforce—people like Alain Tsamas—lives today. For similar reasons, it's ground zero for many of the region's new immigrants and younger artists drawn to the area. And it's home to one of the youngest populations in all of France, left to overcome an array of inequities and stereotypes surrounding them.[4] In the long battle over space in Paris— the centuries-long drive to push the poor further and further away from the center—this is the next frontier. It's also, if the past is any indication, where much of the pushback will come from.

The cityscape immediately bordering Paris to the east—the inner belt ranging from around Saint-Ouen to Montrouge— simply feels like an extension of what remains of working-class Paris. If you can ignore the ring-road highway marking the border, you can come out on the other end and still have a sense of being within Paris proper. There aren't as many Haussmann-style buildings—you'll encounter more apartments made of cheaper, reddish bricks and fewer attempts to imitate the mansard roofs of Paris—but it remains a high-density world with bustling street life. The same mix of inexpensive restaurants and small businesses exist on the other side of the "Périph": fast-food joints churning out kebabs and gooey

French tacos; barbershops and hardware suppliers; locksmiths and bakeries with mass-produced industrial-quality patisserie, most of it frozen and reheated early in the morning. And signs of gentrification are everywhere: new housing developments and restaurants that feel just a bit too flashy for the neighborhoods they're in.

Like northeastern Paris, much of the population here can point to immigrant origins, with shared common spaces keeping alive the capital's ancient hybrid energy. Each of the towns has a particular twist on this, but the scene in central Saint-Denis is especially electric. Three days a week, the city hosts a massive market that puts to shame just about all of its competition on the other side of the ring-road highway: inside a covered hall not far from an ancient basilica where dozens of French kings are buried, a crowd shuffles through a maze of butchers, fishmongers, cheese merchants, fruit vendors, spice vendors, and a couple of stands selling regional specialties from Algeria and France's *départements* in the Caribbean. The action spills outside where, on a recent visit, I saw a nectarine vendor attract a crowd of smiling clients by alternatively boasting about the juiciness of his fruit at the top of his lungs and belting out, *Ooh-la-la-la-la-la-la-la-la-la-la!* At a nearby terrace, people quietly sipped mint tea and snacked on *mhadjeb*, a semolina-based flatbread from Algeria. At another bar, retirees sat reading the papers and gulped down their first drinks of the day.

The name of a nearby street leading up to the tramway—an homage to Gabriel Péri, a Communist member of the French Resistance—provides a hint of who used to run this city. Like many neighboring towns, Saint-Denis was, for decades, part of the old heartland of the Communist Party, the "red belt" that once extended across the major industrial areas surrounding Paris. While many of the factories, docks, and railyards have since closed and the party has gradually lost its grip on local government, this heritage lives on in the names of streets and schools chosen by its former mayors. Further north in the city, toward the university, lie Che Guevera Alley, José Marti Alley, Avenue Stalingrad, and a road named to honor Mexican muralist David Siqueiros. (Needless to say, there are no Avenue Trotskys.) Across the Paris suburbs, there are at least five different Avenue Lénine. A kindergarten, an elementary school, and a high school are all named after Angela Davis. At least two roads and a middle school are named after Rosa Luxemburg. Four streets pay homage to Karl Marx. There are also four different Rues Robespierre—not a commonly celebrated figure of the Revolution—and in Montreuil, there's even a Rue des Fédérés, a bold homage to those killed by French Republican forces in the Paris Commune.

Over the last few decades, the biggest demographic shift in these cities has been the gradual replacement of the old industrial labor force with lower-paid service sector workers. More recently, the latter also tend to share the streets with a small but growing group of creative professionals and budding artists contemplating a life devoted to their crafts: painters, musicians, writers, actors, and filmmakers drawn to Paris who can't afford life inside city limits. Many of the immediate eastern suburbs are bustling with cultural activity—though one, in particular, has become something of a beacon: if a young artist without financial cushion might've moved to Montparnasse in the 1920s or Saint-Germain-des-Prés in the 1940s, today, there's a good chance Montreuil is at the top of their list.

The Squat

On a hot weekday afternoon in July, I went to meet the crew at Art Liquide, one of many different artist squats active at any given moment in Montreuil. Like most of them, it's occupying abandoned industrial infrastructure—in this case, a warehouse that used to stock industrial gas. But the space here is especially massive. It also has the advantage of being hidden from major streets. About a fifteen-minute walk from the city center, it's in a quiet neighborhood across the street from the headquarters of a small industrial cleaning firm. Around the corner sits a social housing project, a small corner store, and a Turkish restaurant.

My guide was Alex, a twenty-nine-year-old drummer who I'd contacted over Facebook. He'd been at Art Liquide for about a year since he and others occupied the building and launched the squat in the first place—a whole process that involved sneaking in and hiding from security guards before declaring the building as a primary residence, a legal maneuver that draws out the eventual (and inevitable) eviction process. He has a beard and long bushy hair that he wears back in dreadlocks.

Alex explained Art Liquide's mission. Around thirty residents work on various creative projects—paintings, drawings, plays, woodworking, musical endeavors, graffiti on the inside walls. But they've also consciously sought to build links with the surrounding community. They hold open-door visits on the weekends and regularly put on concerts open to the public. There's also a definite left-wing undercurrent—the black anarchist flag flies outside and the group's social media account shares images of various protests—though I'm told not everyone maintains that level of political engagement.

People move to squats for different reasons. With its aims of fostering creative self-expression and carving out a space for alternative culture, Art Liquide belongs to a particular subcategory that has become a feature of major western European cities over the last few decades. It's clearly come into its own on this side of the Atlantic, but the tradition draws some amount of inspiration from the movement that swept across the Lower East Side of New York City in the late 1970s and 1980s—a disparate bunch of musicians, painters, immigrants, housing activists, and people on the margins of society who claimed abandoned apartments for themselves, not necessarily with fully developed visions of how to put them to use. By their very nature, squats like Art Liquide are only viable in places where urban space is unutilized. Their preponderance in Montreuil reflects the suburb's current state of development: gentrification has not yet unleashed its full powers.

After a fly-by tour, Alex invited me into a nook overlooking the warehouse where residents joined in on the discussion, coming and going as they chose. A psychedelic painting screaming bright orange and blue pulsated in the corner, accompanied by a red-and-black flag that read "Action Antifasciste." To the right hung the sort of large protest banner often carried by Black Bloc anarchists at the front of demonstrations: "You're Governing Too Close to the Edge." Waiting for a cup of coffee, I sank into a brown leather chair, choosing it over a couple of grimy couches missing cushions. On the ground lay some dirty clothes and a couple of empty bottles of Desperados, a bright yellow, Tequila-flavored lager. A spliff was passed around before finding its final resting place in an ashtray that looked like it hadn't been cleaned since the warehouse was operational. Taking advantage of the fact that I was visibly outside my comfort zone, I posed a tremendously broad question: What's the point of squatting? Why are you doing this?

"I mean, it's a bit like love and revolution," Alex replied. "I can't explain in a hundred words."

Sarah, a twenty-five-year-old native of northeast Paris who moved to the squat a few months after it was created, chimed in.

"It's personal, but I think squatting means, in our society today, that there's a problem of well-being, a feeling of solitude, and a desire for revolution and a new world, but all of this isn't possible alone. There's not this feeling of belonging to a bigger group that pushes you," she said. "The squat is a lot of people passing through, a lot of artists, a lot of opportunities, which is not what you have when you're alone in your apartment."

"I was living in my apartment before and you go nuts—there's no life, no communication, no links, no discovery," she continued. "With the squat, I can exhibit and show what I'm doing, I can make links, do work and push things further, meet other artists or future artists. Otherwise, I might've just kept hiding my sketchbook, you know."

Art Liquide has held a few exhibitions with professional artists and musicians, but most of the full-time residents here are amateurs. Alex plays music from time to time, in a group that plays a mix of reggae, funk, and hip-hop, but it's more of a hobby than anything else. Sarah said squat life encouraged her to draw more, but she doesn't get paid for it either. "It makes me feel good," she said. "It makes me think, that's important for me."

For many of the residents here, this all may prove to be an interlude. A more standardized existence may be around the corner—at a minimum, squatting will have supplied some crucial time to figure things out. But the liberty it provides can sometimes breed deeper devotion to a life in the arts, and squatting culture is filled with legendary names who've passed through the ranks. Just a few years before he achieved global renown, Jean-Michel Basquiat was a teenager from Brooklyn who spray-painted graffiti across Lower Manhattan and benefited from a squatted apartment to experiment with sketches and a dub jazz group, feeding off the energy of others similarly freed from the constraints of paying rent.[5] A pair of celebrated critics of contemporary French society, the comedian Blanche Gardin and the writer Virginie Despentes, each passed through squats in their younger days. In these spaces, burgeoning creators, lost souls, and the contentedly marginal intermingle— the lines between them are blurred.

Sitting on the opposite couch from Sarah was an older guy who didn't share his name. Tattooed, balding, and looking to be somewhere in his mid-forties, he told me he'd been squatting in and around Paris since the late 1990s. He'd been jobless since being laid off from an event planning job during Covid, but was using the extra time to pursue his passion of graffiti. "I don't think of myself as an artist," he said. "I don't make a living from it all."

Describing his hobby's utter lack of visual appeal, he conveyed something resembling pride. "It's on all those disgusting walls you saw in the road with a bunch of tags—letters, not drawings," he said. "When I got to Paris in 1997, it was the big graffiti era. It was about just putting your name down."

He said he often just leaves his tag, "Seultou," an example of French slang known as *verlan*, which involves reversing the syllables of words. His calling card is derived from "Tout Seul," which means "by oneself" or "all alone."

Perhaps looking to redirect the conversation, Alex insisted on the political underpinnings of Art Liquide. "We're all impacted by gentrification," he said. "That's a key part of the fight, too—organizing events and making an occupied building accessible to artists and to the public to come and exchange, discover, and share."

When it comes to the greater battle over gentrification and affordable housing, the squat is just a drop in the ocean. There are far more powerful forces operating all around it. And yet, the net positive seems undeniable: the project has snatched land away from the private market—albeit temporarily—all the while injecting fresh cultural offerings into the neighborhood. These are no small accomplishments. They're all made easier by living in Montreuil, where the support on the ground even caught Alex by surprise.

"We saw right away there were a lot of alternative spaces like the one we wanted to put into place, but the population was really receptive to the idea of having yet another squat in the area," Alex said. "Right away, we had visits from people who stopped us in the street and said it was cool this building was finally occupied because it'd been empty for years and there was this ability to hold events."

The concerts, in particular, attract a distinctively Montreuil-lois mix: "It's funny, there are punks, *gitans*, stoner bobos, but they all get along," said Alex.

Those groups are reflective of the city and neighborhood itself. "It's a pretty residential area, but at the same time, you have squats from Roma people, a lot of young people who rent small parcels of land for themselves, to store cars or things like that. There's the bourgeoisie—well, actually let's say the 'petite bourgeoisie.' They're mostly *nouveau riche*."

Paris used to have large squats like this, including an

especially legendary one near Belleville that shut down in 2014—though they'd be hard to imagine today. Lots are highly valued and accounted for. The squats that do exist are smaller, focused on providing emergency housing, and discrete by design. They're not holding roller-blade discos or raves like Art Liquide.

Still, none of the residents said they regretted not being in Paris.

"It's too fast and people would have difficulty coming to a place like this," said the graffiti aficionado who is most definitely not an artist. "Here, we're open and people around here come for what we are."

"It's more *populaire* [for the people] here," said Sarah. "People are happy to have spaces that offer things that aren't expensive. They're happy to have people doing things. In Paris, someone would end up calling the police because we're making noise."

Alex also acknowledged another somber reality—the fact that the untreated crack epidemic in Paris has created a homeless population with needs that a lot of squatters cannot or do not want to manage. "When you open your space in Paris today, you have to be ready," he said. "When you find yourself in a neighborhood ravaged by crack, it can be really difficult."

The eternal question facing squatters—here and everywhere else—is, what next? The group told me most squats in France only last about a year before they're evicted—and by that measure, Art Liquide is past its expiration date. In fact, when we spoke, they'd just been given final warning to vacate the premises by the city of Montreuil. Theoretically, eviction could've come at any moment.

Alex told me he wasn't sure, but that it would be hard to leave Montreuil.

Fortunately for them, plenty of other squats are likely to sprout up.

"Squats traditionally install themselves in areas that are being renovated," butted in Olivier, a forty-eight-year-old who was recently employed as a social worker to deal with the crack problems in northeast Paris. "Here, you've got major construction projects on the metro nearby and the area is going to be renovated for a bit longer. In general, that's where it happens."

Olivier is a firm believer in the utility of squats. "There's a real social mission in terms of housing and culture," he told me, even if he isn't so optimistic about what this area may soon look like. "In ten years, Montreuil will be filled with hipsters and bobos. Maybe some things like this will stay, but they'll slowly disappear to make space for people with money."

Will there still be squats like this at all? I asked.

"Almost certainly," he said, "but maybe not in the same form."

Of course, squats alone cannot stop gentrification, a process that is usually integral to the functioning of housing markets in high-demand cities under capitalism. In France today, they tend to appear in neighborhoods that have already witnessed some amount of fresh investment—places in the early stage of rent hikes with displacement on the horizon—but if they can help put the brakes on the process, even just a bit, how can that not be a welcome development? One or two squats in a neighborhood might not make a difference, but what about a couple dozen big ones? What about fifty of them? Explicit endorsements are tricky for obvious reasons, but what would it look like if friendly elected officials discreetly encouraged the occupation of space?

True, Art Liquide may not produce any future Modiglianis or Man Rays. But perhaps a couple of the people passing through here will have careers in the visual arts? Not everyone making art or film undergoes the same growth process, but a certain type of creatively inclined person can hone their craft by spending time in spaces like these—places where they have the time to find inspiration and share their work with others, where they can experiment freely, and where they can be insulated from the pressures of the capitalist market.

At any rate, the crew here has almost certainly managed to disrupt the plans of more than a few real estate developers in their day—and that is an extremely satisfying thought.

Into the 9-3

The scenery changes as one moves further into the northeastern *département* of Seine-Saint-Denis, often referred to simply by its zip code, "le 93," or sometimes—among younger residents—as *le neuf-trois*, the "nine-three." The metro network ends around here, counting only a few stops in towns that don't directly border Paris. (A close friend who grew up in the northern suburbs of Paris once told me the banlieue doesn't truly begin until you're outside the reach of the metro.) Still, in certain parts, even the commuter rail network, the RER, is beyond reasonable walking distance. Storefronts start to dwindle. There's a diminishing array of cafés and restaurants. Instead, the horizon is shaped by some of the biggest housing projects in the world.

Known as *cités* or *grands ensembles*, they're the defining markers of the territory—nearly all of them following the brutalist style, with an overabundance of concrete and an absence of ornamentation. There's the Cité Beaudottes in Sevran, a cluster of towers home to a whopping ten thousand residents. In La Courneuve, there's the mesmerizing Cité des 4000, whose name refers to the original number of flats. Aulnay-sous-Bois, meanwhile, hosts the Cité des 3000, rebranded as *La Rose des Vents*, "Rose of the Winds." The Clos-Saint-Lazare in Stains is bounded by dense housing blocs undulating like waves. In Clichy-sous-Bois, there's Chêne Pointu and Sévigné, and in Montfermeil, there's the Cité des Bosquets. Arguably none are as emblematic as Lochères in Sarcelles, a sprawling maze of towers that's home to forty thousand people, technically just over the border in the *département* of Val-d'Oise.

None of these places were built to accommodate vibrant street life. In fact, they were conceived in the 1950s and '60s with just the opposite intention: to produce enclosed bubbles that would contain all the vital services residents could need while primary breadwinners—mostly men—commuted to

Postcard of Lochères in Sarcelles, 1959. *CIM Editions. Patrick Kamoun Collection.*

work elsewhere. While city planners were responding to an urgent need to construct large amounts of housing, that doesn't quite explain the strategy of constructing very specific kinds of developments at far-off distances from city centers. As the journalist Xavier de Jarcy has emphasized, the *grands ensembles* always carried more of a nefarious objective: to discipline urban populations seen as dirty and unproductive.

Following a couple of experimental housing projects in the 1920s and '30s, France's brutishly anti-urban Vichy regime approved the country's first-ever comprehensive city planning law, which transferred critical powers from mayors to the national government. Although officials didn't have time to truly impose their vision of order and rationality, the top-down legal framework remained in place and was gleefully deployed by urban planners after World War II. These people did not like the spontaneity of inner cities—the chance encounters that come from mixing homes, businesses, and spaces that evolve beyond what they're initially designed for. Many were influenced by Franco-Swiss architect Le Corbusier and his Athens Charter, an ultra-technocratic vision of the city that reduced urban life to four functions: dwelling, work, recreation, and transport.[6] Like Le Corbusier, these planners saw urbanism as an experimental science and the *cités* they designed as laboratories,[7] an almost-godlike ambition that can be seen in the numerous aerial photos taken to publicly advertise developments.[8] (The views are often spell-binding from on high, but less amusing if you're one of the mice in the control group.) Despite repeated warnings over the lack of funding and effects of isolating inhabitants in towers, the state kept approving more and more such projects—all the while keeping a strict cap on the budget.

An array of social problems blew apart whatever utopian vision lay at their foundation: the *grands ensembles* often lacked the very services they promised, thanks to chronic underfunding. There weren't as many bakeries, pharmacies, butcheries, libraries, theaters, restaurants, and cafés as in Paris, or even in the centers of other working-class suburbs like Saint-Denis and Saint-Ouen. The developments were premised on a model of full employment and relative economic stability that collapsed mere decades after they went up. That initial period of stability, in retrospect, looks to be more and more the exception rather than the norm of capitalist expansion. (Still battered from deindustrialization, the *département* of Seine-Saint-Denis now has the highest poverty rate, the lowest median income, and one of the highest rates of joblessness in metropolitan France.) But perhaps just as importantly, the vision for the *grands ensembles* discounted the psychological and cultural toll of living in planned communities with little opportunity for spontaneity, exchange with outside residents, or the use of space in ways not already anticipated by architects.

Shortly after the first *cités* opened, the French press coined a word to describe the unique kind of anxiety that comes from living in suburban high-rises in planned communities with little street life: *sarcellite*, or "sarcellitus," derived from the name of the northern city.[9] The term never quite entered the mainstream, but sixty years later, the feelings it sought to capture are still there. When I took a late afternoon stroll through the *cité* that inspired the faux-malady, the sense of monotony was palpable.

Starting from the commuter rail station, the main drag plowed through rows of identical-looking blocks. Inside many of the lots, the grass was overgrown and the benches stood empty. Hardly anyone was outside: a group of men in their twenties sat on the curb drinking beers and listening to French hip-hop, while a few residents ran errands. As cars whizzed by, the biggest crowds could be found on a couple of streets and mini-mall-like hubs, which is where the services are concentrated. These, unlike the rest of the area, were teeming with people and seemed to be stretched beyond capacity. A long line stretched outside the ATM of the Postal Bank. Seven people queued outside a public health center.

Like northeastern Paris and the suburbs at large, the *grands ensembles* have a striking degree of cultural diversity. Many of the women wear Islamic veils and colorful wax-patterned dresses popular among West Africans. I overheard a couple of chefs speaking Turkish and chatted up a couple of Bangladeshi men who'd just arrived in France and were selling corn on the street for one euro a piece. But the unfortunate reality is there are few shared spaces for these people to actually interact with one another. In this part of Sarcelles, there are practically no parks and just a few bars and restaurants—outside of the workplace, life usually takes place indoors, inside the towers.

There's another undeniable fact of life here. In recent years, this city, like other nearby suburbs struggling with poverty and unemployment, has witnessed the increased presence of conservative variants of Islam: forms of the religion that emphasize strict observance and deep fidelity to the community, and claim to be purer and more authentic than other interpretations. France has its own ugly history with Islam—bound up with its colonial past and downright racism—but the spread of these newer varieties of the faith has taken a toll on Sarcelles.

Still likely one of the biggest in Europe, the city's Jewish community has become smaller and more inward-focused over the last decade. A critical turning point came in 2014, when the remnants of a pro-Palestine demonstration transformed into a riot: a small group tried to attack the city's synagogue and ransacked a kosher grocery store and a Jewish-owned pharmacy.[10] Whoever was responsible for the rampage, the events still loom large here. When I walked through the open door into one of the city's remaining kosher butcheries, longtime owner Harry initially downplayed the tensions. "There's mutual respect," said the fifty-six-year-old who first arrived in Sarcelles from Tunisia fifty years ago. "I've always felt good in Sarcelles. The truth is I have nothing to complain about. We've got the kosher restaurants, there's the synagogue—we've got everything we need to be happy."

But as we talked more, Harry opened up about the challenges. He said he has far fewer clients than ever since many of them—nearly all followers of the Jewish faith—are leaving Sarcelles. Although he went to the public schools, he said nearly all Jewish families today send their children to the private religious schools. These institutions are protected by abnormally high fences and locked gates, as is the synagogue. He used to openly wear the yarmulke, but now he wears a baseball hat to cover it. "To be okay, we have to stay together unfortunately, so that there's no tension," he said. "You don't see Jews in public schools, they get picked on."

While the layout of Sarcelles never encouraged dynamic street life, he said it's gotten worse. "The cafés aren't like they used to be, you don't see any women in cafés anymore. It comes down to radical Islam," Harry said.

Laurie, a twenty-two-year-old whose father runs the business next door and told me she considered Harry like an uncle, was even more pessimistic. "We don't mix," she said. "When

I grew up, I was friends with people from India and Pakistan. Today, in the street, we walk by and barely look at each other."

She told me it was hard to imagine staying in the city, let alone France in the long run. "Our country is Israel," she said. "We're all gonna end up there."

The situation in Sarcelles is especially tense and the product of its own particular history, but it did make me think back to something Soumia Chohra had told me months earlier. Growing up in the melting pot of the 18th arrondissement of Paris, she said she was put off by a certain kind of religiosity she encountered in the northern suburbs. She told me she thought France had its own problems with Islam, but that she felt personally uneasy in the banlieue.

"I feel like they're more closed off, they're not as open-minded as us," she'd told me in her apartment back in Paris. "When I'd go to the 9-3—I'm a believer, I'm a Muslim, though I don't wear the headscarf—I saw the women and they're practically all wearing the headscarf. In the 9-3, I can't go get a drink or smoke a cigarette, for example. I feel like they're still old-school. Like I'm a skank or something because I smoke and I go to bars. Sometimes I do drink, but with them, I can't see myself holding a glass of alcohol. It's very taboo. And honestly, here, I can go out and smoke, I can do what I want, and I know I'm not going to be judged."

"I can't see myself living there," she'd said. "It's not mixed enough."

To dismiss criticism of certain challenges plaguing the *cités* of the 9-3 because they make for uncomfortable conversations is to ignore the concerns of residents and their families—an exercise in naivete and condescension. But when reflecting on the difficulties they face, it's important to keep in mind where responsibility lies. Ever since the "problem of the banlieue" emerged as a political topic of its own in the 1980s, it's been commonplace for politicians and media personalities to point the finger at residents of the projects themselves—there are allegedly too many immigrants, too many Muslims, too many workers, or too many low-income people living in the same place at once. This discourse tends to ignore the environment they're consigned to, with people living in stark isolation from one another, with limited access to basic services, and often scraping by at jobs that offer little stability and low pay.

In spite of the many obstacles, the northern and eastern suburbs of Paris continue to punch far above their weight when it comes to cultural influence—not unlike other low-income, majority-minority neighborhoods in the U.S. and U.K. Along with Marseille, this is where French hip-hop came into its own in the 1990s, with groups like Suprême NTM, Secteur Ä, Mafia K'1 Fry, Ministère A.M.E.R., and the producer Jimmy Jay helping to spread the music across the country and throughout the Francophone world.[11] Many popular rappers today still come from the area, like Dinos, Maes, Sifax, and Kaaris.

The lexicon of the banlieue continues to transform the French language. Initially a form of slang used mostly by suburban youth, *verlan* moved squarely into the mainstream in the early twenty-first century via dozens of words: *meuf* (girl), *ouf* (crazy), *chelou* (weird), *vénère* (angry). Other common expressions originate from the banlieue, such as the unclassifiable interjection *wesh*, which comes from Algerian Arabic, and *C'est la hass*, which means something like, "It's a mess." While there may not be a banlieue "accent" per se, France has also seen the development of certain patterns of speech associated with the banlieue—ways of pronouncing words and emphasizing syllables—that transcend regional differences.

The Paris suburbs have also developed into one of the most fertile grounds for footballing talent on the planet, perhaps in part because pitches are one of the rare common spaces in the banlieue.[12] France's original World Cup–winning squad in 1998 featured three stars from the Paris suburbs—Thierry Henry, Patrick Vieira, and Lilian Thuram—and the talent pool has only deepened since then. Some of the biggest stars from the 2018 World Cup–winning squad and the 2022 runners-up have roots in the Parisian banlieue: Kylian Mbappé, Randal Kolo Muani, and William Saliba all hail from Bondy, while Paul Pogba grew up in Roissy and Moussa Sissoko was raised in the Cité des 3000 in Aulnay-sous-Bois. Presnel Kimpembe and Wissam Ben Yedder are from Val-d'Oise. Adrien Rabiot is from Val-de-Marne. Among the stars from the outer *grande couronne* are Mattéo Guendouzi (Yvelines) and Christopher Nkunku (Seine-et-Marne), while Ousmane Dembélé was born in Vernon, a town technically located in Normandy, but accessible on the Paris suburban train network.

Millions are making do in spite of the low pay at work, the lack of services at home, and a landscape built to prevent their neighborhoods from coming into their own—all while living next to one of the richest, most economically productive cities on the planet. With residents already accomplishing so much despite being dealt an unfair hand, one can only wonder, what could their towns look like if some of those trends were reversed? If the region's wealth were better spread around? If they had access to something more closely resembling life in Paris?

Reversing the Brain Drain

Some of the biggest public spaces within the Seine-Saint-Denis are schools. Bringing together hundreds of thousands of students, and tens of thousands of teachers, they provide a window into the challenges faced by residents and the immense amount of energy poured into overcoming them, but also into the intense contradictions imposed by life here: the oscillating sense of frustration and justifiable optimism; the feeling of attachment to one's hometown and the urge to get out; the inferiority complex vis-à-vis Paris and the immense pride that comes from being a *banlieusard*.

Jeroen, a nineteen-year-old who went to middle school and high school in La Courneuve, told me he didn't truly appreciate the specificity of his upbringing until he started his undergraduate law studies in Paris. He now commutes to the Sorbonne from his parents' home in the Cité de L'Inter, a housing complex in the center of town, about a twenty-minute ride on the suburban rail line.

We met at a café in La Courneuve. "There are classrooms where you're supposed to have to a projector to show in class, but the projectors don't exist," he recalled about high school. "Or there are classrooms where they're supposed to have curtains, and it's been ten years since they've been asking for them, but they're not there."

"My last year," he continued, "I remember we didn't have nurses because the last nurse got moved somewhere else after ten years. We went the whole year without a full-time nurse.... When we did have one, she was there just two hours a day."

Many of the students' parents worked in Paris, often in service jobs in restaurants or health care. And many came from families with recent immigrant backgrounds—like Jeroen, who himself is of Sri Lankan descent. I asked about the student body at his school. "I think in my high school there were two white people, if that's what you mean," he laughed. "It's very multicultural. There were Indians, Asians, Arabs, Black people, people with very diverse and different origins."

For fun, Jeroen and his friends would almost always leave for Paris, so long as they had the regional transit pass. "Honestly, I don't know what there is to do in La Courneuve," he said. "It's not like you're gonna go for a walk around here. There's a movie theater, but that's not where we go. There's nothing to do, there are no activities."

In Paris, they'd sometimes go to the park at La Villette in the northeast, but they'd often visit more centrally-located spots along the suburban rail line. "It's cliché, but people would eat at McDonald's, or people would go on walks. It's a calming atmosphere, it's beautiful, you know. We'd go to parks. We often went to the Tuileries. To the Luxembourg Gardens. To Châtelet–Les Halles. We're lucky in La Courneuve because we have the RER B, which goes through most of the touristic parts of Paris."

From the suburbs, Paris retained its aura of splendor.

"We saw it as a source of fresh air," he told me. "And kind of a model of success. For me, Paris meant success. It meant 'I've succeeded in life. I'm in the capital.' We've been to La Chapelle and know there are neighborhoods that aren't great, but still, there are neighborhoods that are very appealing. Maybe because we don't live there. But when we go there, we know that it feels good. It's this image of grandeur, of liberation, of success."

Jeroen acknowledged there is something true about people

of different backgrounds and origins keeping to themselves, but stressed that it's mostly older people who often don't speak French very well. "One shouldn't deny that it exists. There are places it exists in the *cités*, but it's not a majority. I couldn't give you a number, but it's a minority."

He said much of his generation, as diverse as it is, has a different mentality. "Honestly, for young people, there's not this logic of staying together, because we've all kind of grown up in the same schools. We've all studied together, we all speak French very well."

Among this cohort, he felt a real sense of solidarity. "There's a logic of helping each other out, and that's what I miss about high school," he said. "There weren't people fighting against each other to be the 'elite' at the school. There were people who wanted to help each other, and that really had an impact on me."

It can be tough to make the transition to the job market. While numerous studies in France have shown that people with foreign-sounding names suffer from employment discrimination—particularly ones associated with Arabs and Africans—simple mention of this area's zip code on one's application can have adverse effects. One study found that fictitious applicants for entry-level restaurant jobs who claimed to reside in Paris were far more likely to be asked back for interviews than identically qualified people who mentioned the 9-3 in the corner of their CVs.[13] According to another study, six in ten young people in the *département* have said they've suffered from discrimination because of their origins or skin color.[14]

But Jeroen said another big challenge is the brain drain, which is driven by the notion that success is often synonymous with leaving the banlieue. "A lot of people tell me, 'As soon as

I get my diploma or my master's degree, I'm getting out of La Courneuve. It's the first thing I'm doing,'" he said. "I get it, I understand. I even have trouble telling myself that I'll spend my whole life in La Courneuve, which is still pretty run-down today. There's no work, there are no leisure activities. It's not a great place to live, that's a reality."

Jeroen said it's a shame given all the talent and ambition. "You have a lot of people who want to succeed professionally and do end up succeeding," he said. "That will is there. I feel like if you gave people a future that could be created in the banlieue, and that if we made it possible to have more work, for this to be a better place to live, then I think honestly we could better develop it."

"But it needs to happen quickly," he continued. "The problem now is there's sort of two logics. Which is, when you succeed, you want to leave, and when you don't succeed, you end up in this sort of logic of the *cité*, the *cité* forever, and you stay kind of anchored here."

Grand Paris

The divides between Paris and the banlieue have punctuated French press coverage and political debates for much of the last century—though, in more recent years, there's been something of a minor breakthrough with the creation of "Grand Paris." Launched by President Nicolas Sarkozy and then shaped by the governments of his successors, the initiative presented lofty dreams that have since been tamped down: What if the metropolitan area was transformed with new parks and urban gardens? What if there was a mass of environmentally sustainable urban development stretching all the way to Normandy?

Officially, "Grand Paris" now simply refers to the new common governing structure for Paris and many of its suburban cities and towns—an entity that since 2016 has been charged with coordinating policies aimed at 7 million residents living in an area it has designated metropolitan Paris and reducing the imbalances between its component parts.[15]

Even these reduced ambitions are worth pursuing. In the age of hypergentrification, preserving what's left of working-class Paris and improving the livability of the banlieue will require public intervention from entities that view them as equal entities, as fundamentally belonging to the same city. Unfortunately, actually existing Grand Paris is riddled with flaws: it's opaque, ineffective, underfunded, and structurally biased in favor of small towns—all of it to the detriment of the working-class suburbs who have the most to gain.

Since its creation, Grand Paris has been governed in part by a metropolitan council that represents the capital and provides at least one seat for each of the 130 other municipalities involved—in other words, cities like La Courneuve have as much representation as villages like Marnes-la-Coquette, a town of one thousand that is one of the wealthiest in France. What's more, this 208-member body shares power with indirectly elected "territorial councils," a separate layer of politicians appointed by officials elected in municipal elections. As it happens, these low-turnout local polls generally favor conservatives, enabling the right-wing party Les Républicains and their allies to maintain control of the Grand Paris government.

Political parties and the press alike seem content to let this entity operate in the shadows. The government of Grand Paris is largely ignored during electoral campaigns, and its few deliberations rarely receive media attention.[16] The body's president is a technocrat who remains largely unknown among the broader public. Confusion reigns over how the institutions function and what it is they do.

"It's totally undemocratic," Danielle Simonnet, the MP from La France Insoumise who spent years on city council representing eastern Paris, told me. "There's a lot of distance between citizens and the decision process, because it's based on indirect elections. I myself was on city council and I'm an MP, and I don't understand anything. I don't understand it. What is it deciding? What is its authority? I'm not kept up about what they've decided. Go do a poll at the metro. Do you know your elected officials in Grand Paris? What's its authority? You'll get nothing! Nothing at all."

Technically, the metropolis does have power to weigh in on city planning, environmental policies, and housing. But in practice, a tight budget heavily restricts those interventions, and anyway, many of its responsibilities overlap with other elected structures: the region of Île-de-France, the *départements*, and the city governments themselves. Municipal authorities in the Paris region spend about a hundred times more per resident than the metropolis does.[17]

When Parisians and *banlieusards* do refer to Grand Paris, they're more often than not referring to a series of massive transit renovations underway called the Grand Paris Express: the expansion of the metro network in the suburbs and the creation of new lines to better connect parts of the banlieue to one another. This, by far, is the most visible and most significant project associated with Grand Paris—though, ironically, it's not even the product of the metropolitan government. The project is funded by the French state, through a specially created public development corporation.

The transit plan is slated to nearly double the length of the Paris metro network, with the current number of stations expanded by about a fifth, and sixty-eight new stations arriving in the banlieue. Four new lines will be built, including two traversing some of the most impoverished parts of the northeastern suburbs. This expanded network means nurses and retail workers who live in, say, Aulnay-sous-Bois can make it to their jobs in central Paris without torturously long routes involving buses and multiple connections. At the same time, they'll be able to travel within the suburbs without having to pass through Paris.

The problem is that the expansion is happening within the context of hypergentrification, which means the interests of banks and developers are privileged throughout the project. Under the oversight of the Grand Paris Corporation, some of the new stations will have shops built into them—and if existing experiments at rail stations in Paris are any indication, that means many chains and franchises. More importantly, neighborhoods around stations are already seeing new housing developments prop up and prices inch upward—a heating of the private real estate market that suggests a change in the population is on the horizon.

It would be outlandish to oppose investments in economically distressed neighborhoods simply because they increase the value of real estate—an ultra-minoritarian view held by the sorts of radicals who don't particularly care for cities to begin with. On the other hand, it's worth considering whether developments fill existing needs and—if so—whether current residents will be able to benefit from them. In the case of the Grand Paris Express, the lack of a broader investment plan for the banlieue suggests the answer to that second question remains unclear. The ambition of the subway expansion isn't being matched by a similarly grand commitment to social housing that would guarantee the ability of current residents to easily use the network. And while the plan aims to satisfy the demand for improved transit, other major needs in these neighborhoods remain unaddressed. There isn't an influx of cash headed toward schools or hospitals. There isn't a massive plan to build more theaters or parks.

Without a deeper socially conscious program, the areas popping up around the new stations may prove disappointing to those hoping they'll deliver a dose of equality and healthy street life. Otherwise, what might these neighborhoods look like in ten to twenty years? Isolated bubbles of development where middle-class residents keep to themselves? Complexes of condos and chain stores where consultants congratulate themselves about their mortgages and gossip about the problems of the nearby housing projects? Oases for investment that lie somewhere between Phases Two and Three in housing policy expert Phillip Clay's gentrification scheme?

Olympic Illusions

These days, talk of suburban development is inseparable from the 2024 Summer Olympics. While they're branded as "Paris 2024," most of the competitions and nearly all of the new construction projects are taking place in the banlieue, where they're being sold as a boon to the area. Organizers vow the events will usher in new apartments and office space that'll be there long after the TV cameras depart.

Of course, the Olympics have a famously egregious record of displacing low-income populations and inflating the price of previously affordable neighborhoods—just ask the residents of

Atlanta, Athens, or Rio de Janeiro—though organizers in Paris insist their legacy will be different.

They have two main arguments. For one, they point to the limited amount of new construction—and it's true, the French bid was premised on the fact that the games could rely largely on already existing infrastructure. There are only a handful of major new projects: the Olympic Village, split between Saint-Ouen and Saint-Denis; a massive new swimming pool in the latter city; and a Media Village covering three cities further north, including La Courneuve. Secondly, in the areas where new projects are being built, officials promise the resulting effects on housing prices will be cushioned by progressive public policies.

"The difference with Paris and the other big cities that have organized the Olympics is the level of social housing that we have, which preserves us from gentrification," Ian Brossat, the deputy mayor for housing in Paris, told me on the phone. "Once you decide to devote a lot of the Olympic amenities to social housing, you're removing a lot of the effects linked to gentrification."

But Cécile Gintrac isn't so optimistic. A geography teacher and resident of Saint-Denis, she's one of the leaders of the 2024 Olympic Games Vigilance Committee in Saint-Denis, a group critical of many Olympic-related developments. She took me on a tour of the neighborhood known as Pleyel, a sleepy quarter cut off from central Saint-Denis by highways. This business district has never quite taken off, though it's now turned into a massive construction zone ahead of the games. At one of the few cafés in the area—just before picking up her son from school—she tore into the familiar talking points.

Gintrac pointed out the social housing pledge in the nearby

Olympic Village—developers promise at least 25 percent of the new flats will be converted into social housing—is simply in line with the French legal minimum, and there's no guarantee these flats will go to the category most in need.[18] What's more, the portion of social housing being reserved actually falls *below* current rates in the two cities. Either way, she said more central parts of Saint-Denis are already starting to see housing prices rise.

According to Gintrac, the overarching problem is that the new developments don't meet the needs of people who actually live in Saint-Denis today, in the Pleyel area and beyond.

"The question, is, can working-class people stay here?" she said. "Can they have good-quality homes and not be pushed out further away? And for the people who are here, does the infrastructure respond to their needs? It's simple, really. What do people need? They need doctors, they need daycare, they need an environment that doesn't give them cancer or hurt their health. They need green spaces."

Outside the café, ongoing renovations paint the picture of a very different kind of neighborhood taking root. The Pleyel Tower, a once legendary eyesore and rusted-out symbol of the banlieue's economic woes, is being converted into a luxury hotel with a rooftop swimming pool. A new highway interchange meant to accommodate the uptick in traffic now encircles an elementary school. Businesses are likely to move into new office space after the games. "It's going to be a mess," Gintrac said. "It's like a monster with three heads and four arms."

On paper, fresh investment is heading toward a city in need of it, but who stands to gain from the development underway? Working-class residents of Saint-Denis, or tourists looking for a convenient spot to spend the night between the airport and central Paris? Low-income families on the waiting list for social housing, or investors looking to flip studios after the Olympics?

Gintrac herself told me she grew up in the 19th arrondissement of Paris before getting priced out and deciding to raise her family in Saint-Denis. She said the new swimming pool on top of the hotel raised an all-too-familiar question. "My son asked me, 'Will we be able to go there?'" she said, laughing. "I don't think so. It was cute, but I don't think we can afford it."

Is Another Grand Paris Possible?

Perhaps the housing projects and isolated parts of the outer suburbs won't be transformed overnight, but it's clear the residents living in and around them deserve the right to a more equitable, livable city: a place with access to high-quality public services; an array of different small businesses; theaters and concert halls; vibrant street life where the diversity of their communities can shine. They deserve more than an improved metro network, some extra office space, and a mishmash of gyms and pools left over from the Olympics. In short, they merit something closer to what life looks like on the other side of the Périph.

If that's the goal, then efforts to achieve it should probably begin by putting the banlieue on equal footing with Paris—and not just rhetorically, as is all too often the case today. Carrying out that vision will likely depend on institutional reforms to facilitate a more fair and effective distribution of resources, ones that ensure the multimillionaire rentiers living next to private schools in the Bois de Boulogne are increasing their contributions to the upkeep of parks and schools deep in the 9-3. If one follows these aspirations to their logical conclusion, then an obvious solution comes into focus: in order to unlock a shared pool of public money and pave the way for more equitable policies to be directed at the metropolitan area's working majority, it may finally be time to merge Paris and the suburbs into a single entity—to erase the distinctions between them.

One can already imagine a fairer city: metro lines connecting what are now the eastern suburbs and stretching north through Sarcelles, into the bedroom communities of Val-d'Oise; scores of sleepy city centers transformed into thriving neighborhoods lined with apartments zoned for social housing and small businesses to serve residents; parcels of land serving little social utility transformed into parks and affordable housing projects; the construction of well-funded schools named not after distant Soviet icons or American civil rights leaders, but Francophone champions of universalism whose attention to difference speaks more closely to the realities of the area's diverse population. Imagine elementary schools paying homage to anti-colonial writer Frantz Fanon, Tunisian-born abortion rights activist Gisèle Halimi, or the immigrant trade union leaders of the 1960s and 1970s.

Traditionalists might scoff at the mere thought of redefining the borders of Paris, but the last major extension of the city limits, in 1860, is a reminder that expansion is both possible and long overdue. Any new boundaries would likely be up for debate, but a city that assumed, for instance, the current limits of Grand Paris—most towns in the "little crown" and a few in the "big crown"—would make for a reasonable size to manage. It would occupy about the same area as Berlin or New York City, but would still be smaller than London or Rome.

This would certainly not be a silver bullet. France's powerful national government retains broad authority and bears ultimate responsibility for the lack of public services in the banlieue. A commitment to more investment in schools, healthcare, and education depends heavily on state funding and the choices made by parties who hold the presidency and legislative majorities. Conquering and administrating state power on the national level remains an obvious path for remedying injustice—this is how most people conceive of social progress, and especially in France, with its deep Jacobin heritage.

But the creation of an expanded Paris could go a long way in addressing inequities. Municipal budgets are financed, in large part, through property taxes, driving major disparities in spending power between city governments. If there was a single municipal government, it could tap into a lucrative tax base to better implement the policies that do fall within its purview. It would have authority to manage elementary schools in a more equitable fashion. It could impose more humane development policies—such as crafting more parks in the suburbs or driving the highly polluting and symbolically violent ringroad highway fully underground. A larger Parisian government could enforce more equitable housing policies, building and reserving social housing for residents in areas that need and want them. It could also set far-reaching cultural policies aimed at reducing the gap between the capital and periphery: imagine a wave of plays, concerts, and festivals at renovated theaters and city squares in places like La Courneuve, Sevran, and Aulnay-sous-Bois.

A few political outliers have proposed a fusion of Paris and the banlieue—most prominently, the ex-Macronist mathematician and former MP Cédric Villani, who came up short in a bid to unseat Mayor Anne Hidalgo in 2020—but today's power brokers have shown little interest in the idea. As one might expect, the region's conservatives aren't enthralled by the prospect of sharing resources with poorer cities. But the parties of the Left have also shown some degree of resistance to merging municipalities, perhaps out of an attachment to the limited powers that come from managing various public entities of their own.[19] Back in 2014, local elected officials from the Communists and Socialists joined forces with their right-wing counterparts to limit the authority of Grand Paris to intervene into housing policy.[20] The other two big parties, the Greens and La France Insoumise, haven't said much on the topic.

But before they began winning local seats on a regular basis, these parties' more ambitious forbearers once called for just this.

Following the municipal elections of 1912, a time in which the rambunctious marches of Georges Cochon were at their fever pitch and the issue of housing front and center on the political agenda, France's Socialist Party proposed a merger between city and suburbs. To create "an administration that conforms with the interests of the working class," read an article in the party's newspaper *L'Humanité*, now was the time, "more than ever," to create a single "grand Parisian municipality."[21]

Apolitical academics and insurrectionary anarchists would probably agree on the following: expanding the city of Paris would mean reviving a tradition extending back to the uprisings of 1789 and 1871, renewing the principle that Parisians must organize government for themselves when the state is neglecting the interests of the city's working masses. Since the medieval era, the French word *commune* has denoted the country's most basic administrative unit—the equivalent of town, village, or municipality—though, until several decades ago, the city of Paris was denied the right to organize itself as such.

Instead, it was ruled over by national authorities wary of a place that might exert too much influence on its own. The original "Paris Commune," which took shape after the storming of the Bastille, sought to remedy this injustice. And well before the word became associated with the global class struggle, the second Commune sought, at the most basic level, to bring government closer to the people—here was an entity charged with representing the will of the Parisian majority instead of the bankers and industrialists who'd reigned under Haussmann and company. In other words, Parisians needed to take matters into their own hands. Given the state of the suburbs today, how could one argue the state is fulfilling its responsibility to citizens?

Of course, a merger of the city and suburbs will require buy-in from political forces with weight to throw around and pressure from the people who'd stand to benefit from it—a mix of institutional backing and outside pressure that isn't in the cards today. But if you look a little more closely, there are flickers of unrest—flashes of protests, walkouts, and strikes—that suggest a climate more amendable to sweeping change is closer than most care to believe. If officials think they're past the era of urban working-class insurrection—that they've moved beyond a scenario in which working people in Paris and the suburbs think of themselves as belonging to a common camp with shared interests—they're almost certainly mistaken.

And the city has always evolved in response to the social forces doing battle within it. Whatever the more immediate bread-and-butter demands of the day have been, sustained collective action from Parisian workers has a proven track record of ushering in deeper transformations of the cityscape and its web of governing laws. The rich may have held the upper hand over the last few decades, but if the interests of labor were to recover confidence and knock off a string of cascading victories, changes to existing regulations and boundaries would be all but destined to follow suit. The scales of the class struggle can tip back in the other direction—and when they do, residents of the banlieue will be expecting their fair share. Like their predecessors who occupied apartments and carried out mass strikes, they'll be expecting to live in a city that's built for them.

For Alain Tsamas and his coworkers at Monoprix, a sense of shared interest and commitment to collective action are not abstract notions.

Frustrated by staff reductions and the lack of pay hikes, Alain and other members of his union, the CGT, decided to go on the offensive in late 2019—forming a collective that operates outside their union's existing structures and holds regular demonstrations and strikes at the supermarket chain. This combative approach was inspired, in part, by the movement launched by housekeepers at hotel chain Ibis in the western neighborhood of Batignolles, a twenty-two-month-long strike led by mostly African immigrant women that ultimately won pay hikes and a reduced work strain. Like those strikers, Tsamas and his colleagues have appealed to groups of sympathetic unions at other employers, aiming to grind out the bosses over time.

"Beyond the label of employees, we're creators of wealth," Tsamas told me. "Because that money comes from us. If there are no employees, there's no wealth."

It's been an uphill battle at times. Tsamas told me he was surprised that the picket lines often generate more positive feedback in wealthy neighborhoods than in eastern Paris—the opposite of what he and his colleagues anticipated. He thought of it as a sign of the precarity and powerlessness felt by many low-wage workers, some of the very obstacles they're trying to surmount.

"I think it's because people tell themselves, 'I'm not making enough to satisfy myself. And if these people come make their mess, I [have to suffer the consequences],'" Tsamas explained. "In the nicer neighborhoods, the bobo neighborhoods, they have nothing to lose, everything is already acquired, they don't worry about the cost of living, they might have secondary residences."

"In the working-class neighborhoods," he continued, "if there's a strike, the thinking might be, 'I can't do my groceries, maybe stores might close. I don't have enough to go further away because of the transit costs.' All this psychology plays a part."

But Tsamas and his colleagues haven't let up, sticking with their strategy of intermittent strikes. On one Saturday afternoon, Alain invited me to a walkout at a store in the 15th arrondissement. The crowd of supporters wasn't massive, but the sense of working-class solidarity was palpable.

Employees from other Monoprix stores turned out, joined by airport workers, postal workers, and sympathetic college students. One of the leaders of the grueling Ibis hotel strike, Rachel Keke—now an elected member of the National Assembly, representing an eastern suburb—showed up and took selfies with the crowd. After Tsamas turned on an amplifier and launched a well-known protest song on loop, most of the supermarket staff started to walk out, leaving managers scrambling to run two checkout lines.

Béatrice, who was on strike and, like Alain, works in the butchery department, insisted she was in this for the long haul. She's been employed at this same store for the last twenty-two years and still makes just over minimum wage, commuting from the far-off suburb of Épinay-Sur-Seine, in the *département* of Val d'Oise. On workdays, she wakes up at 4 in the morning to catch the train at 5:05.

Béatrice told me the movement was about getting what they deserve. "We need to shake things up, and maybe by shaking things up, we'll get heard from on high and we'll be understood and get something," she said. "We're saying 'enough is enough.' We've been fighting too long for this. At some point, they need to take responsibility."

She said she was grateful for the support from other workers, part of the network they've helped build together.

"The collective is there to support them. We all support each other," she told me. "It's about solidarity. . . . They have the same problems as us, they're fighting for higher salaries and better working conditions. People need to put in their heads that the government needs to listen to all the workers, not just shareholders. They need to understand we're going through too much."

CONCLUSION:
THE RIGHT TO PARIS

Those committed in one way or another to the mission of making cities more egalitarian, more democratic, and more accessible—as well as more enjoyable—commonly reference the "right to the city." When he coined the phrase back in 1967, the French philosopher and sociologist Henri Lefebvre defined it as "the right to urban life, to renewed centrality, to places of encounter and exchange, to life rhythms and time uses, enabling the full and complete usage of these moments and places."[1]

Famously described by the author as both a "cry and demand," it's an empowering notion, but conceptually amorphous, which perhaps accounts for some of its staying power. Everyone from radical academics and housing activists to elected officials and NGO leaders have embraced it as either a goal or animating principle behind their work.

Marxist geographer David Harvey has called to adopt it

as both a "working slogan and political ideal"—a collective
response to global capital's domination of urban space.[2] Operating on a more practical level, activists in the U.S. have rallied
around the phrase as they fight against evictions and push for
the construction of affordable housing. And as slums swallow
up land across the Global South, the World Social Forum has
deployed the term to press for access to clean drinking water
and improved infrastructure.

Governments have also latched on to the phrase, ostensibly
to showcase their commitment to equitable urban development
and enhanced public input in city planning. Brazil's 2001 city
statute recognizes the "right to sustainable cities" and "right
to urban land." In 2010, Mexico City adopted a "right to the
city" charter meant to usher in a fairer, more democratic, and
environmentally friendly capital.[3] The United Nations Human
Settlement Programme, or UN-Habitat, has incorporated the
idea into its research and policy recommendations. In 2016,
even the UN General Assembly endorsed a roadmap for urban
development that referenced policymakers' use of the term—in
a characteristically vague paragraph emphasizing the need to
build "cities for all."[4]

Institutions downplay the concept's radical roots. But in the
version deployed by many of the activists on the outside looking in—the one that still packs some punch—a couple of simple
ideas are at work.

For one, the growing share of people living in cities today
deserve a right to basic services. That includes the right to
quality affordable housing, the foundation on which ordinary
people can comfortably experience and enrich urban life. (In
concrete terms, protecting that right implies measures to keep
buildings out of the hands of predatory developers.) But resi-

dents also deserve access to quality education: well-funded public schools with reasonable class sizes and decent pay for teachers. They merit access to hospitals and clinics that guarantee quality healthcare for those in need. Properly funded public transit can ensure that easy movement across cities isn't a privilege reserved for the wealthy, while public parks and a bevy of cultural and recreational services multiply the opportunities for rich and rewarding time outside of work.

Secondly, residents ought to have a say in how all these affairs are managed. The "right to the city" depends on a kind of perpetual enforcement from below. Instead of far-off government bureaucrats or local officials detached from their constituents, the people most affected by urban policies should be the ones deciding them in the first place. Ambitiously worded charters and flowery institutional visions ring hollow without mechanisms that guarantee democratic oversight.

These are commonsense ambitions shared by millions of city dwellers worldwide. And they're at the core of some of the most dynamic organizing happening in Paris today, from the groups fighting evictions and calling on the state to lodge migrants to the low-wage workers standing up for pay hikes to cover the rising costs of living.

This rights-based framing also happens to be an effective way of pushing back against the idea that critics of gentrification oppose urban investment in all forms. Combating rent hikes and tenant displacement doesn't mean rejecting development at large, but it does mean casting aside the phony all-or-nothing choices gentrifiers and their allies like to impose: Do you want this luxury hotel or nothing at all? Do you want nicer restaurants or would you prefer the status quo? Opposing gentrification means reorienting the terms of the debate around a positive vision of what the neighborhood might otherwise look like—at a minimum, this includes viewing the city as a place where current residents can easily meet their needs and, if they so please, stay for as long as they want.

And yet, something feels incomplete about simply reaffirming the "right to the city" in twenty-first-century Paris, given the exceptionally unfair geography of the metropolitan area. The banlieue was always a blind spot in the grandiose vision held by Henri Lefebvre, who perhaps didn't foresee just how many working-class people would flee Paris, or at the very least, didn't anticipate how quickly this might happen. His initial emphasis on "renewed centrality" has lost much of its luster—something he did acknowledge in a later 1989 essay, when he wrote that the "historic center" of cities had ultimately "disappeared as such," amid a much bigger urbanization overtaking the world.[5] Today, urban sprawl is extending across North America and Europe, while the rapidly expanding mega-cities of the Global South are giving birth to "a planet of slums," as the writer Mike Davis argued so compellingly.[6]

What's perhaps more at stake today, then, is the "right to Paris": whether the millions of people currently living in the broader metropolitan area can afford to inhabit neighborhoods that meet their needs and offer the humanizing effects of rich, intricate street life. This question applies as much to the last remaining belt of resistance within the city limits as it does to those living in the banlieue. While they resemble their Parisian counterparts in so many ways, low-income inhabitants of the Paris suburbs are forced to make do in a far more alienating environment. Isolated in towers and deprived of access to quality services, millions are being denied the dense neighborhood life that has sustained working-class Paris over the years—that mesmerizing web of "encounter and exchange" that inspired Henri Lefebvre. Within the limits of Paris proper, hypergentrification has placed that very way of living under threat.

In the end, the fate of working-class Paris will be determined by the nature of public policies: inaction means prolonged inequalities as gentrification washes away whatever lies in its path.

If one takes the expression to embody the struggle for improved living standards and greater democracy, there is a compelling case to be made that the "right to the city" has been at the core of what Parisian laborers have been fighting for all along. History retains the names of the largely bourgeois leaders of the Revolution—as well as their debates over abstract liberal principles—but the sans-culottes of Paris were animated by a desire to improve living conditions and to have a say in running the deeply unequal city around them. Their demands for price controls and sovereign rule were reflected most vigorously by the Paris Commune and its armed sections, the radical institutions that emerged as levers of pressure against national legislative bodies.

The revolts punctuating the first half of the nineteenth century can be viewed in a similar light: the city's emerging working class articulated calls for democratic reform alongside pleas for direct economic relief—oftentimes at odds with the rest of France's rural, conservative population. After Parisian barricades ushered in a Second Republic in 1848, the capital's laborers briefly won the concession of national workshops to combat unemployment—a policy that conveyed their high expectations of what they felt a genuinely republican state owed them. As other researchers have observed, the Paris Commune of 1871 was, in many respects, a rebuttal to the Baron de Haussmann's drive to expel the working masses from the center of Paris.[7] The Communards were reclaiming neighborhoods that once belonged to them.

The tenant movements of the early twentieth century similarly fought for the rights of workers and low-income Parisians to stay within a city that was becoming increasingly expensive. As organized labor bolstered its ranks, and as Parisians flocked to Socialist and Communist parties vowing to conquer state power on behalf of working people, the pressure forced governments to protect the city's housing market from speculation. Even once the specter of anti-capitalist revolution appeared to fade after World War II, French officials were careful to keep living costs in check for the metro area's working population.

Clearly, the balance of power has shifted more squarely in favor of capital in recent decades. Deindustrialization, globalization, and financialization present challenges that would've confounded the likes of Louise Michel and Georges Cochon. Today's labor unions and tenant movements aren't as powerful as they once were. But even in their relatively weakened state, even with reduced numbers, they mark a form of continuity with the working-class struggles of the past—flickering flames of resistance that carry the promise of conflagration so long as they continue to burn. Like their predecessors in the faubourgs or the old slums of the banlieue, today's working Parisians may not all have been born in the capital. Some have traveled great distances to arrive. But this is their home—and if you ask around, most feel that they deserve to be able to stay here.

Gentrifiers and their allies want urbanites to believe the composition of cities is decided by the market alone: supply and demand; interest rates; the willingness of banks to extend loans; the broader economic picture. If longtime residents are priced out of their neighborhoods, it may be sad and unfortunate, but these outcomes are, in some sense, a natural part of urban development—or so the logic goes.

The reality is that the question of who gets to live in a city—and who does not—is eminently political. It always has been. Authorities can either embrace the commodification of housing head-on, or they can move to protect low-income residents from the ravages of the capitalist market. Cities bear the weight of these choices.

Vienna's extensive social housing regime is a prime example of what the latter route can offer. The system is the product of the Social Democratic Workers' Party's hold on local government, the Red Vienna era after World War I that saw the advent of an ambitious welfare state. The waning affordability of Paris today reflects a different set of policy choices, with deregulation wreaking havoc but remaining tenant protections providing real resistance. The obscene housing costs that define so many major American cities are no less the fruit of political decisions, a collective move to step aside and let the market rip. Failure to intervene in the housing market is, of course, a radical decision of its own.

The transformative vision underlying Henri Lefebvre's original call for a "right to the city" shouldn't be forgotten either. The goal can't simply be to carve out a space for working people in a city dominated by the rich, but rather to remake the city in the interests of working people. The history of Paris is littered with unrealized attempts to do just this. Much of the city's greatness stems from these initiatives. There will be more of them.

ACKNOWLEDGMENTS

I'm forever grateful to Sandra Pareja for believing in this project and for offering such valuable guidance and feedback from the very beginning. Thank you to the teams at The New Press and Saqi Books—in particular, the editors Marc Favreau and Mitchell Albert. Thanks as well to Emily Albarillo, Rachel Vega DeCesario, and Elizabeth Briggs for helping bring this book to fruition. Thanks to Brian Baughan for the excellent copy edits. Thanks to Brian Ulicky and Emily Janakiram for their work on publicity and marketing.

I'm very grateful to M Jesuthasan for fact-checking certain sections of the book.

Thank you to all the people who shared their stories with me, opening up about their lives to a stranger. I hope I did you justice.

Other authors provided insight and encouragement at key stages in the pitching process. Thank you to Jess McHugh, Sarah Jaffe, and Joel Warner.

Other friends helped me refine certain ideas and more generally appreciate the qualities of the city. Thank you to Ethan Earle, Harrison Stetler, Théo Bernard, Chloé Jouvin, Benoît Gautier, Hélène Goutany, Nicolas Lovatin, Adèle Dumour, Irène Voyatzis, Antoine Formica, Charlotte Guerre, Dalia Cohen, and Erin Ogunkeye, among others.

As a freelance journalist, I'm grateful to the editors who've commissioned my work over the years. I'm especially appreciative of Shuja Hader for agreeing to take on a long feature about the Paris housing crisis for *The Nation* in the summer of 2020.

I'm immensely grateful to my subscribers on Patreon for supporting my work. They made it easier to devote time to this project.

My high school English teacher John Martin helped instill a passion for writing. Dave Jamieson taught me a great deal about reporting. My friend Matt Sitman has always encouraged me to take more risks as a writer.

Thank you to my family.

Finally, thank you to Benjamin Lesire-Ogrel, connoisseur of the *banlieue* and northeastern Paris, but more importantly, a wise, funny, caring, and adventurous companion.

NOTES

Introduction

1. "Prix de l'immobilier au m² Goutte d'Or-Château Rouge (Paris 18ème)," SeLoger, https://www.seloger.com/prix-de-l-immo/vente/ile -de-france/paris/paris-18eme/goutte-d-or-chateau-rouge/48276.htm.

2. "Prix m2 immobilier quartier Goutte d'Or-Château Rouge (Paris) en février 2023," *Le Figaro immobilier*, https://immobilier.lefigaro.fr/prix -immobilier/goutte-d-or-chateau-rouge/quartier-3704052642970624.

3. "Paris et l'ouest parisien : des territoires quasiment inaccessibles à l'achat pour la majorité des locataires franciliens," INSEE Ile-de-France research note no. 113, January 28, 2020, figure 1, https://www.insee.fr /fr/statistiques/4294778; Marc Lomazzi, "Immobilier: Paris franchit les 10000 euros le m2," *Le Parisien*, September 5, 2019.

4. "Prix de l'immobilier au m² Paris," SeLoger, https://www.seloger .com/prix-de-l-immo/vente/ile-de-france/paris.htm.

5. INSEE Ile-de-France research note no. 113, January 2020.

6. "Evolution en 2021 des loyers d'habitation du secteur loca-tif privé dans l'agglomération parisienne," Observatoire des Loy-ers de l'Agglomération Parisienne, August 2022, p. 5, https://

www.observatoire-des-loyers.fr/sites/default/files/olap_documents/rapports_loyers/Rapport%20Paris%202022.pdf; Exchange rates EUR-USD, EUR-GBP accessed via Xe.com on February 24, 2023.

7. "Les salaires dans le secteur privé en 2020," INSEE Première research note no. 1898, April 26, 2022, https://www.insee.fr/fr/statistiques/6436313.

8. UBS Global Real Estate Bubble Index, October 12, 2022, p. 5, https://www.ubs.com/global/en/wealth-management/insights/2022/global-real-estate-bubble-index.html.

9. The Economist Intelligence Unit, Worldwide Cost of Living 2021 report summary, p. 4, https://www.eiu.com/n/campaigns/worldwide-cost-of-living-2021/.

10. Paul Abran, Clémence Bauduin, "Démographie à Paris : la capitale perd 12 400 habitants en moyenne par an," *Le Parisien*, December 30, 2022; "90 % des Parisiens qui quittent la capitale s'installent dans une commune urbaine," INSEE Ile-de-France research note no. 143, November 22, 2021, https://www.insee.fr/fr/statistiques/5871250.

11. "Paris, 2050 : quels impacts des évolutions démographiques sur les besoins en équipements ?" INSEE Ile-de-France research note no. 83, May 15, 2018, https://www.insee.fr/fr/statistiques/3543915.

12. From 2010 to 2020, New York City grew by 8 percent. Annie Correal, "New York City Adds 629,000 People, Defying Predictions of Its Decline," *New York Times*, August 12, 2021. Over the same stretch, London grew by 10 percent. "London's Population," Greater London Authority, https://data.london.gov.uk/dataset/londons-population.

13. The national statistics agency has two measures for the Paris metropolitan area: the *unité urbaine* (around 11 million inhabitants) and the larger *aire d'attraction* (around 13 million).

14. The categories of *ouvriers* and *employés*, broad groups of non-managerial professions that can be roughly translated as "manual workers" and "service workers" respectively. The French term *classe ouvrière*, used in translations of Marx and classic Communist literature to designate the historic agent of social change, has declined in use, in part, because it's associated exclusively with industrial and/or blue-collar labor. When I write "working class" in English, I'm thinking of something much closer to the contemporary French term *classes populaires*. This term has the benefit of capturing the diverse forms that

low-wage labor takes today. In other words, a cashier at McDonald's is no less "working class" than someone on the assembly line at a Renault auto plant. Nevertheless, my use of *ouvriers* and *employés* as short-hand for "working class" comes with limits of its own. These broad categories don't include teachers, librarians, artists, technicians, paralegals, and other wage-earners who are instead classified under the census categories of "intermediate professions" (*professions intermédiaires*) and *cadres*.

15. In 1999, 35 percent of the working population residing in Paris was manual workers (*ouvriers*) and service workers (*employés*). "Population active, emploi, chômage : Les ressources humaines d'une capitale économique," Atelier Parisien d'urbanisme report, November 2013, p. 6, https://www.apur.org/sites/default/files/documents/Population_active_emploi_chomage.pdf. The same categories represented just 26 percent in 2016. "Dynamiques démographiques et sociales à Paris," Atelier parisien d'urbanisme report, September 2020, p. 29, https://www.apur.org/sites/default/files/dynamiques_demographiques_sociales.pdf.

1. The Other Side of the Hill

1. Some portions of this chapter appeared, in different form, in "The Death of Working-Class Paris," *The Nation*, November 10, 2020.

2. Claire Ané, Véronique Chocron, "L'accès au logement social se complique, hormis pour les jeunes et les parents isolés," *Le Monde*, October 6, 2022.

3. "Attribution des logements sociaux de la Ville de Paris," Paris.fr, May 30, 2022, https://www.paris.fr/pages/attribution-des-logements-sociaux-de-la-ville-de-paris-120.

4. Ruth Glass, introduction to *London: Aspects of Change* (London: MacGibbon & Kee, 1964), xviii–xix.

5. Neil Smith, "Toward a Theory of Gentrification: A Back to the City Movement by Capital, Not People," *Journal of the American Planning Association* 45, no. 4 (1979): 538–48.

6. Neil Smith, *The New Urban Frontier: Gentrification and the Revanchist City* (New York: Routledge, 1996).

7. Phillip L. Clay, *Neighborhood Renewal: Middle-Class Resettlement*

and Incumbent Upgrading in American Neighborhoods (Lexington, MA: Lexington Books, 1979).

8. P.E. Moskowitz, *How to Kill a City: Gentrification, Inequality, and the Fight for the Neighborhood* (New York: Bold Type Books, 2018 [2017]), 34.

9. Océane Herrero, "Paris : un fast food Five Guys prendra-t-il la place de Gibert Jeune dans le Ve arrondissement ?" *Le Figaro*, January 28, 2022.

10. Neil Smith, "New Globalism, New Urbanism: Gentrification as Global Urban Strategy," *Antipode: A Radical Journal of Geography* 34, no. 3 (2002): 427–50.

11. Samuel Stein, *Capital City: Gentrification and the Real Estate State* (New York/London: Verso Books, 2019), ebook.

12. Paul Tostevin, "The Total Value of Global Real Estate," Savillis, September 2021, https://www.savills.com/impacts/market-trends/the -total-value-of-global-real-estate.html.

13. Diane Lacaze, "Paris vaudrait 700 milliards d'euros," BFM TV, October 15, 2013.

14. Stein, *Capital City*, 88.

15. See Grace Watkins et al., "Gentrification in Los Angeles: Describing and Mitigating the Effects of Neighborhood-Level Displacement," April 6, 2021, ArcGIS StoryMaps, https://storymaps.arcgis.com/stories /c62eefccdc424603ba4603deff2119d7. Michael Kimmelman, "Los Angeles Has a Housing Crisis. Can Design Help?," *New York Times*, June 22, 2021; Los Angeles County Economic Development Corporation, 2021 Economic Forecast, 2022 Economic Forecast.

16. Hideo Nakazawa, "Introduction: Tokyo's Gentrification in Context," *Japanese Journal of Sociology* 30, no. 1 (2021): 3–5.

17. Benjamin Haas, "My Week in Lucky House: The Horror of Hong Kong's Coffin Homes," *The Guardian*, August 29, 2017.

18. Josef Filipowicz, "Room to Grow: Comparing Urban Density in Canada and Abroad," *Fraser Institute Research Bulletin*, January 2018, https://www.fraserinstitute.org/sites/default/files/room-to-grow -comparing-urban-density-in-canada-and-abroad.pdf.

19. Jay Caspian Kang, "Want to Solve the Housing Crisis? Build More, and Build Higher," *New York Times*, September 2, 2021.

2. The Melting Pot

1. "Une population immigrée aujourd'hui plus répartie sur le territoire régional," INSEE Ile-de-France research note no. 70, October 17, 2017, https://www.insee.fr/fr/statistiques/3136640.

2. Clément Lépidis, "Le passé arménien de Belleville," *Hommes & Migrations*, no. 1168 (1993): 48–50.

3. "Paris," United States Holocaust Memorial Museum, https://encyclopedia.ushmm.org/content/en/article/paris.

4. Éric Hazan, *L'invention de Paris* (2002; repr., Paris: Seuil, 2004), 281.

5. "Les quartiers parisiens de la politique de la ville, principales données de l'Observatoire des quartiers prioritaires - Contrat de ville 2015–2020," Atelier parisien d'urbanisme report, January 2016, 100–102, https://www.apur.org/fr/nos-travaux/quartiers-parisiens-politique-ville-principales-donnees-observatoire-quartiers.

6. "Quartier Prioritaire : Grand Belleville 10ème - 11ème – 20ème," Système d'information géographique de la politique de la ville public data set, https://sig.ville.gouv.fr/Cartographie/QP075020#thematique-header-11.

7. "Prix de l'immobilier au m² Belleville (Paris 20ème)," SeLoger, https://www.seloger.com/prix-de-l-immo/vente/ile-de-france/paris/paris-20eme/belleville/48286.htm.

8. Claude Calvarin, "La naissance d'une cité ouvrière sous le Second Empire : Le territoire du comte de Madre," *Histoire Urbaine* 1, no. 36 (2013): 105–32.

9. Romain Lescurieux, "Paris : Le siege du PCF, un bloc de béton dont 'la magie fonctionne toujours,'" *20 Minutes*, November 19, 2020.

10. Lucine Endelstein, "Religion, transformation des quartiers populaires et recomposition des identités diasporiques," *Espace populations sociétés*, no. 1 (2006): 83–94.

11. Aude Mary, *En territoire tamoul à Paris. Un quartier éthnique au métro La Chapelle* (Paris: Editions Autrement, 2008).

3. City of Barricades

1. Daniel Roche, *Le peuple de Paris* (Paris: Aubier, 1981), 52.

2. Louis-Sébastien Mercier, *Tableau de Paris*, vol. 1, *Nouvelle edition corrigée et augmentée* (Amsterdam, 1782), chap. 4, p. 10, https://gallica .bnf.fr/ark:/12148/bpt6k65717195/f11.item.texteImage.

3. Honoré de Balzac, *The Girl with the Golden Eyes*, trans. Ellen Marriage (1835), https://www.gutenberg.org/files/1659/1659-h/1659-h .htm.

4. David Garrioch, *The Makings of Revolutionary Paris* (Berkeley: University of California Press, 2002), 85. The nobility made up around twenty thousand people.

5. Anne Clerval, *Paris sans le peuple* (Paris: Editions La Découverte, 2013), ebook, 71.

6. Garrioch, *Revolutionary Paris*, 86; Laurence Croq, "L'autre noblesse (Paris, XVIIIe siècle)," *Genèses* no. 76 (2009): 16. As Croq writes, the neighborhoods of Saint-Eustache and Saint-Roch were more "mixed" elite neighborhoods, but the Faubourg Saint-Germain welcomed in "almost only" nobles of the sword.

7. Michel Vovelle, "Le peuple de Paris en révolution," in *Paris, le peuple : XVIIIe-XXe siècle*, ed. Jean-Louis Robert and Danielle Tarta-kowsky (Paris: Éditions de la Sorbonne, 1999), 113–29.

8. Victor Hugo, *Les Misérables*, trans. Isabel Hapgood (1862; repr., New York: Thomas Y. Crowell & Co., 1887), vol. 3, book 1, chap. 12, https://www.gutenberg.org/files/135/135-h/135-h.htm.

9. Jean-Jacques Rousseau, *The Confessions of Jean-Jacques Rousseau* (1782; repr., London, 1903), book 4, https://gutenberg.org/files/3913 /3913-h/3913-h.htm.

10. Arlette Farge, "L'ivresse dans le Paris populaire du xviiie siècle," *Revue de la BNF 53*, no. 2 (2016): 37–45.

11. For more, see Thomas Le Roux, "Une rivière industrielle avant l'industrialisation: la Bièvre et le fardeau de la prédestination, 1670–1830," *Géocarrefour 85*, no. 3 (2010): 193–207.

12. Haim Burstin, *Une révolution à l'oeuvre : Le faubourg St-Marcel, 1789–1794* (Seyssel, France: Champ Vallon, 2005), 21.

13. Burstin, *Une révolution à l'oeuvre*, 19. See Annexe I of Christine Piette and Barrie Ratcliffe, "Les Migrants et la Ville: Un nouveau regard sur le Paris de la Première moitié du XIXe siècle," *Annales de démographie historique* (1993): 289. Administrative subdivisions of the

city created by the Constituent Assembly in 1790, the revolutionary sections that came to be known as the Finistère, L'Observatoire, and the Sans-Culottes, covered the area corresponding to the Faubourg Saint-Marcel.

14. Auguste Luchet, *Paris. Esquisses dédiées au peuple parisien et à M.J.A. Dulaure. Membre de la société des Antiques de Paris* (Paris: J. Barbezat, 1830), 11.

15. Raymonde Monnier, "Les classes laborieuses du Faubourg Saint-Antoine sous la Révolution et l'Empire," *Annales historiques de la Révolution française* 51, no. 235 (1979): 121–22.

16. Raymonde Monnier, *Le Faubourg Saint-Antoine (1789–1815)*, 2nd ed. (1981; repr., Paris: Société des études robespierristes, 2012), 38–39.

17. Monnier, *Le Faubourg*, 43. This figure is from 1790. Monnier estimates six workers per boss in 1791.

18. Françoise Brunel, "Raymonde Monnier, *Le Faubourg Saint Antoine (1789–1815)* [compte-rendu]," *Revue d'histoire moderne et contemporaine* 31, no. 3 (1984): 524.

19. George Rudé, *The Crowd in the French Revolution* (1959; repr., New York: Oxford University Press, 1967), 73–75.

20. Rudé, *The Crowd in the French Revolution*, 105–6.

21. Piette and Ratcliffe, "Les Migrants et la Ville," 267–68.

22. Bernard Marchand, *Paris, histoire d'une ville : XIXe-XXe siècle* (Paris: Seuil, 1993), 28.

23. Claire Lemercier, "Classer l'industrie Parisienne au xixe siècles," *Actes et communications de l'INRA* 21 (2004): 237–71, https://halshs .archives-ouvertes.fr/halshs-00412049/document.

24. André Cochut, "Paris industriel," *Revue des Deux Mondes, Nouvelle période* 16 (1852): 638–70, https://fr.wikisource.org/wiki /Paris_industriel.

25. Maurizio Gribaudi, *Paris ville ouvrière: Une histoire occultée (1789–1848)* (Paris: La Découverte, 2014), 179.

26. Paris Chamber of Commerce, "Statistique de l'Industrie à Paris resultant de l'Enquête faite pour la Chambre de Commerce pour les années 1847–1848" (Paris: 1851), 32. "We designate . . . under articles of Paris, this varied mass of diverse products that Parisian industry, and above all this most divided industry, supplies for the consumption of all

countries, and which distinguish themselves by taste and an incessant search for novelty" (my translation). https://gallica.bnf.fr/ark:/12148/bpt6k86332h/f29.item.

27. Paris Chamber of Commerce, 1851 study, 20, https://gallica.bnf.fr/ark:/12148/bpt6k86332h/f17.item.

28. Jacques Houdaille, "Les porteurs d'eau à Paris en 1793," *Population* 50, nos. 4–5 (1995): 1245–47.

29. Dominique Kalifa, *Paris: Une histoire érotique, d'Offenbach aux Sixties* (Paris: Payot, 2018), 212.

30. See Maurice Alhoy, *Physiologie de la lorette* (Paris: Aubert, 1841), https://gallica.bnf.fr/ark:/12148/bpt6k1132844/f3.item.

31. Lucy Santé, *The Other Paris* (2015; repr., New York: Farrar, Strauss and Giroux, 2016), 114.

32. A. Husson, "De la population indigente secourue à domicile dans la ville de Paris," *Journal de la société statistique de Paris* 5 (1864): 289, http://www.numdam.org/item/JSFS_1864__5__288_0.pdf.

33. Marchand, *Paris, histoire d'une ville*, 31.

34. Marchand, *Paris, histoire d'une ville*, 31.

35. Camille Lestienne, "En 1832 l'épidémie de choléra avait déjà vidé Paris," *Le Figaro*, April 3, 2020.

36. Marchand, *Paris, histoire d'une ville*, 40.

37. Heinrich Heine, *De la France* (Paris: Eugène Renduel, 1833), 162. Quoted in Éric Hazan, *L'invention de Paris*, 328.

38. Gribaudi, *Paris ville ouvrière*, 78.

39. Gribaudi, *Paris ville ouvrière*, 76–78.

40. René Le Mée, "Le choléra et la question des logements insalubres à Paris (1832–1849)," *Population* 56, nos. 1–2 (1998): 379–97.

41. Honoré Frégier, *Des classes dangereuses de la population dans les grandes villes* (1840; repr., Geneva: Slatkine-Megariotis Reprints, 1977) 7, https://gallica.bnf.fr/ark:/12148/bpt6k54922/f21.item.

42. See Mark Traugott, *The Insurgent Barricade* (Berkeley: University of California Press, 2010).

43. Thomas Bouchet, "La barricade des Misérables," in *La barricade*, ed. Alain Corbin and Jean-Marie Mayeur (Paris: Éditions de la Sorbonne, 1997), 125–35.

44. Hugo, *Les Misérables*, vol. 4, book 12, chap. 5.

45. Lucie-Marie Albigès and Martine Illaire, "Rue Transnonain, une maison à Paris sous Louis-Philippe," *Histoire par l'image*, October 2003, https://histoire-image.org/etudes/rue-transnonain-maison-paris-louis -philippe.

46. Karl Marx, *The Eighteenth Brumaire of Louis Bonaparte (1852)*, chap. 1, https://www.marxists.org/archive/marx/works/1852/18th-bru maire/ch01.htm.

47. Walter Benjamin's famous quip from his unfinished *Arcades Project* has been taken out of context and blown out of proportion. In his essay "Paris, Capital of the 19th Century," he writes that Haussmann "wished to make the erection of barricades in Paris impossible for all time," and that "new streets were to provide the shortest route between the barracks and the working-class areas." The full essay appears in *Perspecta* 12 (1969): 163–72.

48. Jules Janin, *L'été à Paris* (Paris: L. Curmer, 1844), 48, https://gallica .bnf.fr/ark:/12148/bpt6k102791c/f63.item.

49. David Harvey, *Paris, Capital of Modernity* (New York/London: Routledge, 2003), 135.

50. Harvey, *Paris, Capital of Modernity*, 134.

51. Harvey, *Paris, Capital of Modernity*, 130-31.

52. David Jordan, *Transforming Paris: The Life and Labors of Baron Haussmann* (New York: Free Press, 1995), 233.

53. Jordan, *Transforming Paris*, 239.

54. Rupert Christiansen, *City of Light: The Making of Modern Paris* (New York: Basic Books, 2018), 61, ebook.

55. Hazan, *L'invention de Paris*, 177.

56. Baron Haussmann, *Mémoires du baron Haussmann: Tome 3* (Paris: 1890–1893), 54, https://gallica.bnf.fr/ark:/12148/bpt6k220530f/f70.item.

57. Marchand, *Paris, histoire d'une ville*, 88.

58. John Merriman, *Massacre: The Life and Death of the Paris Commune* (New York: Basic Books, 2014), 15–17, ebook.

59. Charles Baudelaire, *Les fleurs du mal: The Complete Text of* The Flowers of Evil, trans. Richard Howard (1982; repr., Jaffrey, NH: David R. Godine, 2003), 90.

60. Pierre Solda, "Émile Zola et l'haussmannisation de Paris," in *Paysages Urbains de 1830 à nos jours,* ed. Peter Kuon and Gérard Peylet (Pessac, France: Presses Universitaires de Bordeaux, 2004), 95–108, https://books.openedition.org/pub/28963?lang=en.

61. Jacques Rougerie, *La Commune et les Communards* (Paris: Gallimard, 2018), 19.

62. Michel Cordillot, "Eugène Varlin," *Le Maitron Dictionary of the French Workers' Movement,* https://maitron.fr/spip.php?article24876.

63. Jacques Rougerie, *Paris libre 1871* (1971; repr., Paris: Seuil, 2004), 21.

64. Merriman, *Massacre,* 21–23.

65. Rougerie, *Paris libre,* 9.

66. Xavière Gauthier, *On les appelait pétroleuses* (Tunis: Editions Elyzad, 2021), 29.

67. Rougerie, *La Commune et les Communards,* 27–28. For a map of the participation, see Rougerie, *Paris libre 1871,* 144.

68. Rougerie, *La Commune et les Communards,* 28–29.

69. Karl Marx, *The Civil War in France (1871),* chap. 5, https://www.marxists.org/archive/marx/works/1871/civil-war-france/ch05.htm.

70. Rougerie, *Paris libre,* 153–56.

71. Merriman, *Massacre,* 103–4.

72. Merriman, *Massacre,* 92–93.

73. Merriman, *Massacre,* 106–8.

74. Rougerie, *Paris libre,* 208.

75. Rougerie, *Paris libre,* 257.

76. Michèle Audin, "25 mai 1871, des milliers de morts et un marriage," *L'Humanité,* May 25, 2021, https://www.humanite.fr/en-debat/il-y-150-ans/25-mai-1871-des-milliers-de-morts-et-un-mariage-708211.

77. Franck Frégosi, "La 'montée' au Mur des Fédérés du Père Lachaise," *Archives des sciences sociales des religions,* no. 155 (2011): 166. A banquet was organized in 1878, but the first significant gathering took place in 1880.

78. Audrey Viault, "Les chants de la Commune," BNF Gallica blog, May 28, 2021, https://gallica.bnf.fr/blog/28052021/les-chants-de-la-commune.

79. Eugène Pottier, "Elle n'est pas morte!" 1886, in *Manière de voir (Le Monde diplomatique* magazine), no. 106, 2009.

4. Art and Affordability

1. Jean-Paul Caracalla, *Montparnasse: L'âge d'or* (1997; repr., Paris: La table ronde, 2017), 109.

2. Caracalla, *Montparnasse*, 112.

3. Caracalla, *Montparnasse*, 114.

4. Marc Chagall, *My Life* (New York: Orion Press, 1960), 103.

5. Caracalla, *Montparnasse*, 118.

6. "Témoignages sur Soutine et Modigliani," France 2 and the National Audiovisual Institute (INA), December 30, 1994, https://www.ina.fr/ina-eclaire-actu/video/i00008470/temoignages-sur-soutine-et-modigliani.

7. Olivier Renault, *Montparnasse: Les lieux de légende* (Paris: Paragramme, 2013), 10.

8. Sue Roe, *In Montparnasse: The Emergence of Surrealism in Paris, from Duchamp to Dalí* (New York: Penguin Random House, 2018), 17, Adobe ebook.

9. Roe, *In Montparnasse*, 117, 129. He moved twice in Montparnasse. First to the Rue Delambre, then to the Rue Campagne-Première.

10. Sylvia Beach, *Shakespeare and Company* (New York: Harcourt, Brace and Company, 1959), 15.

11. Noel Riley Fitch, *Sylvia Beach and the Lost Generation: A History of Literary Paris in the Twenties and Thirties* (1983; repr., New York/London: W.W. Norton & Company, 1985), 59.

12. Fitch, *Sylvia Beach and the Lost Generation*, 74.

13. Ernest Hemingway, "Living on $1,000 a Year in Paris," *Toronto Star*, February 4, 1922, https://americanliterature.com/author/ernest-hemingway/essay/living-on-1000-a-year-in-paris.

14. Michael Reynolds, *Hemingway: The Paris Years* (New York: W.W. Norton, 1989), 15–16.

15. Agnès Poirier, *Left Bank: Art, Passion, and the Rebirth of Paris, 1940–50* (Bloomsbury, 2018), 264–69.

16. Poirier, *Left Bank*, 217.

17. Ellery Washington, "James Baldwin's Paris," *New York Times*, January 17, 2014.

18. Poirier, *Left Bank*, 285.

19. James Baldwin, "The New Lost Generation," *Esquire*, July 1, 1961.

20. "Paris Home Price Indices since 1200," data set maintained by the Conseil Général de l'environnement et du développement, Ministère de la Transition écologique, https://www.igedd.developpement-durable .gouv.fr/house-prices-in-france-property-price-index-french-a1117 .html. For a more detailed explanation, see a presentation from J. Friggit for Paris city officials, "Le prix des logements à Paris de 1200 à 2015 et sa prospective," November 26, 2015, https://www.cgedd.developpement -durable.gouv.fr/IMG/pdf/prix-immobilier-paris_cle6f1be3.pdf, p. 5.

21. Danièle Voldman, "La loi de 1948 sur les loyers," *Vingtième siècle : Revue d'histoire* no. 20 (1988): 95.

22. "En 1948 les Français ont dépensé 30 milliards pour leurs loyers 204 milliards pour leur tabac," *Le Monde*, March 8, 1949.

23. Patrick Kamoun, *V'la Cochon qui déménage : prélude au droit au logement* (Vauchrétien, France: Éditions Ivan Davy, 2000), 71.

24. Michelle Perrot, "Les ouvriers, l'habitat et la ville au XIXe siècle," in *La question du logement et le mouvement ouvrier français* (Paris: Les Éditions de la Villette, 1981), 20.

25. However, in May 1912, Georges Cochon himself ran for city council in the 20th arrondissement, angering many of his allies in the Renters' Union and leading to his expulsion from the organization. He was not elected.

26. Kamoun, *V'la Cochon qui déménage*, 95.

27. Kamoun, *V'la Cochon qui déménage*, 80.

28. Jean-Marc Stebé, *Le logement social en France* (1998; repr., Paris: Presses Universitaires de France, 2019), 61–62.

29. Kamoun, *V'la Cochon*, 98.

30. Simone Morio, *Les contrôle des loyers en France (1914–1948) : documents pour l'étude comparative des politiques du logement* (Paris: Centre de sociologie urbaine, 1976), 22–23.

31. Danièle Voldman, "L'encadrement des loyers depuis 1900, une question européenne," *Le Mouvement Social* 245, no. 4 (2013/14): 140–41.

32. Simone Morio, *Le contrôle des loyers en Franc*, 121.

33. Danièle Voldman, *Locataires et propriétaires : une histoire française* (Paris: Payot & Rivages, 2016), 168. For a more detailed chronology, see Morio, *Le contrôle des loyers en France*, 226–36.

34. Susanna Magri, "Le mouvement des locataires à Paris et dans sa banlieue, 1919–1925," *Le Mouvement Social*, no. 137 (1986): 63.

35. See Morio, *Les contrôle des loyers en France*, for more.

36. Danièle Voldman, "La loi de 1948 sur les loyers," *Vingtième Siècle : Revue d'histoire*, no. 20 (1988): 93.

37. Michel Pinçon and Monique Pinçon-Charlot, *Sociologie de Paris*, 3rd ed. (2008; repr., Paris: *La Découverte*, 2014), 65.

38. Voldman, *Locataires et propriétaires*, 246–47.

39. "Paris Home Price Indices since 1200," Conseil Général de l'environnement et du développement, Ministère de la Transition écologique, https://www.igedd.developpement-durable.gouv.fr/house-prices-in-france-property-price-index-french-a1117.html.

40. George Orwell, *Down and Out in Paris and London* (London: Victor Gollancz, 1933), 7.

41. See Lucy Santé's list from *The Other Paris* (New York: Farrar, Strauss and Giroux, 2016), 23.

42. Leon-Paul Fargue, *Le Piéton de Paris* (1932; repr., Paris: Gallimard, 2021), 140.

43. Leon-Paul Fargue, *Le Piéton de Paris*, 18.

44. Henri Calet, *Les deux bouts* (1954; repr., Geneva: Editions Héros-Limite, 2016), 9.

45. Calet, *Les deux bouts*, 167.

46. Calet, *Les deux bouts*, 76.

47. Carol O'Sullivan, "Picturing Characters: Zazies à gogo," in *Seeing Things: Vision, Perception and Interpretation in French Studies*, ed. Simon Kemp and Libby Saxton (Oxford: Peter Lang, 2002), 271.

48. Clément Lépidis, *La main rouge* (1978; repr., Paris: Seuil, 2015), 100, ebook.

49. Lucy Sante, *The Other Paris*, 60–64.

50. Robert Doisneau and Blaise Cendrars, *La banlieue de Paris* (1949; repr., Paris: Denoël, 1983).

51. Yvan Gastaut, "Les bidonvilles, lieux d'exclusion et de marginalité en France durant les trente glorieuses," *Cahiers de la Méditerranée*, no. 69 (2004): 233–50.

52. Henri Cartier Bresson, "Terrain vague dans le Marais" (1953), in *Henri Cartier-Bresson Revoir Paris*, ed. Anne de Mondenard and Agnès Sire (Paris: Editions Paris Musée, 2021), 124.

53. "Porte de Vanves," in Izis Bidermanas, *Paris des rêves* (1950; repr., Paris: Flammarion, 2016).

54. Anne Clerval, *Paris sans le peuple* (Paris: La Découverte, 2013), ebook, 60–63.

55. Clerval, *Paris sans le peuple*, ebook, 57–58.

56. Willy Ronis, "1er mai, place des Fêtes" (1948), in Willy Ronis and Didier Daeninckx, *Belleville-Ménilmontant* (Paris: Editions Hoëbeke, 2017), 74–75.

57. Clerval, *Paris sans le peuple*, ebook, 74.

58. See Ville de Paris, Direction de l'Aménagement Urbain, "Plan Programme de l'Est de Paris," November 28, 1983, pp. 9, 19, and 40, https://50ans.apur.org/data/b4s3_home/fiche/56/01_plan_programme _est_paris_ap_1234_32539.pdf.

59. "Population active, emploi, chômage : Les ressources humaines d'une capitale économique," Atelier Parisien d'urbanisme report, November 2013, 5. https://www.apur.org/sites/default/files/documents /Population_active_emploi_chomage.pdf.

60. The expansion of federally funded highways disfigured cities like Detroit, Houston, the twin cities of Minneapolis and St. Paul, and New Orleans, among others. Rachael Dottle, Laura Bliss, and Pablo Robles, "What It Looks Like to Reconnect Black Communities Torn Apart by Highways," *Bloomberg*, July 28, 2021, https://www.bloomberg.com /graphics/2021-urban-highways-infrastructure-racism/.

5. Storming the Gates of Disneyland Paris

1. Eve Szeftel, "Jean-Baptiste Eyraud, bien charpenté," *Libération*, April 27, 2022.

2. Pauline Gauer, "Pour 550 euros, des retraités louent une chambre de misère, moisissures et rats inclus," *StreetPress*, July 8, 2022, https:// www.streetpress.com/sujet/1657286886-hotel-marche-paris-retraites

-chambre-misere-moisissures-rats-logement-insalubre-expulsion.

3. Céline Carez, "La révolte des locataires de la rue de Meaux, menacés d'expulsion à Paris, *Le Parisien*, July 5, 2022.

4. Eve Szeftel, "Les 'Dalo' lèvent le camp à Bastille après avoir obtenu gain de cause," *Libération*, May 15, 2022.

5. Kate Connolly, "Berlin's Rent Cap Is Illegal, Germany's Highest Court Rules," *The Guardian*, April 15, 2021.

6. Dave Braneck, "Berliners Voted for a Radical Solution to Soaring Rents. A Year On, They Are Still Waiting," *Euronews*, September 26, 2022, https://www.euronews.com/my-europe/2022/09/26/berliners-v oted-for-a-radical-solution-to-soaring-rents-a-year-on-they-are-still -waiting.

7. "Les derniers chiffres du logement social à Paris," Atelier Parisien d'urbanisme research note, February 2022, https://www.apur.org/fr /nos-travaux/derniers-chiffres-logement-social-paris.

8. The share of households living in socially rented homes in London fell from 35 percent in 1981 to 21 percent in 2020. "Housing Tenure over Time," Trust for London, https://www.trustforlondon .org.uk/data/housing-tenure-over-time/. Rachel Holliday Smith, "What is NYCHA? Your Questions Answered About New York City Public Housing," *The City*, February 23, 2021, https://www. thecity.nyc/2021/2/22/22296354/what-is-nycha-your-questions -answered-about-new-york-city-public-housing.

9. Stephen Barnett et al., *European Pillar of Social Rights: Cities Delivering Social rights*, Eurocities, November 2020, https://eurocities.eu/ wp-content/uploads/2020/11/EUROCITIES-report-EPSR-principle-1 9-on-housing-and-homelessness.pdf.

10. Atelier Parisien d'urbanisme research note, February 2022.

11. According to the French government, 53 percent of concerned municipalities did not hit their most recent social housing targets. "L'article 55 de la loi solidarité et renouvellement urbain (SRU), mode d'emploi," Ministère de la Transition écologique et de la Cohésion des territoires, August 23, 2021, https://www.ecologie.gouv.fr/larticle-55 -loi-solidarite-et-renouvellement-urbain-sru-mode-demploi.

12. Aitor Hernández-Morales, "How Vienna Took the Stigma Out of Social Housing," *Politico*, June 30, 2022, https://www.politico.eu/arti cle/vienna-social-housing-architecture-austria-stigma/.

13. "Housing Sector Country Snapshot: Austria," OECD, September 24, 2021, https://www.oecd.org/housing/policy-toolkit/country-snapshots/housing-policy-austria.pdf.

Twenty-three percent of households reside in social housing provided by the municipal government, 21 percent in social housing provided by limited-profit groups.

14. "Attribution des logements sociaux de la Ville de Paris," *Paris.fr*, May 30, 2022, https://www.paris.fr/pages/attribution-des-logements-sociaux-de-la-ville-de-paris-120.

15. Atelier parisien d'urbanisme research note, February 2022.

16. "Paris : 34 logements sociaux inaugurés sur un ancien terrain de la famille al-Assad, dans le XVIe arrondissement," *Le Parisien*, June 29, 2022.

17. Zemmour won 17.5 percent of the vote in the 16th arrondissement, but just 7.1 percent nationally. First-round presidential election results, 16th arrondissement of Paris, *Paris.fr*, April 2022, https://cdn.paris.fr/paris/2022/04/11/df279dc4b4df0bb44be90aab13966067.pdf.

18. Denis Cosnard and Isabelle Rey-Lefebvre," La Ville de Paris se prepare à contrôler les loyers à la place de l'Etat," *Le Monde*, March 10, 2022.

19. "1er barometre de l'Observatoire de l'encadrement des loyers à Paris," Fondation Abbé Pierre, October 2021, https://www.fondation-abbe-pierre.fr/sites/default/files/2021-fapdg_encadr-loyers-final.pdf.

20. See sums allotted to the "compte foncier logement" in "Le budget primitif 2022," Ville de Paris, 85, https://cdn.paris.fr/paris/2022/07/18/91c13670573d55e6296cf13db8b5eb43.pdf.

21. "À Paris, quatre residences secondaires sur dix appartiennent à des Franciliens," INSEE Ile-de-France research note no. 122, November 12, 2020, https://www.insee.fr/fr/statistiques/4945664.

22. "18600 logements durablement vacants à Paris en 2020," Atelier parisien d'urbanisme report, July 2022, 5. For breakdown by arrondissement, see p. 11.

23. "18600 logements durablement vacants à Paris en 2020," 6.

24. "Airbnb condamnée à 8 millions d'euros d'amende à Paris pour des announces sans numéro d'enregistrement," *Le Monde*, July 1, 2021.

25. Jason French, Sam Schechner, and Matthias Verbergt, "How

Airbnb Is Taking Over Paris," *Wall Street Journal*, June 26, 2015, http://graphics.wsj.com/how-airbnb-is-taking-over-paris/.

26. "Paris se vide de ses élèves : la carte des écoles primaires qui ferment," *Le Monde*, August 28, 2018 (updated July 4, 2019), https://www.lemonde.fr/education/visuel/2018/08/28/demographie-scolaire-a-paris-ces-ecoles-primaires-qui-ferment_5347198_1473685.html.

27. Philippe Baverel, "Paris : la librairie Les Mots à la bouche va déménager dans le XIe," *Le Parisien*, February 9, 2020.

28. Philippe Baverel, "L'Open café, c'est fini à Paris," *Le Parisien*, April 6, 2022.

29. Luc Lenoir, "Le photographe René Robert, mort dans l'indifférence en pleine rue," *Le Figaro*, January 25, 2022.

30. "Les personnes sans-abri à Paris la nuit du 20 au 21 janvier 2022," Atelier parisien d'urbanisme, June 2022, https://cdn.paris.fr/paris/2022/06/30/a40bf4df41fc4546e5243773365b2d81.pdf.

31. Denis Cosnard, "Le gouvernement bloque le projet de centre pour toxicomanes du 16e arrondissement de Paris," *Le Monde*, June 17, 2022.

32. In 2020, Afghans made up the largest group of first-time asylum seekers in France, with 10,100 individual requests. Interior Ministry, June 2021, https://www.immigration.interieur.gouv.fr/Info-ressources/Etudes-et-statistiques/Chiffres-cles-sejour-visas-eloignements-asile-acces-a-la-nationalite/Archives/Statistiques-publiees-en-juin-2021.

33. See "Les oubliés du droit d'asile : enquête sur les conditions de vie et l'accès aux droits des exiles fréquentant 5 structures d'accueil à Paris," Fédération des Acteurs de la Solidarité Ile-de-France, December 2021, https://www.federationsolidarite.org/wp-content/uploads/2021/12/Rapport-oubliedroitasile-2021-vfinale-web-sansreco.pdf.

34. "Évacuation de migrants à Paris : Darmanin juge les images 'choquantes,'" *Le Parisien*, November 23, 2020.

35. "Campement de migrants : près de 400 tentes déployées place de la République," *Le Figaro*, March 25, 2021.

36. Juliette Bénézit, "Utopia 56, ou la stratégie de 'visibilisation' des migrants," *Le Monde*, December 26, 2020.

37. "About Sixty Exiled People Claim Their Right to Exist," Utopia 56 statement, July 20, 2022, https://utopia56.org/une-soixantaine-de-personnes-exilees-revendiquent-leur-droit-dexister/.

6. The Worlds of the Banlieue

1. Eurostat, *Urban Europe: Statistics on Cities, Towns and Suburbs* (Luxembourg: Publications Office of the European Union, 2016), 199, https://ec.europa.eu/eurostat/documents/3217494/7596823/KS-01 -16-691-EN-N.pdf/0abf140c-ccc7-4a7f-b236-682effcde10f ?t=1472645220000.

2. "Près de 60 % des actifs travaillant à Paris ne résident pas dans la capitale," INSEE Ile-de-France flash no. 55, February 23, 2021, https:// www.insee.fr/fr/statistiques/5057486.

3. "90 % des Parisiens qui quittent la capitale s'installent dans une commune urbaine," INSEE Ile-de-France research note no. 143, November 22, 2021, https://www.insee.fr/fr/statistiques/5871250.

4. Seine-Saint-Denis is the youngest *département* in metropolitan France, with 36 percent of residents under age twenty-five. Hajera Mohammad, "La Seine-Saint-Denis, département où les difficultés sociales persistent selon l'Insee," *France Bleu Paris*, February 13, 2020, https://www.francebleu.fr/infos/faits-divers-justice/la-seine-saint -denis-reste-le-departement-le-plus-jeune-de-france-metropolitaine -1581584826.

5. Laura van Straaten, "The Jean-Michel Basquiat You Haven't Seen," *New York Times*, February 13, 2017. See also Lucy Sante, "An Intimate Look at Jean-Michel Basquiat's Early Days," *Village Voice*, February 8, 2017.

6. Pierre Longeray, "Une histoire des 'cités de banlieue' françaises," *Vice*, February 19, 2019, https://www.vice.com/fr/article/bjq7j3/une -histoire-des-cites-de-banlieue-francaises.

7. Xavier de Jarcy, *Les Abandonnés : Histoire des 'cités de banlieue'* (Paris: Albin Michel, 2019), 187–88, Adobe ebook.

8. Raphaële Bertho, "The *Grands Ensembles*: Fifty Years of French Political Fiction," trans. James Gussen, *Études photographiques* 31 (2004): 8–10.

9. "Quand sévissait la 'sarcellite,'" *Le Figaro*, March 18, 2006.

10. Olivier Faye, "Sarcelles sous le choc des violences antisémites," *Le Monde*, July 22, 2014.

11. Rossana Di Vincenzo and François Chevalier, "La carte des rappeurs franciliens qui représentent fièrement leur quartier," *Téléra-*

ma, November 21, 2017 (updated December 8, 2020), https://www
.telerama.fr/sortir/la-carte-des-rappeurs-franciliens-qui-representent
-fierement-leur-quartier,n5347365.php.

12. Simon Kuper, "From Pogba to Mbappe: Why Greater Paris Is the
World's Top Talent Pool," ESPN, December 27, 2017, https://www
.espn.com/soccer/blog/espn-fc-united/68/post/3320634/greater-paris
-biggest-talent-pool-in-football-paul-pogba-kylian-mbappe-anthony
-martial.

13. "Vivre dans le 93, vrai obstacle à l'embauche," *Le Parisien*, June 18,
2013.

14. Hajera Mohammad, "Seine-Saint-Denis : 84% des jeunes du
département déclarent avoir été victimes de discrimination," *France
Bleu Paris*, November 9, 2021, https://www.francebleu.fr/infos/societe
/seine-saint-denis-84-des-jeunes-du-departement-declarent-avoir
-ete-victimes-de-discrimination-1636109737.

15. The area making up "Grand Paris" doesn't extend across the
entirety of the Paris metropolitan area (the *unité urbaine)* as defined by
the national statistics agency, which explains the population discrep-
ancy between the two.

16. Philippe Subra and Wilfried Serisier, "La Métropole du Grand
Paris, enjeu caché des élections municipales de 2020," *Métropolitiques*,
June 17, 2021, https://metropolitiques.eu/La-Metropole-du-Grand-Pari
s-enjeu-cache-des-elections-municipales-de-2020.html.

17. "Communes, EPT, MGP : État des lieux et enjeux des relations finan-
cières dans le coeur d'agglomération," L'Institut Paris Région, December 2021, 51, https://www.institutparisregion.fr/fileadmin/NewEtudes
/000pack2/Etude_2749/Architecture_financiere_MGP.pdf.

18. "Athletes' Village," Société de livraison des ouvrages olympiques,
https://projets.ouvrages-olympiques.fr/en/athletes-village/.

19. Olivier Morin, "Le loup de la fusion aux portes du Grand Paris,"
L'Humanité, July 26, 2017.

20. Michel Cotten, "Le Grand Paris est bien mal parti," *Slate.fr*,
October 16, 2014, https://www.slate.fr/story/93463/grand-paris-mal
-parti; Simon Ronai, "Grand Paris : état des lieux de la construction
métropolitaine après six mois de guerre de positions," *Métropolitiques*,
June 1, 2015, https://metropolitiques.eu/Grand-Paris-etat-des-lieux-d
e-la.html.

21. Alain Rustenholz, *De la banlieue rouge au Grand Paris : D'Ivry à Clichy et de St-Ouen à Charenton* (Paris: La Fabrique, 2015), 15.

Conclusion: The Right to Paris

1. Henri Lefebvre, *The Right to the City* (1968), trans. Eleonore Kofman and Elizabeth Lebas (1996), accessed online via The Anarchist Library, https://theanarchistlibrary.org/library/henri-lefebvre-right-to -the-city#toc13.

2. David Harvey, "The Right to the City," *New Left Review* 53 (2008): 23–40.

3. David Adler, "Do We Have a Right to the City?," *Jacobin*, October 6, 2015.

4. "Resolution Adopted by the General Assembly on 23 December 2016," United Nations General Assembly, https://habitat3.org/wp -content/uploads/New-Urban-Agenda-GA-Adopted-68th-Plenary -N1646655-E.pdf.

5. Henri Lefebvre, "Quand la ville se perd dans une métamorphose planétaire," *Le Monde diplomatique*, May 1989, 16–17, https://www .monde-diplomatique.fr/1989/05/LEFEBVRE/41710.

6. Mike Davis, *Planet of Slums* (New York/London: Verso Books, 2006).

7. See John Merriman, *Massacre: The Life and Death of the Paris Commune* (New York: Basic Books, 2014); David Harvey, *Paris, Capital of Modernity* (New York/London: Routledge, 2003); and Jacques Rougerie, *Paris libre 1871* (1971; repr., Paris: Seuil, 2004).

INDEX

266 INDEX

Monnier, Adrienne, 119

Monoprix grocery chain, 5, 190–92, 229–31

Montagne Sainte-Geneviève, 101

Montfermeil, 206

Montmartre, ix–x, 3, 27, 72, 118, 133; annexation during Haussmannization, 102; and the Paris Commune of 1871, 107, 111

Montparnasse, 118–21, 133, 145, 197

Montreuil, 197–205

Montrouge, 195

Moroccans, xii, 49, 52

Moskowitz, P.E., 17–18

Les Mots à la Bouche (LGBT bookstore in the Marais), 181

Mouillart, Michel, 27

A Moveable Feast (Hemingway), 121

Muani, Randal Kolo, 213

Muslims, 12, 209, 210–11; celebration of Eid al-Adha, xii; conservative Islam, 48, 209, 210–11; and French republicanism, 48–49

The Mysteries of Paris (Sue), 88–89, 99–100

The Naked and the Dead (Mailer), 122

Napoleon Bonaparte, 81, 89

Napoleon III, 47, 94–100, 104

National Archives, 73

National Assembly, 104, 107, 128, 146–47, 168, 174, 230

National Guard, 107–8, 111

National Institute of Statistics and Economic Studies (INSEE), xvi–xvii, xviii, 39, 177, 193

Neuilly-sur-Seine, 193

"The New Lost Generation" (Baldwin), 122–23

New Wave cinema, 116, 135, 139

New York City: gentrification and housing, 17–18, 21, 66; immigrants and cultural diversity, 46; Lower East Side artist squats of the late 1970s and 1980s, 199, 201; Manhattan real estate prices, 17–18; population density, 8; social housing, 165

Nice, France, 167, 177

Niemeyer, Oscar, 59

NIMBY ("not in my backyard") agenda, 23

19th arrondissement, 13, 51, 63, 143, 153, 163, 166, 183, 186, 224

"le 9-3" (Seine-Saint-Denis), 205–13, 214, 216, 231

Nkunku, Christopher, 213

nobility, French, 73

Normandy, France, 54, 56, 192, 213

Notre Dame Cathedral, 71–74, 99–100, 178

Notre-Dame de Lorette, 85

Les Nuits de Paris (Restif de la Bretonne), 71

Occitan language, 47

Occupation of Paris, 117, 121

octroi, 72

Odéon Theatre, 134

ABOUT THE AUTHOR

Cole Stangler is a journalist based in Marseille, France. A contributor to *The Nation*, *Jacobin*, and the international news network France 24, he has also published work in the *New York Times*, the *Washington Post*, *The Guardian*, *Foreign Policy*, and other outlets.

PUBLISHING IN THE PUBLIC INTEREST

Thank you for reading this book published by The New Press; we hope you enjoyed it. New Press books and authors play a crucial role in sparking conversations about the key political and social issues of our day.

We hope that you will stay in touch with us. Here are a few ways to keep up to date with our books, events, and the issues we cover:

- Sign up at www.thenewpress.com/subscribe to receive updates on New Press authors and issues and to be notified about local events
- www.facebook.com/newpressbooks
- www.twitter.com/thenewpress
- www.instagram.com/thenewpress

Please consider buying New Press books not only for yourself, but also for friends and family and to donate to schools, libraries, community centers, prison libraries, and other organizations involved with the issues our authors write about.

The New Press is a 501(c)(3) nonprofit organization; if you wish to support our work with a tax-deductible gift please visit www.thenewpress.com/donate or use the QR code below.